ACCLAIM FOR

THE GOSPEL IN PARABLE

"Donahue presents the major parables in the Synoptic Gospels as representative of the particular theological themes of each writer. . . . This book contains striking insights into the meaning of individual parables along with suggestions for preaching the parables today."

—PHEME PERKINS
Boston College

"This is a superb book. . . . The work of a seasoned scholar who likewise possesses the heart of a pastor. It incorporates years of careful study and reflection; it is also eminently readable. Specialists will overlook it at their peril; pastors and seminarians will find it rich in scholarly insight and homiletical wisdom. It deserves a wide readership."

—JACK DEAN KINGSBURY
Union Theological Seminary, Richmond

"John Donahue not only helps us read the parables in the Synoptic Gospels with intelligence but demonstrates their usefulness in the preaching and the living out of their message. This book exudes profound scholarship as well as a readability that is not always common in the world of scriptural studies. . . . There is, in short, a keen pastoral edge to his work which nicely complements careful scholarship."

—LAWRENCE S. CUNNINGHAM
University of Nortre Dame

". . . stimulating and suggestive. . . . This book makes a significant contribution to the study of the parables. . . . Preachers and teachers—especially those who follow the lectionary—will want to consult this book each time they discuss a parable."

—M. THOMAS NORWOOD, JR.
The Christian Century

"Donahue's excellent volume sets out 'to wed recent parable study to the results of redaction criticism of the Synoptic Gospels.' . . . The result is a first-rate commentary on the parables of the Synoptic tradition, which incorporates a survey of recent scholarly opinion with personal, often very helpful insights."

—SCHUYLER BROWN
Interpretation

Metaphor, Narrative, and Theology in the Synoptic Gospels

THE GOSPEL
IN
PARABLE

JOHN R. DONAHUE, S.J.

FORTRESS PRESS

Cover illustration: "The Return of the Prodigal Son" by Rembrandt
Cover design: Jim Gerhard

First paperback edition 1990

Library of Congress Cataloging-in-Publication Data

Donahue, John R.
  The gospel in parable.

  Bibliography: p.
  Includes index.
  1. Jesus Christ—Parables. 2. Bible, N.T. Gospels—
Criticism, interpretation, etc. I. Title.
BT375.2.D66   1988   266'.806   87-45888
ISBN 0-8006-0852-6 (cloth)
ISBN 0-8006-2480-7 (paper)

CONTENTS

Preface ix

1. How Does a Parable Mean?
   Introduction 1
   The Parable as Text 4
   The Parable as Narrative 20
   The Parable as Context 25

2. The Parables of Mark
   Introduction 28
   Parables and the Mystery of the Kingdom: Mark 4 29
   The Drama of Salvation History in Mark 12 52
   Community Life "between the Times": The Parables
      of Mark 13 57

3. The Parables of Matthew
   Introduction 63
   Ethics and Discipleship: Matthew's Redaction of
      Mark 4 64
   The Justice of the Kingdom in Matthew 70
   Matthew's Debate with "the Synagogue across the
      Street" 85
   The Eschatological Crisis and the Parables of
      Matthew 24 and 25 96

4. The Parables of Luke
  Introduction   126
  Luke's Theological Program: The Good Samaritan
    in Context   128
  Table Fellowship with the Marginal and Luke's
    Gospel in Parable   140
  A "Gospel within a Gospel": The Parables of Luke 15   146
  The Parables of Luke 16 and Rich and Poor in
    Luke's Gospel   162
  Trial by Prayer: The Parables of the Widow and the
    Judge and the Pharisee and the Tax Collector   180

5. The Gospel in Parable
  The Gospel of Mark: Christology and Discipleship
    in Parable   194
  Eschatology, Ethics, and the Good News of the
    Kingdom: Matthew's Gospel in Parable   199
  Parables and Paradigms for a Community in Mission:
    Luke's Gospel in Parable   204
  Proclaiming the Gospel in Parable   211

  Abbreviations   217

  Bibliography   220

  Index of Parables   234

  Index of Citations   236

  Index of Authors   251

PREFACE

Not another book on the parables! So exclaimed a colleague, himself the author of a fine book on the parables, when I mentioned that I had the present work in mind. During its gestation, I felt often that his exclamation was a prediction. Still, behind his surprise was a well-grounded sense that there was no dearth of excellent studies of the parables (see Bibliography).

Yet the parables, like all great literary and artistic works, are ever old and ever new and resist capture by any one movement or period, not to say by any one book. This work arose from a concern that an area of parable study remained relatively uncharted. For the past century the parables have served as the royal road to the life, teaching, and self-understanding of Jesus. Their primary literary context, however, is their location in the different Gospels. My purpose is to wed recent parable study to the results of redaction criticism of the Synoptic Gospels. From my work with the parables over a number of years, my conviction is that they offer a Gospel in miniature and at the same time give shape, direction, and meaning to the Gospels in which they are found. To study the parables of the Gospels is to study the gospel in parable.

The subtitle of my study is in debt to Paul Ricoeur's description of the parables as a combination of the metaphoric process and the narrative form (see below, pp. 10–11). My initial chapter takes its title in conscious echo of John Ciardi's wonderful book *How Does a*

Poem Mean? I first used this too many years ago for an undergraduate
class in Latin poetry, with the hope that the students would see
Horace as something other than a thicket of difficult grammar. In
seeking to ask *how a parable means*, I offer a survey of recent reflection
on parable, metaphor, and narrative. In the central chapters my
method is to study the parables as texts—but as texts in the literary
and theological context of a given Gospel. The final chapter, virtually
an epilogue, tries to draw together different threads and to offer
suggestions for proclaiming the parables today. Commentary on the
texts of the parables makes up the bulk of the work. My plea is that
readers work with the Bible at hand. Whether readers agree with
my suggestions is far less important than their own engagement with
the biblical images and texts.

   This work has arisen from years of teaching the parables primarily
to students in training for ministry to different Christian communities,
and also from giving a great number of workshops on the parables.
To teach the parables for over a decade is to realize their power to
challenge and fascinate people. Students from the most varied
backgrounds and with wide differences in formal training in biblical
studies can raise probing questions and make original suggestions.
Much that I presume to claim as original arose from dialogue with
students, especially those at the Vanderbilt Divinity School and the
Graduate Theological Union. To them I feel a great debt of gratitude.
My hope is that this work will be of value for people in training for
ministry, for those in the active ministry, and for all who are caught
up in the world of the parables.

   While attempting to mediate the results of exegesis to a group
larger than biblical specialists, I have tried to remain faithful to the
canons of exegesis. The lengthy Bibliography, limited for the most
part to titles available in English, represents an attempt to acquaint
readers with important books and articles on the parables.

   Like all who study the parables, I have been influenced by the
seminal work of Joachim Jeremias and the creative discussion in the
United States since the late 1960s associated with names like J.
Dominic Crossan, Robert Funk, Norman Perrin, Amos Wilder, and
Dan O. Via—all of whom gave a new direction to parable study.
Recent works by Kenneth Bailey, Madeleine Boucher, Jan Lambrecht,
Pheme Perkins, and Mary Ann Tolbert have also been stimulating

and helpful. When teaching the parables, I urge students to engage many different works and perspectives. My own work is an invitation for readers to learn as I did from these authors.

To name all those to whom I owe a debt of gratitude would keep us too long at the starting gate. I must, however, thank faculty colleagues at Vanderbilt such as Sallie McFague, Walter Harrelson, and Douglas Knight, who encouraged this work at its inception. The Dean of the Jesuit School of Theology at Berkeley, T. Howland Sanks, S.J., and fellow faculty there constantly encouraged me to complete the work. I also appreciate the interest of other faculty at the Graduate Theological Union, especially William Herzog and Antoinette Wire, who at opportune times sustained the flagging enthusiasm of a weary author. I am also grateful to Evelyn Thibeaux, a Ph.D. candidate in New Testament, for invaluable assistance in the final editing of the manuscript and to the Graduate Theological Union which granted her a Newhall Fellowship to assist faculty research. John A. Hollar of Fortress Press has been more than a dedicated editor. He has been a friend who encouraged the work at every stage and showed wonderful patience in the face of many delays. Special gratitude is owed to the Woodstock Theological Center at Georgetown University, which provided a research fellowship and supportive environment to complete the work.

This book is dedicated to the memory of my parents. They loved laughter, language, and stories. Their long lives were themselves parables that continue to be good news to all who knew and loved them.

THE GOSPEL IN PARABLE

1

HOW
DOES A
PARABLE
MEAN?

INTRODUCTION

Biblical statements about God and God's actions in the world are expressed in a language of images that moves in the rhythmic cadences of Hebrew poetry. God is not simply powerful but one who "kills and brings to life; he brings down to Sheol and raises up" (1 Sam. 2:6). God does not simply free a people but leads them out of a house of bondage "with a mighty hand and an outstretched arm" (Deut. 5:15). The Hebrew Bible images a God who lays the foundations of the earth and shuts in the sea with doors (Job 38:4, 8), who seeks an unfaithful people with the longing of a rejected lover (Hosea 2) and remembers a people with a mother's love (Isa. 49:14–15). The biblical God speaks through images that touch hidden depths of human experience and cover the whole gamut of human emotion. Nor is biblical literature ashamed of its wealth of images, not always easily reconciled with each other.

Jesus of Nazareth is both heir to this tradition and the genesis of a new tradition. He does not simply warn his disciples of the pitfalls of following him but says, "If the salt has lost its saltness, how will you season it?" (Mark 9:50). Though not technically classed as poetry by later Western standards, the speech of Jesus reveals characteristic devices of Hebrew poetry such as repetition along with contrasting (antithetical) and complementary (synthetic) parallelism. Jesus says:

> For nothing is covered
> that will not be revealed.
> (Matt. 10:26)

and

> For my yoke is easy, and
> my burden is light.
> (Matt. 11:30)

At times the language of Jesus strikes us not simply as a forceful collocation of images but as a series of riddles that put our ordinary perceptions askew and challenge our understanding:

> Leave the dead to bury their own dead.
> (Matt. 8:22)

> To him who has will more be given;
> and from him who has not, even what
> he has will be taken away.
> (Mark 4:25)

> Unless you turn and become like children,
> you will never enter the kingdom of heaven.
> (Matt. 18:3)

Through its concreteness the language of Jesus captures our attention, through its rhythmic cadences it resonates in our memories, and through its puzzles and enigmas it engages our quest for understanding.

Among the many sayings in the Synoptic Gospels (Matthew, Mark, and Luke), those which best embody the speech of Jesus and which are most distinctive of him are the more than forty parables attributed to him. These parables manifest such a range of images that the everyday world of rural, first-century Palestine comes alive in a way true of few ancient cultures. The parables embrace images of the dynamism of nature and deviousness of human nature and range from short narrative vignettes to full-blown dramatic stories.

The parables and the poetry of Jesus, however, are unlike nineteenth-century nature poetry which draws the reader to aesthetic contemplation of the beauty of nature. Through the language of Jesus we are in contact with his imagination as it brings to expression his self-understanding of his mission and his struggle with the mystery of his Father's will. As Robert Tannehill notes, "The sayings do not invite contemplation of themselves as objects of value but require us to contemplate our lives."[1]

One major problem in making contact with the imagination of Jesus and in letting his sayings touch our lives is that the original context of the parables and sayings is no longer accessible to us. Most fundamentally, the parables were spoken, and, whether to disciples or to opponents, they share in the dynamics of oral, interpersonal dialogue. Things such as the situation that evoked their original utterance, the tone in which they were spoken, and the bodily expressions with which they were heard—a shrug, a sigh, or a snarl—all are lost to us. We now have the parables only *as text*, nor do we have a stenographic record of the original text of any one parable but only Greek adaptations and translations. As Joachim Jeremias has shown, the text has been so altered in transmission that the original "text" of any parable is a reconstructed one.[2] Also reconstructed, even though with a solid basis, is the original context of the parables, the kingdom proclamation of Jesus. In proclaiming the advent of God's kingdom (Mark 1:14–15), Jesus proclaims God's sovereign rule and God's summons to people to open their hearts to the claims of God present in his teaching and ministry. From these parables Jeremias is able to reconstruct the lineaments of this proclamation: now is the day of salvation; God is merciful to sinners and will deliver his loved ones from coming tribulation; the catastrophe is imminent, however, and it may already be too late, so now is the time for decision. Virtually every subsequent attempt to reconstruct the proclamation of Jesus is in debt to Jeremias's careful discussion of the history of the transmission of the parables and his reconstruction of Jesus' proclamation of the kingdom in parable, even though his work should be supplemented by the examination of the kingdom proposed by John Riches and the excellent studies of the parables as sayings of Jesus by James Breech, J. Dominic Crossan, and Bernard Brandon Scott.[3]

A more secure context for interpreting the parables is that of the individual Gospels. In fact, it is the only context that is directly

1. Tannehill, *Sword of His Mouth*, 17.
2. Jeremias, *Parables*, 23–114.
3. Riches, *Jesus and the Transformation of Judaism*, 87–111; Breech, *Silence*; Crossan, esp. *In Fragments* and *In Parables*; Scott, *Jesus, Symbol-Maker*.

accessible to us. Such con-textual study of the parables (see below, pp. 25–27) is simply an aspect of redaction criticism that seeks the author's intention not only in the way a given tradition is altered but also through observation of the location of a specific pericope in relation to surrounding material, often called composition criticism.

The parables of Jesus, therefore, as we find them in the Gospels are texts that exist in a definite context. Though I may suggest possible meaning(s) for a given parable in the ministry of Jesus, this is not my primary aim. I will treat the parables principally in the context of the individual Gospels and present them both as an entree to the theology of a given Gospel and as a reflection of its major themes.[4] Since the parables for the most part were not actually written by the evangelists but have a certain independence as texts, and since people today meet them in sermons and study as independent texts, I will propose also a literary analysis of the major parables. We have immediate access to the *text* of a parable in the *context* of a Gospel, and I would claim that a study of text and context provides a valid method of examining the Gospels in parable. Nor is it my purpose to treat every parable in each Gospel; instead, I wish to treat a significant number that provide a virtual compendium of the theological motifs of a given Gospel, either on the basis of a discernible redaction of the tradition (e.g., Matthew's editing of Mark's parable of the Wicked Tenants, Matt. 21:33–45 = Mark 12:1–11) or because of their location in a definite context (e.g., the Good Samaritan in the context of Luke 10).

THE PARABLE AS TEXT

Virtually all persons who write on the parables treat the same pericopes, usually the longer narratives such as the Sower, the Laborers in the Vineyard, and the Prodigal Son. Yet those sections in a Gospel explicitly called parable are quite diverse (e.g., Mark 3:23–27; 7:14–17), and some of the most vivid "parables" of the Christian tradition are not explicitly called such (e.g., the Good Samaritan, Luke 10:29–37, and the Unjust Steward, Luke 16:1–8).

---

4. With the exception of a few technical studies, recent general works on the parables have not stressed the relation of the parables to the theology of the individual Gospels. See the scholarly works by Carlston, *Parables*; Kingsbury, *Matthew 13*; and Lambrecht, *Once More Astonished*.

This ambiguity arises because in its original sense "parable" is not a fixed literary form. Behind our English "parable" stands the Greek *parabolē* (from the preposition *para,* "alongside of," and *ballein,* "cast, place, or throw"). Etymologically parable means that one thing is understood in juxtaposition or comparison with another. In the Greek translation of the OT (the Septuagint), *parabolē* normally translates the Hebrew *māšāl.* Though the etymology of this term is unclear, its root meaning suggests "to be like or similar," and the term is used to describe a wide variety of literary forms, such as proverbs (1 Sam. 10:12; Prov. 1:1, 6; 10:1; 26:7–9), riddles (Judg. 14:10–18), taunt songs (Mic. 2:4; Hab. 2:6), allegories (Isa. 5:1–7; Ezek. 17:3–24), and, in the intertestamental literature, long revelatory discourses such as the similitudes of Enoch (*1 Enoch* 39—71).[5] Surprisingly the parable of the trees (Judg. 9:7–15) and that of the ewe lamb (2 Sam. 12:1–4), which in form and function are most like many NT parables, are not called parables. This same variety characterizes the Gospel parables where *parabolē* can mean proverb (Luke 4:23, "Physician, heal yourself"), wisdom saying (Luke 5:36–39), allegory (Mark 12:1–11; Matt. 22:1–14), and the more familiar narrative parable. Pericopes not explicitly called parables should also be considered as such, either because of introductory formulas "it is like" (Matt. 11:16), "the kingdom of heaven is like" (e.g., Matt. 13:31, 33) or "may be compared to" (Matt. 18:23) or "to what shall I compare?" (Luke 7:31; cf. Mark 4:30), or because the context clearly indicates that a given section is a parable (Luke 15:11–32; cf. 15:1).

Among the canon of those authors who are indispensable for study of the parables, C. H. Dodd has offered the most comprehensive and adequate definition of the NT parables:

> At its simplest the parable is a metaphor or simile drawn from nature or common life, arresting the hearer by its vividness or strangeness, and leaving the mind in sufficient doubt about its precise application to tease it into active thought.[6]

5. See Herbert, "The 'Parable' (*MĀŠĀL*) in the Old Testament"; Polk, "Paradigms, Parables, and *Mĕšālîm*; and Stewart, "The Parable Form in the Old Testament and the Rabbinic Literature." Sider ("The Meaning of *Parabolē*") minimizes the influence of the Hebrew Bible or the Septuagint and argues that *parabolē* is used in an Aristotelian sense of illustration by analogy. Texts such as Mark 4:10–12 and 7:15–17 scarcely support his position.

6. Dodd, *Parables,* 5.

Dodd's definition has two distinct advantages. First, it is arrived at inductively and descriptively, a result of Dodd's own broad knowledge of classical literature and intense engagement with the NT. When reading the parables, we feel that Dodd describes what we are actually reading. Second, it provides useful categories under which I may summarize the major aspects of the nature and function of parables, as they have been discussed since Adolf Jülicher (1888), but primarily in the last two decades. Dodd, in effect, diagnoses four major aspects of parabolic language: *(a)* its poetic and metaphoric quality, *(b)* its realism, *(c)* its paradoxical and engaging quality, and *(d)* its open-ended nature. One aspect that Dodd did not stress but that has been the focus of contemporary discussion is the parable "as narrative." My presentation of the parable "as text" will follow Dodd's description and then add a section on parable as narrative. Each aspect of Dodd's definition involves literary observations that spawn a theological reflection. This combination has implications for the re-presentation and proclamation of parables today.

". . . is a metaphor or simile"

In most general terms, parables are in the realm of figurative or tropical language where communication takes place through images and the suggestive power of language rather than through literal and precise speech.[7] At least since Aristotle, literary critics have attempted to classify and describe the different figures of speech (tropes) that characterize imaginative discourse. Chief among these has been the language of comparison, simile and metaphor. As Aristotle notes and etymology supports, metaphor (from the Greek *meta*, "across or over," and *pherein*, "carry or bring") involves the transference of things proper to one reality over to another.[8] In the words of I. A. Richards, "when we use metaphor we have two thoughts of different things active together and supported by a single word, or phrase, whose meaning is a resultant of their interaction."[9] For example, Jesus' statement, "You are the light of the world" (Matt. 5:14), evokes different images for the mission of the disciples—guidance,

---

7. Boucher, *Parables*, 25–31; idem, *Mysterious Parable*, 11–25.
8. Aristotle *Poetics* 1457b; *Rhetoric* 1405a–1407a; 1411a–1413b. See Grube's helpful edition of Aristotle's work in this area: *Aristotle: On Poetry and Style*.
9. Cited in McFague, *Speaking in Parables*, 43.

opposition to the unknown and darkness, pointing the way on a journey. In more technical language, metaphor brings together two discrete elements that are united by a point of comparison (the *punctum* or *tertium comparationis*). The basis of metaphorical predication is a perceived similarity or analogy between different things. Aristotle remarked that "the right use of metaphors is a sign of inborn talent and cannot be learned from anyone else; it comes from the ability to observe similarities in things" (*Poetics* 1459a). The disciples could scarcely be called "the treasure hidden in the field," since there is no point of similarity. The distinction between metaphor and simile, as well as other figures of speech, is complex. At the risk of oversimplification, metaphor is called an implied comparison, while simile is expressed by the use of some particle such as "like" or "as." According to Norman Perrin, metaphor contrasts two fundamentally different categories of reality and hence produces a shock to the imagination, while the simile is essentially illustrative.[10]

The attempt to describe more carefully the language of the parables began with the massive two-volume study of Jülicher (1888 and 1899).[11] Jülicher broke with the centuries-old tradition of interpreting the parables in allegorical fashion and argued that their "point" or meaning must be sought in the historical context of the teaching of Jesus. In his study Jülicher was strongly influenced by Aristotle's *Rhetoric* and viewed the parables primarily as rhetorical devices rather than poetic ones. Jesus, therefore, used the parables primarily to teach or to defend his teaching. In locating the parables in the context of Jesus' teaching, Jülicher showed the problematic nature of allegorical exegesis which extended from the allegory of Mark 4:13–20 to his own day. He argued that a parable is a developed simile where the point of comparison is clear, while allegories are developed metaphors that foster inauthentic speech and arbitrary interpretation. Each parable is thought to have only one point of comparison and this is to have the widest possible application, usually in the sphere of ethics. The Jesus who emerges from Jülicher's work proclaims "a

---

10. Perrin, *Jesus and the Language*, 99–100; 128–129; 135–36. Perrin acknowledges the insights of Wilder and Funk; see below, n. 13.
11. Jülicher, *Gleichnisreden*. See the summaries of his position and influence in Jones, *Art and Truth*, 1–40; and Perrin, *Jesus and the Language*, 92–97. Perrin's book presents the best survey of parable research subsequent to Jülicher.

manifesto of nineteenth-century German liberal theology."[12] While
subsequent research altered Jülicher's portrayal of Jesus by stressing
the eschatological rather than the ethical meaning of the parables
(Dodd and Jeremias), the influence of Jülicher has been lasting. He
bequeathed to scholarship the descriptive categories of "similitude"
or short comparison (Gleichnis: e.g., the Hidden Treasure, Matt.
13:44), "parable" or extended comparison (Parabel: e.g., the Unmerciful Servant, Matt. 18:23–35), and "example story" (Beispieler-
zählung: e.g., Luke 10:29–37). Jülicher's adamant opposition to
allegory and his insistence on a single point of comparison became
a dogma of parable exegesis only slightly less rigid than the dogmatism
that earlier allegorical exegesis had buttressed.

A major turning point in the study of the parables came with the
seminal works of Amos Wilder and Robert Funk, both published in
the mid-1960s, which examined the parables as poetic forms where
a deep appreciation of metaphor opened the way to new understandings of their literary and theological importance.[13] Wilder was one
of the first NT scholars who saw the need to be engaged with the
aesthetics of biblical language. As one who received a cosmopolitan
education—poet, theologian, and exegete—he was uniquely equipped
for the task. Writing recently from a vantage of over six decades of
reflection on the Bible, he states his "continuing conviction that both
scholars and general readers have failed to do justice to what one
can call the operations of the imagination in the Scriptures—to the
poetry, the imagery, and the symbolism," and he attributes opposition
to a literary approach to an "occupational cramp" among his
colleagues:

> If, in interpreting the Psalms or the Book of Revelation, they treated
> poetry as prose, it was because their philological tradition was interested
> in minutiae and analysis, while their theological tradition was interested
> in ideas.[14]

Among the literary genres discussed by Wilder in his path-breaking

12. Tolbert, Perspectives, 24.
13. Wilder, "The Parable," in Language, 79–96 (also in Jesus' Parables, 71–87);
Funk, "The Parable as Metaphor," in Language, Hermeneutic, 133–62; see also Perrin,
Jesus and the Language, 127–41.
14. Wilder, Jesus' Parables, 15. Wilder's preface (15–38) provides a superb introduction to his own life and thought. See also Wilder, "New Testament Studies, 1920–
1950." Wilder's contributions to NT studies are described in Crossan, A Fragile Craft.

The Language of the Gospel is parable. Wilder broke with the dominant view of parable as a "pedagogical strategy" and argued that, like the art forms of any age, parables convey basic assumptions about existence. He sees Jesus' language as primarily metaphoric and writes:

> A simile sets one thing over against another: the less known is clarified by that which is better known. But in the metaphor we have an image with a certain shock to the imagination which directly conveys vision of what is signified.[15]

Shortly after Wilder's work, Funk published "The Parable as Metaphor," also a landmark in parable exegesis.[16] Funk integrates insights from secular literary criticism, from the later Heidegger's understanding of language as "the house of being," and from the German "new hermeneutic" school (especially Ernst Fuchs and Gerhard Ebeling), with its stress on the sayings of Jesus as language events that do not communicate primarily the teaching of Jesus but his own self-understanding and his radical challenge to others. Funk begins with Dodd's definition of parable and argues that in a metaphor two discrete but not entirely comparable elements are juxtaposed and that this juxtaposition produces an impact upon the imagination and induces a vision of reality that cannot be conveyed by discursive speech. What is pointed to by the metaphorical predication is ultimately beyond the power of language to express; metaphorical language cannot be translated into discursive language but must be experienced so that "interpretation of parables should take place, therefore, in parables."[17]

With Funk and Wilder, and in subsequent writings, "metaphor" is no longer mainly a literary figure but a theological and hermeneutical category. Metaphor is especially suited to express two necessary qualities of religious experience: immediacy and transcendence. A religious experience—that sense of awe in the face of the holy or of being grasped by mystery—is always immediate and individual, and in the great religious literature of human history it is expressed in physical and sensuous imagery. At the same time,

---

15. Wilder, *Language*, 80.
16. Funk, *Language, Hermeneutic*, 133–62. See the discussion of Wilder and Funk in Perrin, *Jesus and the Language*, 127–41.
17. Funk, *Language, Hermeneutic*, 196.

religious experience involves a sense of being drawn out of oneself
to the transcendent and confesses the limits of language to express
the experience.

As metaphors, the parables of Jesus point to an order of reality
other than that described in the parable. Often it is an element of
the parable itself, such as the extraordinary harvest (Mark 4:8) or
the order of payment (Matt. 20:8), where the ordinary has gone
askew and thereby shocks us into realizing that the parables lead
into another way of thinking about life. Jesus thus spoke a language
of the familiar and concrete which touched people in their everyday
lives but which pointed beyond itself and summoned people to see
everyday life as the carrier of self-transcendence. Therefore a great
number of Jesus' parables are explicitly kingdom parables, and many
scholars locate all the parables in the context of the kingdom
proclamation. The message of the kingdom, which itself, as Perrin
notes, is a "tensive symbol," is that God is powerful and active and
that the world is in a process of transformation.[18] The new age has
begun and God has entered history in a new way. In effect, the
message of the kingdom is that the world points beyond itself. The
use of parable with the native power of metaphor to point beyond
itself means that in effect the medium is the message. Jesus himself
is parable; so also the Gospel presentations of him. Thus, theological
language is radically parabolic.[19]

While reflection on the parable as metaphor continues, a number
of cautions are in order. First, it is not totally accurate to equate the
parables of Jesus with metaphor. For the most part, parables are
extended similes, since they have an introductory "like" or "it may
be compared to." More important, the word "metaphor" is normally
found in the predication of an image or attribute in a sentence (e.g.,
you are the salt of the earth), while the parables are extended
narratives. More properly, parables should be called "metaphoric,"
since it is the dynamics of metaphor rather than the figure itself
which empowers them. Generically they are "stories" or narratives,
so that Paul Ricoeur's description of parables as a combination of

18. Perrin, *Jesus and the Language,* 196.
19. Metaphor and parable have become a vital part of contemporary exegesis and
theology. The historical Jesus, the Jesus of Mark, and the Gospel of Mark itself have
all been called parabolic. See McFague, *Metaphorical Theology,* 42–66; Kelber, *Oral
and Written Gospel,* 117–29; and below, chap. 5, n. 4.

the metaphoric process with the narrative form is the most adequate way of talking about the parables as metaphors.[20] Second, there has been an escalation of theological language about parable and metaphor. One hears phrases such as metaphor shattering worlds, creating new visions, and calling existence into question.[21] The impression arises that at times salvation comes from metaphor alone! Often there is a carry-over from the referent of metaphor to the language itself. Jesus' language is powerful, not because of its aesthetic brilliance or paradoxical quality, but because of the experience of God it mediates and the kind of life Jesus himself lived. What he spoke of in parable he lived. For example, one can think of his association with tax collectors, sinners, and other marginal groups as an enacted parable of the Lost Sheep (Luke 15:1–7). Finally, while studies drawing on contemporary literary criticism have been most fruitful for understanding parables, comparison of parables with the literary genres of antiquity indicates that they are very close to proverbs and maxims which form so much of the wisdom tradition of antiquity. Madeleine Boucher has cogently argued that the rhetorical dimension of parables should not be abandoned.[22] They did function in teaching and argumentation, even if the content is not as broad and simple as Jülicher argued.

An Afterthought on Parable and Allegory

An enduring aspect of Jülicher's legacy has been a polemic against allegory. Allegory is faulted on two major grounds: (*a*) it gives independent significance to details of the parable, and (*b*) the interpretation of these details is determined not by their original context or meaning but by the way they function as coded language to illustrate the already held beliefs of the interpreter. Allegory illustrates meaning rather than creates it.[23] Allegory also allows for an almost infinite variety of arbitrary interpretations. At the same time, allegory is "a protean device, omnipresent in Western literature," and is undoubtedly like metaphor, since it says one thing and

20. Ricoeur, "Biblical Hermeneutics," 29–145, esp. 30–33.
21. Tolbert (*Perspectives*, 42–43) criticizes such "inflated language."
22. Boucher, *Parables*, 32–40.
23. For the standard criticisms of allegory, see Dodd, *Parables*, 2–9; Jeremias, *Parables*, 19–22; D.O. Via, *Parables*, 2–25; and Crossan, "Parable as Religious and Poetic Experience."

means another.[24] Yet the adamant rejection is not fair to NT parables or to the manner in which they can be represented.

Many of the images in the parables, such as king, vineyard, and servant, have overtones from their biblical heritage which suggest that in these cases the individual elements may in fact stand for something else, such as God, Israel, or the prophets. While it may be true to say that the parables do not have a virtually unlimited sequence of applications, the "unpacking" of possible OT allusions or references does not constitute allegorizing. Also it is more accurate to speak of "one central focus" in the parables than "a single point of application." Especially in the narrative parables the secondary characters, such as the older brother (Luke 15:25–32), are an important part of the dynamics of the parable. As a poetic and literary form, parables also allow multiple interpretations.

Finally, Jülicher and his successors, while understandably wary about the use of allegory to buttress dogmatic principles, were not open enough to the power of allegory. Allegory is the mainstay of apocalyptic literature, as the Book of Revelation testifies, and is often an index that a community is undergoing persecution.[25] In some Christian communities, such as the black church, allegory has remained a vibrant form of proclamation. Perhaps some distinctions are in order that would nuance Jülicher's view. First, one must distinguish between allegorical interpretation of nonallegorical material and the detection and proper interpretation of allegorical material such as OT allusions or common cultural conventions, such as the use of sowing for preaching (cf. 1 Cor. 3:5–9). One must also distinguish between *proper* and *improper* use of allegory in proclamation. In the light of Funk's oft-quoted statement that a parable can be interpreted only by a parable, interpretation of parables also by allegories cannot be ruled out.[26] The criterion of proper interpretation is not the genre chosen but whether the interpretation is faithful to the original meaning and context(s) of the parable.

From a literary perspective, therefore, parables are metaphoric in

---

24. Fletcher, *Allegory*. Among NT scholars, Boucher argues most strongly that parable and allegory are similar. See also, Klauck, *Allegorie und Allegorese*; and Weder, *Die Gleichnisse Jesu als Metaphern*. See the discussion of these works by Carlston, "Parable and Allegory Revisited."
25. Fletcher, *Allegory*, 22.
26. Funk, *Language, Hermeneutic*, 196.

combining in one assertion two orders of reality and in using the language of concrete imagery to suggest an analogy or comparison with the thing signified. Theologically, metaphor and parable become the language par excellence for theology, since they point beyond what is expressed to what is beyond expression. For this reason the making of metaphors is unceasing. The metaphoric nature of parables has implications for the manner in which they are represented in proclamation. First, engagement with the concrete metaphor is essential. The parables are not carriers of ideas where the image is the husk to be discarded in the quest for the kernel of meaning. The nuances and implications of the images must be unfolded in the manner in which Ricoeur presents a meditation on finding while reflecting on the pearl of great price (Matt. 13:45–46).[27] It is also necessary to unsediment "dead" metaphors. Like treasures hidden at the bottom of the sea, the images of the Gospels are encrusted with centuries of interpretation and must shine anew. Finally, the preacher must allow the parable to exercise its own power on the hearers and not be reduced to moral precepts or theological ideas.

". . . drawn from nature or common life"

While metaphor provides the fundamental category for understanding parables, the other elements of Dodd's definition throw light on the special characteristics of Gospel parables. While metaphor tells us that the use of images points to another order of reality, the realism of the parables tells us that the raw material of Jesus' language was the everyday world of nature and human activity. In contrast to much similar literature, such as Hellenistic fables or even the stylized debates of the rabbinic parables, the parables of Jesus are characterized by realism. Through the parables we are given a glimpse of the everyday life of first-century Galilee: the world of farming and fishing, of weddings and feasts, of landed gentry and restive tenants, of travelers knocking in the night, and of a widow standing up to a callous judge. It is a world without cosmetic adornment where even the hero of the parable can be a pragmatic schemer (Luke 16:1–8) or a seemingly capricious landowner (Matt. 20:1–16). Much of the appeal of the parables comes from their concreteness. They embody

27. Ricoeur, "Listening to the Parables of Jesus," 239–45.

that quality of great literature which William Wimsatt has called the "concrete universal" where a work of literature or art presents "an object which in a mysterious and special way is both highly general and highly particular."[28] The parables present stories about ordinary individuals and ordinary events, but told in such a way that people from every age and culture have seen their own life with its hopes and challenges replayed in these short vignettes.

With his accustomed insight Wilder has underscored the religious significance of this realism:

> In the realism of the parables we recognize Jesus the layman. It is not only human life that is observed, but nature as well or man in nature. This realism, moreover, has to do with things going on. This is a world in which as a matter of course things happen, men and women do things, one thing leads to another. And all this is real and significant. Jesus, without saying so, by his very way of presenting man shows that for him man's destiny is at stake in his ordinary, creaturely existence, domestic, economic and social. This is the way God made him. The world is real. Time is real. Man is a toiler and an "acter" and a chooser. We have stories indeed, but they are close to things as they are.[29]

The realism of the parables means that Jesus places the point of contact between God and human beings in the everyday world of human experience. The Jesus of the parables does not speak God language, and even the language of his religious heritage, the Hebrew Bible, is rarely quoted. The parabolic language of Jesus is therefore potentially available to all who have ears to hear. The scandal of the realistic language is a counterpart to the emptying of Jesus in the incarnation as found in an early Christian hymn (Phil. 2:5–11). The parables claim that the arena in which God summons human beings to the risk of decision is the world of everyday existence, that same world in which the life of Jesus unfolded in dialogue with the mystery of God.

The realism of the parables, with its theological and christological implications, affects the way the parables should be proclaimed. Often, much Christian proclamation is ineffective because it speaks a religious dialect which becomes unintelligible to many both inside

---

28. Wimsatt, *The Verbal Icon*, 71.
29. Wilder, *Language*, 82.

and outside the community. The secularity of the parables remains a caution against placing an unnatural divorce between the "Sunday morning" world of religious life and the world of daily human exchange. Ultimately nothing is purely religious or purely secular. Jesus took up in his parables the daily experiences of his hearers and let them see in these the bearers of God's presence. Preachers not only must hear the words of Scripture but must hear the hearers of the Word. Paradoxically, then, in presenting the parables it is not enough simply to restate or paraphrase the parables. The vibrancy of the original images must be recaptured often in language as realistic as the original language. Even the old wine of the parables must shatter new wineskins.

"... arresting the hearer by its vividness or strangeness"

The realism of the parables is but one side of the coin. In terms of image and subject matter the parables are realistic, but in the unfolding of the parable the realism is shattered. Funk says that the parables present disorientation of everydayness, exaggerated realism, distended concreteness, incompatible elements often subtly drawn— which prohibit the parable from coming to rest in the literal sense.[30] Ricoeur observes that the parables follow a pattern of orientation, disorientation, and reorientation.[31] A prime key to the meaning of a parable arises when the realism of the parable begins to break down. The harvest is truly extravagant (Mark 4:8), the mustard tree is not really "the greatest of all shrubs" (Mark 4:32), and fathers in a first-century Near Eastern environment do not run (Luke 15:20).

This aspect has been developed in Crossan's series of intriguing and literate presentations of the parables.[32] In almost every case Crossan sees the parable as presenting a paradox, a seeming absurdity which conceals a deeper truth. The one who loses life will save it; unless you are born "from above" you cannot enter the kingdom. The paradoxical language of Jesus is, for Crossan, an extension of the prohibition of images of God in biblical thought. God cannot be

---

30. Funk, *Language, Hermeneutic,* 160–61.
31. Ricoeur, "Biblical Hermeneutics," 122–28; see also McFague, *Metaphorical Theology,* 46–47.
32. See my Bibliography for Crossan's major works.

captured by a verbal image any more than by a plastic one. For Crossan, the most fundamental message of Jesus' parables is that things are not as they seem, that you must be open to having your tidy vision of reality shattered. By their paradoxical qualities the parables become metaphors of the transcendent. Only when one stands before the limits of language is one able to accept the advent of God's kingdom as gift.

Allied to the insights of Crossan are those of Ricoeur, upon whom Crossan draws and who is also concerned with the strangeness of the parables. After describing parables as a combination of the narrative form with the metaphoric process, Ricoeur turns to the question of why parabolic language is "religious." The language of the parables is paradoxical and exaggerated (hyperbolic) and at the same time realistic. It is thus an instance of "extravagance which interrupts the superbly peaceful course of action and which constitutes what I have called the extraordinary within the ordinary."[33] No particular genre or type of language is religious of itself; it becomes religious when a particular use of it is pushed beyond its immediate significations to the point of the wholly other. Thus religious language is "limit language" not in the sense of imposing limits but in the sense of pushing toward the limits of intelligibility where one stands at the threshold of mystery. For Ricoeur, the extravagance and paradox of the parables, and their ability to disorient and reorient our lives, are a sign that religious language "dislocates our project of making a whole of our lives—a project which St. Paul identifies with the act of 'self-glorification,' or, in short, 'salvation by works.' "[34] It is this trait which transforms the parables into a poetics of faith. Parable thus provides a bridge between the proclamation of Jesus and the theology of Paul.

In presenting parables, then, the preacher must recapture their religious dimension. Though realistic and pointing beyond themselves to the self-disclosure of God, this realism and referential character must not be allowed to compromise their strangeness and mystery. The revelation of God in parable cannot be reduced to a series of theological platitudes or moral maxims. Here we touch on one of the major problems of preaching on the parables: the tendency to

33. Ricoeur, "Biblical Hermeneutics," 118.
34. Ibid., 125.

soften their shock by moralizing them, that is, turning the good news into good advice. Though the parables take the sphere of human action and present vivid pictures of good and evil acts, as religious language they present not simply a series of ethical paradigms or exhortations, though they are often so interpreted, but a *vision of reality which becomes a presupposition to ethics*. We will note this in detail in the following chapters; here a few general instances will suffice.

The parables join together what we would normally pull asunder: unforgivable debt with unlimited forgiveness; rebellion with acceptance; the outsider with the insider. The presupposition to a Christian ethic is to hear the message of the parables which often shatters the preconceived world of rights and duties, sin and virtue, and opens us to the advent of God's kingdom as gift, a gift that can then be expressed in action. Jesus proclaimed the parables in the context of the kingdom: God's entry into history with an offer of forgiveness to the "sick" and the marginal. And the church proclaimed the parables in the context of "gospel": the narrative of Jesus' life as a testimony to this gift and a sign of its power. Parabolic preaching must retain some of the vividness and strangeness of the parables. It must itself find a limit language of paradox whereby people who hear that things are not the way they seem to be may experience what they have not dared to hope.

". . . leaving the mind in sufficient doubt about its precise application to tease it into active thought"

The final component of Dodd's definition describes the openendedness of the parables or what, in contemporary terms, has been called their polyvalence, that is, their ability to admit of multiple interpretations.[35] For example, is the "point" of the parable of the Pearl (Matt. 13:45–46) the search, the joy of finding, or the willingness to risk all? Rather than claiming that the parable allows only one point of application that can be recovered with absolute certainty, commentators now admit that parables admit of multiple meanings. This is evident in the NT itself where different evangelists give a parable a different interpretation. For Matthew (Matt. 18:12–14),

35. See esp. Tolbert, *Perspectives*.

the Lost Sheep functions to exhort church leaders to care for the weak in the community; in Luke, it justifies Jesus' mission to the lost (Luke 15:4–7).

Another reason for the polyvalence of the parables is their dialogic nature. Whether spoken to confront opponents or to encourage disciples, the parables take up the world of the hearer. Eta Linnemann's concept of "interlocking" provides a creative way of describing the parable as dialogue which engages the hearer.[36] For Linnemann, the parables "work" because the world of the hearer is somehow reproduced in the parable. The Pharisees, for example, knew of God's mercy and reflected on the necessity of works of charity. In a parable such as the Laborers in the Vineyard it is precisely the values that Jesus shares with the Pharisees and that reappear in the parable which enable the parable to have its shock effect.

The classic example of such interlocking is the parable of the ewe lamb in 2 Sam. 12:1–4 along with the following dialogue of vv. 5–10. This parable follows the section in which after his adultery with Bathsheba and the impending birth of a child, David stages the death of her husband Uriah. The prophet Nathan then tells the parable of a man who possessed "one little ewe lamb," which is described in the language of tender care for a child (he brought it up, it grew up with him and his children, it used to eat his morsels, drink from his cup, and lie in his bosom, and it was like a daughter to him, 2 Sam. 12:3). In contrast there was a rich man who had many herds. When a traveler came, the rich man took the poor man's lamb and prepared it for the traveler. In a moment of startling obtuseness David then roars that the rich man should die, and Nathan exclaims, "You are the man." The question of David's reaction is closely connected with David's sin. His sin is not the more obvious one of murder or adultery but one of injustice and violation of a trust. As king he is bound to uphold justice in the land and to care for the weak. It is for this reason that he reacts so violently to the manifestation of brutal power by the rich man in the parable. It is this world of injustice and concern for the weak in society which is taken up into Nathan's parable. David's sin was equally an exercise of brutal power—"might

---

36. Linnemann, *Jesus*, 23–30.

makes right"—and a violation of all the norms of justice by which society was held together. The parable functions for David like a trap. His world and its values appear in the parable, and the moment of revelation comes when the prophet summons David to see himself in the parable. The parable of the Two Debtors which Jesus tells to Simon the Pharisee (Luke 7:41–43) functions in similar fashion as a trap and elicits a grudging acceptance from Simon. So too today, when we read the parable of the Pharisee and the Tax Collector (Luke 18:9–14) and smugly identify with the humble prayer of the tax collector, we are in effect adopting the attitude of the Pharisee, "I am not like others" (Luke 18:11, au. trans.).

The parable is a question waiting for an answer, an invitation waiting for a response. It does not really "exist" or function until it is freely appropriated. Theologically this means that the parable is a form of discourse that appeals not only to the fascination of the human imagination with metaphor, or to the joyous perception of a surprise or paradox, but to the most basic of human qualities: freedom. Jesus chose a form of discourse that appealed to human freedom and risked himself with human freedom. The narratives in the Gospels where Jesus is challenged to give an authenticating sign (e.g., Mark 8:11–13), as well as the taunt "Come down now from the cross, that we may see and believe" (Mark 15:32) show that the language and life of Jesus was an appeal to a free response and did not compromise freedom for the sake of adherence or commitment.

This aspect of the parables has implications for how the parables are presented today. The preacher or teacher is faced with the challenge of interpreting an ancient text, that is, giving people enough information that they can hear the text and see that it has meaning for their lives today. The normal tendency is to offer an application, and usually this is in the moral arena. People are exhorted to be good Samaritans or to return to God in repentance after wandering in a far country. Such preaching, however, too often presents a closure on the potential polyvalence of the parable. For the parable to be open-ended and to have the world of the hearer of today taken up in a parable, people almost need "permission" to identify with the less attractive characters in the parable, to grumble with the vineyard workers or feel the chagrin of the elder brother, and thereby open themselves to the message of judgment or forgiveness. Rather than presenting the parables with immediate applications, it might be better for preachers and readers to leave the parable open-ended and ambiguous. The risk of freedom must be taken by those who preach and by those who hear the parables.

THE PARABLE AS NARRATIVE

As noted, the term "parable" is applied to a wide variety of literary forms from short comparisons to longer stories. In contemporary scholarship and proclamation, parable most often describes the longer narratives. A recent description of a short story provides a striking parallel to the way scholars speak of the narrative parables:

> It [the short story] is fiercely condensed, almost like a lyric poem; it explodes in a burst of revelation or illumination; it confines itself to a single over-powering incident: it bears symbolic weight.[37]

Therefore study of the parables has concentrated not only on their metaphorical quality but on how narrative analysis contributes to interpretation. Such an investigation has taken two major directions. One, called structuralism or semiotics, attempts, under the influence of Russian formalism and French structuralism, to write a narrative grammar of the parables.[38] The other, often called rhetorical criticism, general literary criticism, or aesthetic criticism, uses modes of literary criticism widely used by secular scholars working on ancient or contemporary literary texts.[39] While the first method has issued in a number of significant studies, to approach the parables in this manner requires mastery of a specialized and technical vocabulary and a method of exegesis that is a virtual sub-discipline in NT studies. The second uses a vocabulary that is more intelligible to both the specialist and the generalist—"plot," "character," "point of view"—even though these terms usually have a highly specialized meaning for a given critic. It also offers a method that can be more easily adapted to a wide variety of biblical material. This second approach informs the present work.

37. Howe and Howe, *Short Shorts*, ix. Both the introduction by Irving Howe (ix–xvii), which develops this definition, and the collected stories offer an excellent approach to parabolic narrative.
38. See esp. the treatments in *Semeia* 1 (1974). Perkins uses aspects of this method in treating individual parables (*Hearing*, 52–54).
39. Perkins, *Hearing*, 50–52; and Robertson, s.v. "Literature, The Bible as," *IDB Sup*.

A major contribution to narrative analysis of the parables are the "narrative laws" evolved by Rudolf Bultmann through comparison of the parables with other folk literature.[40] They touch on three major aspects of the parables: narrative style, characterization, and plot or the manner in which the narrative unfolds. Stylistically *the parables are characterized* by the following:

- The narration is concise—only the necessary people appear and much information is communicated by suggestion.
- Groups of people tend to be treated as single characters.
- The law of stage duality applies—only two characters interact at the same time.
- The hearer is asked to focus on only one perspective at a time.

In terms of *character portrayal* the following apply:

- There is little description in terms of attributes, feelings, or emotions; what people do indicates their characters.
- Rarely are explicit motivations given.
- Secondary characters are not described in any detail.
- Where a window is given into a character, it is often in the form of a soliloquy or of direct speech, often in a question form which engages the reader.

Certain *plot devices* are also present:

- Repetition is a way the action is maintained.
- The parable follows the law of "end stress," with the final verses often containing the denouement.
- There is a lack of conclusion, and certain issues are left unresolved.

These laws convey the cameo quality of the parables where important elements stand out strongly from the background. They also caution against reading too much into the parables through psychologizing, since inadequate information is offered for such approaches. Moreover, they provide a way of unpacking the parables and anticipate much of the contemporary discussion of parables as narrative.

Though analysis of narrative is complex, the guidelines offered by

40. Bultmann, *Synoptic Tradition,* 188–92; see the summary in Linnemann, *Jesus,* 8–16.

two literary critics (Robert Scholes and Robert Kellogg) and by the combined study of a literary critic (Donald Michie) and a NT scholar (David Rhoads) provide a kind of manual for a narrative analysis of the parables.[41] Scholes and Kellogg describe four elements of narrative: meaning, character, plot, and point of view. Rhoads and Michie also treat four elements: rhetoric (the "how" of narrative comprising literary and stylistic devices), setting, plot, and character. Since meaning and point of view best emerge in the study of individual parables, as does the rhetoric, a few comments about plot and character, the constants of narrative analysis, are in order.

Plot

Plot is described as "the arrangement of incidents" (Aristotle *Poetics* 1450b) or as "the dynamic, sequential element in narrative literature."[42] The dynamic element is perceived by careful observation of the actions and movements in the story, and the sequential element focuses on how one part is connected with another either through continuation of a previous part or through anticipation of some future action. As the plot of a story or parable unfolds, it follows a discernible pattern which can be called the story line or structure.

Certain techniques help to uncover the structure and dynamics of the plot. Every story begins with a situation of tension or potential conflict, often indicated by short phrases such as "A man . . . had two sons" (Luke 15:11) or "A man going on a journey called his servants and entrusted to them his property" (Matt. 25:14). In each case the readers' curiosity is captured; each phrase spawns further questions—what about the two sons? what happened while the man was away? The drama of the plot consists in the intersection of elements which either further or impede the resolution of the tension, and here attention to the minor characters is important. In describing plot and structure, it is helpful to divide a parable into acts or scenes which are often indicated by time changes or by the arrival of new characters. One should also ask how a scene is both like and unlike the ones that precede and follow, and juxtaposition and contrast of scenes are a help to discerning plot development. Another important

---

41. Scholes and Kellogg, *Narrative*. See Scholes, *Elements of Fiction*, for an introduction to narrative analysis; for the NT, see Rhoads and Michie, *Mark as Story*.
42. Scholes and Kellogg, *Narrative*, 207.

clue for unlocking plot development has been suggested by Mary Ann Tolbert. She looks at the places where narrative or narrative discourse shifts to dialogue or direct discourse.[43] This occurs often at dramatically important places in the parables. Careful attention should be given to the presence of one of the most prevalent narrative devices of antiquity, the overarching structure of A, B, A' or, in its more developed form of chiasm, A, B, C, B', A' and other concentric patterns.[44]

A final element of plot development concerns the general movement of the plot, whether it is "tragic" or "comic," categories introduced into the discussion by Dan O. Via's groundbreaking work. In a tragic plot the character moves from good fortune to bad usually through some character flaw or misguided judgment, and usually arrives too late at some recognition of the cause of the fall. Comedy not only involves the opposite movement from a situation of threat or danger to one of well-being but often pokes fun at the more serious side of human conduct. The parables of Jesus offer examples of both tragic (e.g., the Unmerciful Servant, Matt. 18:23–35) and comic plots (e.g., the Unjust Steward, Luke 16:1–8).[45]

Character

Characters are agents (actors or "doers") in a narrative, the people about whom the story is told and whose actions or speech or failure to act and speak make the plot move. Characterization refers to the way a narrator brings characters to life in a narrative. The narrator achieves characterization by telling us what the characters are like through explicit description (e.g., the judge who neither feared God nor regarded man, Luke 18:1) or by showing, that is, letting the character emerge from his or her actions or speech (as in the case of the shepherd or the woman in Luke 15:1–10).[46] Characters tend to be either "rounded," with well-developed and individualized traits, or "flat," with undeveloped or typical and predictable traits. In every narrative there are main characters (e.g., the king and the unmerciful

---

43. Tolbert, *Perspectives*, 74–78; adopted by Perkins in *Hearing*.
44. See Dewey, *Markan Public Debate*, 5–39, for discussion of this technique and other aspects of rhetorical criticism.
45. D.O. Via, *Parables*, 137–44; 155–62.
46. On the distinction between showing and telling, see Rhoads and Michie, *Mark as Story*, 101.

servant, Matt. 18:23–35) and secondary characters (e.g., the fellow servant[s], Matt. 18:29, 31), determined either by their perdurance throughout the narrative or by their importance to the dramatic structure of the plot.

In the case of the parables, characterization normally comes through showing rather than telling, and the individuals involved have a minimum of personality traits. Moral descriptions such as "foolish" (Matt. 25:2) or "unjust" (Luke 16:8) are the exception rather than the rule. One of the important tasks in defining the central character in the parable is to ask upon whom the plot centers or whose actions determine the further unfolding of the plot. Often the traditional titles given to the parables (e.g., the Prodigal Son, the Wicked Tenants, etc.) obscure the main character and distort plot development.[47] Another important locale for characterization is soliloquy or interior monologue where the narrator gives the reader a glimpse into the thoughts of the characters.[48]

Narrative analysis of plot and character provide another entree to the parable as text. As with the study of the elements of parable, so narrative analysis yields a theological reflection with implications for pastoral presentation of the parables. Most fundamentally, the parables as narrative are a vivid instance of the narrative quality of biblical revelation. While we would not claim that the Bible is all narrative, it is the stories of the Bible which give it its distinctive shape. A people freed from Egypt told and preserved the stories, and the stories formed and preserved a people during centuries of exile and oppression. The stories became Torah and Testament for Jew and Christian, and both claim that they must return often to these stories to find their heritage and their hope. The Judeo-Christian vision is enshrined in narrative, and the narrative quality of this vision precludes reduction of it to a collection of ideas about God or a structured ideology. The narrative quality of Christian revelation is also allied to its public character. The parables told by Jesus about the kingdom of God, and the Gospel stories told by the church about Jesus as the anointed (Christ) of God, have a transcultural, universal appeal. Though from a particular time and place, they are retold in

47. Even though one of the major thrusts of my book is to challenge the traditional titles of the parables, I will continue to use them for ease of reference and familiarity.
48. Scholes and Kellogg, *Narrative,* 177.

every time and place. The parables of Jesus prod the religious complacency of the industrialized and prosperous First World and give hope to oppressed minorities that the blind rich will be brought low (see Luke 16:19–31).

As in so many other aspects of parable research, it was Amos Wilder who got to the heart of the religious significance of narrative. He notes that "the narrative mode is uniquely important in Christianity" and that Christian faith is confessed simply by the recital of the story of the Bible. The effect is that "the life of a Christian is not like a dream shot through with visions and illuminations, but a pilgrimage, a race, in short, a history. The new Christian speech inevitably took the form of a story."[49] Human life itself is a story lived out in time where memory re-creates the past and hope envisions a future. To read a parable or a Gospel is to align our stories with those told by Jesus and about him. The path *from* parable *to* gospel though shrouded in historical darkness is no less secure.

The narrative parables should then be proclaimed as narrative. The one challenged to preach the parables is often tempted to give either the "point" or the application of the parable without leading others through the drama of the parable. The story must be re-presented before it can be truly present. Often this is best done by a paraphrase of the story after indicating some of the elements of plot and character that may allow the story to be heard in a fresh way. In place of Martin Dibelius's famous adage about Christian literature, "In the beginning was the sermon," we might say, "In the beginning was the story."[50]

THE PARABLE AS CONTEXT

There is really no such thing as an absolute meaning to a parable. As a mode of discourse it was originally a communication between a speaker, Jesus, and any number of potential hearers. It existed in the social context of Jesus' ministry and the religious context of his mission and proclamation. As metaphors the parables point beyond this context to another order of reality. In a sense the original context of the parables is irretrievable, since we can never be in the historical

---

49. Wilder, *Language,* 64–65.
50. Dibelius, "Die alttestamentlichen Motive in der Leidensgeschichte des Petrus- und des Johannes-Evangeliums," in *Botschaft und Geschichte* 1:223.

position of Jesus' audience. The original context is always a reconstruction and this reconstruction involves a whole series of judgments
about the life and ministry of Jesus.[51]

Since almost all NT scholars hold that Jesus proclaimed the kingdom
of God, the parables are often viewed in this context. The recent
study of John Riches, *Jesus and the Transformation of Judaism*, provides
an excellent example of the way in which continued study of the
kingdom helps us to understand better the teaching of Jesus.[52]
Riches's work represents an advance over earlier studies by uncovering the social context of kingdom statements as well as their
theological meaning. Following Gerd Theissen, he notes that Jesus
stands among the many reform movements active in first-century
Judaism.[53] Neither Riches nor Theissen, however, devotes much
space to a study of the social setting of the parables or the social
settings and values within the parables themselves. Nor will the
present study do this. It should, however, be on the agenda for
continued study of the parables.

The context that is of prime interest to us is the literary context of
the parables in the three Synoptic Gospels. This explains this section's
emphasis on the parable *as context* rather than *in context*. In the
Gospels the parables are texts that are to be read "along with" other
texts. What we propose is "an expanding contextual analysis." This
will involve first attention to the immediate context of each parable,
study of the pericopes preceding and following to see whether the
location of a parable provides a clue to the evangelists' intentions.
Similarly, the proximate context is important. That is, how does the
parable in its immediate context fit into the larger context of a section
of a Gospel (e.g., the Lukan travel narrative [Luke 9:51—19:27] or
the Matthean apocalyptic discourse [Matthew 24—25]). Following
the principle that Scripture should be interpreted through Scripture,
the final context will be the canonical context, in which we will ask
whether the parable has points of contact with perspectives, motifs,

---

51. As noted (see above, n. 2), the major figure in this reconstruction was Jeremias.
The "new hermeneutic" which followed the work of Jeremias used the parables as a
window to Jesus' understanding of human existence, and this approach has been
continued in the work of Crossan, Breech, and Scott (see above, n. 3).

52. See above, n. 3; see also Chilton, *God in Strength*.

53. Theissen, *Sociology of Early Palestinian Christianity*.

or themes found in other parts of Scripture. Obviously the enterprise here will be suggestive rather than exhaustive.

Two other contexts can be simply mentioned as areas for further investigation. One would be what German scholars call the *Wirkungsgeschichte* of a parable, that is, a history of its effect or impact on theology and church life. Often the way the Christian community has handed on the story of the parables is a mirror of its own story. The final context is that in which we read, appropriate, and proclaim the parables. Here we are touching on the much larger question of a full-blown theory of hermeneutics and the way in which we as readers actually confer meaning on the parables. Such reflection would lead us to dialogue with those who are employing the "reader response" theorists in literary criticism and the insights of Hans Georg Gadamer in theological hermeneutics.[54] Despite the extensive number of works published on the parables, much remains to be done. Without attempting a full-blown hermeneutical justification, we will occasionally suggest ways in which a given parable in context may have a bearing on our contemporary context.

54. For a discussion of reader response criticism or "reception theory" by a literary critic, see Eagleton, *Literary Theory*; 74–88; by NT scholars, Keegan, *Interpreting the Bible*; and Fowler, "Who Is 'the Reader' of Mark's Gospel?" 31–54. See also McFague, *Metaphorical Theology*, 56–66 (on Gadamer).

2

THE
PARABLES
OF
MARK

INTRODUCTION

Commentators generally identify six Markan parables: the Sower
(4:3–8), the Seed Growing Secretly (4:26–29), the Mustard Seed
(4:30–32), the Wicked Tenants (12:1–11), the Fig Tree (13:28–29),
and the Doorkeeper (13:34–37).[1] Mark also contains a large number
of parabolic sayings, such as the Sons of the Bridechamber (2:19–
20), the Patched Garment and the Old Wineskins (2:21–22), the
Beelzebul parables (3:23–27; called explicitly *parabolai* in Mark
3:23), the things that defile (7:14–15; also called a *parabolē*, 7:17),
and the sayings of Mark 4:21–25. Mark uses the term *parabolē*
thirteen times, to describe short comparisons (3:23–27), longer
narratives (4:3–9; 12:1–9), riddles (4:11; 7:17; cf. 10:25), and
illustration or meaning of the parable (13:28, "From the fig tree
learn the parable" [RSV: "learn its lesson"]), as well as allegory
(4:13–20; 13:34–37).[2] Two of the six Markan parables are explicitly
called kingdom parables (4:26–29, 30–32), and all except the Seed
Growing Secretly are taken over by Matthew and Luke. The world
of the Markan parables is that of the village, and their images come
from farming and the processes of nature.[3] Mark has only one
dramatic parable (i.e., where characters interact, 12:1–9) which does

---

1. Kelber (*Oral and Written Gospel*, 58–59) calls these "parabolic stories."
2. Boucher, *Mysterious Parable*, 17–25.
3. Goulder. "Characteristics of the Parables." 51–53.

not stand in one of the two great blocks of teaching material (chaps. 4 and 13). My approach will be to study the six major parables as "texts" and then to ask how they fit into the major theological themes of the Gospel of Mark.

PARABLES AND THE
MYSTERY OF THE KINGDOM:
MARK 4

A cursory glance at Mark 4 discloses a composition of different elements.[4]

4:1–2   An elaborate, scenic introduction

4:3–9   The parable of the Sower

4:10–12 Private instruction on the reason for speaking in parables to "those who were about him with the twelve"

4:13–20 The allegory of the seeds

4:21–25 Four sayings that have parallels in the Q tradition (i.e., material common to Mark and Luke, but not in Matthew);[5]

4:26–29 The parable of the Seed Growing Secretly

4:30–32 The parable of the Mustard Seed

4:33–34 Concluding sayings on the reason for speaking in parables.

---

4. The literature on Mark 4 and esp. on 4:10–12 is vast. See the following: Boucher, *Mysterious Parable*, 42–63; Bowker, "Mystery and Parable: Mark iv. 1–20"; Carlston, *Parables*, 97–109, 137–162; Dahl, "The Parables of Growth"; Lambrecht, *Once More Astonished*, 84–109; Marcus, *The Mystery of the Kingdom of God*; idem, "Mark 4:10–12 and Marcan Epistemology"; and Trocmé, "Why Parables?"

5. Throughout this work I follow the generally admitted "two source theory"— that Matthew and Luke in composing their Gospels used as a source Mark and a collection, mainly of sayings of Jesus (roughly 235 verses), not found in Mark, which has been called Q. The classic exposition of this theory in English is Streeter, *The Four Gospels*. See also Kümmel, *Introduction*. This theory has been attacked in recent years, especially by Farmer (*The Synoptic Problem* and "Modern Developments"). The attacks exact more from the two source theory than the data allow. Also, adherents of the two source theory generally admit that traditions often existed in both written and oral forms, so that, for example, Matthew and Luke, even when following Mark, could have access to an earlier oral version of a given saying. For a strong defense of the two source theory, see Fitzmyer, "The Priority of Mark and the Q Source in Luke." Excellent commentaries on the Q material are Edwards, *A Theology of Q*; and Manson, *Sayings*. See also Kingsbury, *Jesus Christ in Matthew, Mark and Luke*, 1–27. For a survey of recent theories of composition within Q, see Kloppenborg, *The Formation of Q*, esp. 41–101; and "Tradition and Redaction in the Synoptic Sayings Source"; also Neirynck, "Recent Developments in the Study of Q."

Aspects of Mark 4 suggest composition from elements of different traditions: the elaborate introduction of 4:1–2 with the threefold emphasis on the *teaching* of Jesus (4:1, he began to teach; 4:2a, he taught them in parables; and 4:2b, in his teaching he said to them); in 4:1–2 Jesus is teaching publicly, while in 4:10–12 he teaches his disciples privately; the audience shifts—in 4:33 he seems to be addressing the crowds again, while in 4:35 he speaks to the disciples. There are different introductory formulas, such as "he said to them" (4:2, 11, 13, 21, 24, 33) and simply "he said" (4:26, 30). While only one parable is given in 4:3–9, in 4:10 the disciples ask Jesus "concerning the parables." At first glance the statement in 4:11–12 that the parables were given to outsiders to prevent their hearing conflicts with the statement in 4:33 that Jesus adapted his parabolic teaching to the hearing of the crowds. The material of the chapter is also diverse: three seed parables united by catchwords (sowing, 4:3, 4, 31, 32; seed, 4:26, 31); a saying based on Isa. 6:9–10 which itself is used in different contexts in the NT (Acts 28:26; John 12:40); an allegory of the seeds (4:13–20) which may have followed 4:3–9 in the pre-Markan tradition; and four gnomic sayings which are well attested both in the Q tradition and (for three of them) in the *Gospel of Thomas*.[6]

Structure of Mark 4

Mark 4 has a clear structure where the important material in the center of the chapter is bracketed or framed by similar material—a technique extensively used in other parts of Mark. For example, in 3:20–21 [22–30] 31–35, the Beelzebul controversy and the saying about sin against the Spirit are framed by narratives of the relationship of Jesus to family and disciples; and in 5:21–24 [25–34] 35–43, the story of a woman who touched Jesus' garment is framed by the cure of the daughter of Jairus.[7] Both Joanna Dewey and Jan Lambrecht have also found instances in Mark 4 of a concentric structure.[8] I will

---

6. On the relation of the Gospel parables to the *Gospel of Thomas*, see below, chap. 3, n. 52. Parallel texts from the *Gospel of Thomas* are listed in Funk, *New Gospel Parallels*, 195–96; and Crossan, *Sayings Parallels*, nos. 47, 115, 144.

7. For a complete list, see Donahue, *Are You the Christ?* 58–59. For their literary function, see Rhoads and Michie, *Mark as Story*, 51.

8. Dewey, *Markan Public Debate*, 147–52; and Lambrecht, *Once More Astonished*, 86–89. My structure, though similar, differs from their proposals.

first indicate my proposed structure and then give the supporting reasons.

A		4:1–2	Introduction	2 vv.	(46 words)
B		4:3–9	Sower	7 vv.	(105)
	C	4:10–12	Reason for speaking in parables	3 vv.	(52)
	D	4:13–20	Allegory of seeds	8 vv.	(146)
	C'	4:21–25	Enigmatic sayings	5 vv.	(74)
B'		4:26–32	Seed parables	7 vv.	(117)
A'		4:33–34	Conclusion	2 vv.	(26)

The chapter is carefully composed in concentric parallelism so that the central motifs are highlighted.[9] The introduction and the Sower (4:1–9, A, B) occupy 9 verses (151 words and 17½ lines of Greek text in the Nestle-Aland 26th edition). The conclusion (4:33–34) and the two preceding parables (4:26–32, B', A') likewise occupy 9 verses (143 words and 17½ lines of text). This quantitative parallelism has a correspondence in content with an introduction (A) followed by a seed parable (B), while the chapter concludes with seed parables (B') and a conclusion by the narrator (A'). The middle section also has a relation of structure and content. Both section C and C' occupy the same space (8 and 8½ lines, 52 and 74 words, respectively), and the longest pericope in the chapter is D' (4:13–20, 146 words and 18½ lines). At the center of this middle section and therefore of chapter 4 as a whole stands the allegory of the seeds (4:13–20).

The first striking element of this structure is that the introduction, conclusion, and seed parables (A, B//A', B') frame the material that is most clearly addressed to the disciples (C/D/C'). The question of the audience in the chapter is obscure. Clearly 4:1–9 is addressed to the crowds with an explicit change of audience in 4:10 ("when he was alone, those who were about him with the twelve"). Commentators generally claim that the rest of the chapter (4:11–32) is then

9. Even though verse counting is an anachronism, since division by verses represents a late addition to the text of the NT, the number of verses gives a rough estimate of the amount of time taken to proclaim a certain text (as in oral performance) or of the space it occupies on a papyrus. My counting of lines is based on the Greek text of Nestle-Aland, 26th edition.

addressed to the disciples.[10] The text, however, does not clearly support this. The conclusion of the chapter (4:33–34), "With many such parables he spoke the word to them," recalls the address to the crowds in 4:2 ("He taught them many things in parables"), and the distinction between teaching "to them" (the crowds) and the disciples (v. 34) recalls a division that runs through the chapter. At 4:26 (the introduction to the Seed Growing Secretly) a change of audience is indicated by the shift from "he said to them" to simply "he said." The formula "to them" (*autois*) does not designate a specific group (disciples versus crowds) but the nearest referent of previous sayings. In 4:11, 13, 21, and 24 it refers to the disciples, while in 4:33 it refers to the "crowds" who have apparently heard the three previous parables (4:26–32). More important, the parables from 4:26–32 are explicitly kingdom parables. In Mark, Jesus proclaims the kingdom publicly and openly (1:15; 3:24; 10:14; 12:34), while its deeper nature is explained to disciples (4:11; 9:1, 47; 10:23–25). The three kingdom parables of chapter 4 are addressed to the crowds.

The material in 4:10–25 is therefore addressed to disciples, and there is also an inner connection between the framing sections 4:10–12 and 4:21–25. While 4:11 presents a favorable view of the disciples—"to you has been given the mystery of the kingdom"—in 4:12 the disciples are warned that they can become outsiders for whom everything happens in riddles. Similarly, 4:21–22 is a positive exhortation to the disciples; 4:23–25 is a warning. The challenge of discipleship is clearly a major concern of the chapter.

While the structure of chapter 4 reflects Mark's composition and interpretation of tradition, its component parts had earlier settings and meanings. In Gospel studies it is customary to distinguish *three settings or stages*: (*a*) the setting of the life of Jesus, (*b*) the setting of the life of the early church, and (*c*) the setting of the evangelist (or author in the case of literature outside the Gospels). While our primary concern is for the third stage, we will now turn to the elements of Mark 4 to study them as independent texts and to suggest some meanings in their settings prior to incorporation into the Gospel.[11]

---

10. See Kelber, *Kingdom in Mark*, 28–41; and Pesch, *Das Markusevangelium* 1:225–28, 266–67.
11. For a discussion of these three stages in the growth of tradition, see Marxsen, *Mark the Evangelist*, 15–29; and Perrin, *What Is Redaction Criticism?*

The Sower (Mark 4:3–9 = Matt. 13:3–9; Luke 8:5–8)

The seed parables of Mark 4 form a relatively independent group, united by both theme and structure (B and B'). The first of these, the Sower, paints a deceptively simple and idyllic picture, narrated in the manner of a folk tale with a minimum of detail and with repetition for effect. In what seems a haphazard manner, a sower scatters seed. The parable describes the failure of three of the sowings: that on the path is devoured by birds (v. 4); that on rocky ground is scorched by the sun because it has no roots (vv. 5–6); and that among the thorns is choked (v. 7). Yet one-fourth of the seed yields a harvest that is not simply bountiful but truly extraordinary, since a tenfold yield was a good harvest, while a yield of 7½ constituted an average one.[12] As a text, the parable is polyvalent; there are different options for interpretation. The common designation of it as the parable of "the Sower" is least apt, for the sower is simply mentioned and does not appear as a dramatic character; he neither rejoices in the bountiful yield nor orders it to be harvested. Nor is it a parable of the four seeds as the allegory of 4:13–20 suggests.

Concentration on different aspects of the parable has yielded fruitful interpretations. Dodd stresses that since a good harvest emerged, Jesus proclaims that *now* is the time to reap the fruit of the harvest.[13] Jeremias calls attention to the difference between the time of sowing and that of harvest as well as to the discrepancy between the three failures and the great harvest.[14] In the parable, then, Jesus assures his disciples that what God has begun in his ministry, despite apparent failure, will have ultimate success. J. Dominic Crossan treats the Sower in conjunction with the Mustard Seed, and while admitting the contrast between the failure and the harvest, he emphasizes the miracle of the harvest rather than its size. This calls attention to the giftlike nature, the graciousness, and the surprise of the advent of the bountiful harvest—all suggestive of the advent of the kingdom.[15] It is like that, surprise and gift.

Closer examination of the movement and images of the parable

---

12. Jeremias, *Parables*, 150 n. 84.
13. Dodd, *Parables*, 145–47.
14. Jeremias, *Parables*, 149–51.
15. Crossan. *In Parables*, 51; see also, idem, "The Seed Parables of Jesus."

suggests another interpretation. The first three sowings convey a rhythmic temporality. Each begins with the mention of a seed, proceeds to the situation that the seed encounters—path, rocky soil, thorns—and concludes with the failure of the seed to mature. The parable does not hurry to its conclusion, and the description of the three sowings takes seventy-three words in the Greek text. The parable achieves a dramatic effect, not by simply listing the three failures in contrast to the one great harvest but by depicting a progression in the growth of the seed. The first seed has virtually no chance of survival and is devoured before any roots are put out. The second seed seems to be growing—"immediately it sprang up" (v. 5)—but withers under the heat of the sun. The third grows higher, to a stage when the buds are almost ready, but is choked off at the last minute. This rhythmic and ascending progression involves the hearer in the unfolding mystery of growth. A natural conclusion to the parable would be that the fourth seed "brought forth grain" and the harvest was good.

The expectation of the hearer is shattered, and the rhythmic progress of nature, which lulls the hearer into acceptance, is broken in v. 8 which, though condensed into twenty-four words, explodes with verbs of motion. The seeds fell (*epesen*) and brought forth (*edidou*) grain, growing up (*anabainonta*), increasing (*auxanomena*), and they yielded (*epheren*) thirtyfold, sixtyfold, and a hundredfold. The contrast between a 75 percent failure and an extraordinary harvest suggests that there is no comparison between the expectation of the kingdom and its effect. But the manner in which the final verse explodes, after the lull of the previous three verses, conveys the advent of the kingdom in Jesus' teaching and activity (cf. Mark 1:14–15) as something that shatters the way in which we feel that life normally operates and the patterns it follows.

The Seed Growing Secretly
(Mark 4:26–29)

This parable along with the Mustard Seed provides the framework of images for the middle section of chapter 4. It is found only in Mark; its omission by Matthew and Luke has long been a problem in exegesis. It is also the first parable that Mark explicitly calls a kingdom parable. Like the Sower, it admits of multiple foci for interpretation. There is an initial contrast between the inactivity of the farmer who simply scatters the seed and then returns to his rhythm of daily activity and the dynamic activity of the seed. The description of the seed as sprouting and growing, without the farmer knowing how, suggests that the central thrust is the mystery of growth. On the other hand, the earth produces "of itself" (v. 28, *automatē*), which underscores the power of the earth and the seed. The final verse announces that the ripening of the grain is the signal for the harvest to begin so that no time should be lost: "at once he puts in the sickle" (v. 29).

Such a range of possibilities intrinsic to the text itself has produced an equally high range of interpretations. Nineteenth-century liberalism embraced this parable as the image of the hidden growth of the kingdom within human hearts and society. C. H. Dodd places the emphasis on the harvest, which suggests that the end time is realized in the advent of Jesus.[16] Joachim Jeremias calls it the parable of "the Patient Husbandman" and stresses the contrast between the inactivity of the farmer and the certainty of the harvest.[17] It is a parable of assurance that the final eschatological harvest already begun in the ministry of Jesus is coming and one can do nothing to hasten its arrival. Also suggested is that it countered a zealot-like desire to hasten the arrival of the kingdom through violence; patient waiting, not activity, brings the harvest.[18]

Here I want to focus on certain aspects of the movement and images of the parable. As in the Sower, a lulling effect is conveyed by the portrait of the farmer who follows the natural rhythms of life—sleep and rise, day and night (4:27)—juxtaposed with the rhythms of growth (first the blade, then the ear, then the full grain in the ear, 4:28). Such rhythmic balancing suggests the rhythm of the times in Eccles. 3:1–9 (esp. 3:2, "a time to plant, and a time to pluck up what is planted"), two times in alternation—God's time and human time. In Mark 4:29, these times intersect when the grain is ripe and the harvest has come, with overtones of the eschatological judgment (cf. Joel 3:13). Now is the time for the rhythm of nature to cease and the farmer to resume activity. In this manner Jesus

16. Dodd, *Parables*, 141–44.
17. Jeremias, *Parables*, 151–53.
18. Ibid., 152.

proclaims the kingdom. His hearers "interlock" as they see their daily lives mirrored in the parable (see above, p. 18). God's power and activity have their times and rhythms, and human activity does not hasten their full manifestation. Yet the hearers are summoned to think of a new time when God's reign and time may intersect their lives and shatter the tranquil rhythms of life. Only then is the time for immediate response.

The Mustard Seed
(Mark 4:30–32 = Matt. 13:31–32;
Luke 13:18–19)

Examining the tradition history of this parable is an aid to its interpretation.[19] The parable appears in the triple tradition (i.e., a passage in Mark that is taken over by Matthew and Luke), but the differences in the respective versions suggest that there may also have been a Q version of the parable.[20] Mark, followed by Matthew, says that the mustard seed was the "smallest" of all seeds (Mark 4:31 = Matt. 13:32). Luke (13:19) simply says the kingdom is like "a grain of mustard seed." Mark, followed again by Matthew, says that the seed became the greatest of all shrubs (Mark 4:32 = Matt. 13:32), while Luke says that it became a tree (13:19). Mark alone states that the shrub "puts forth large branches" (4:32). Mark says that the birds of the air nest *in the shade* of the tree (4:32), while Matthew and Luke say the birds nest *in the branches*, which is more natural. While some of these differences may be explicable in terms of differences in the oral tradition, according to the normal criteria of the two source theory, when Matthew and Luke *agree in disagreeing* with Mark, they depend on the sayings source, Q.[21] Since Matthew and Mark agree in designating the final growth as a tree and placing the birds' nests in the branches, many scholars posit a Q version of the parable which would be much like the present text of Luke. Matthew seems to have used both Mark and Q, which explains the agreements of Matthew with Mark (the designation of the seed as the smallest and the phrase "greatest of all shrubs").

19. A helpful exposition is McArthur, "The Parable of the Mustard Seed."
20. It appears also in the *Gospel of Thomas* 20 in a form that may be close to the original. See Crossan, *In Parables*, 45–49.
21. See above, n. 5.

This complicated tradition history suggests that the three evangelists freely adapted an original parable to their own purpose. In the original version, probably close to that of Luke and the *Gospel of Thomas* 20, the thrust is on the contrast between the small seed and the final tree. There is a certain extravagance in this version, since the mustard seed does not really grow into a tree. This extravagance and contrast suggest that the kingdom of God is like this—small, with barely visible beginnings and hidden growth, with disproportionate and surprising results.

The allusions to different texts of the OT also enrich the possible meanings of the parable. The specific point of contact is that the birds nest (*kataskēnoun*, v. 32) either in the branches of the tree or under its shadow. The pertinent texts are the hymn to God as creator (Ps. 104:12), the allegory of the sprig (Ezek. 17:22–24), the allegory of the cedar (Ezekiel 31), and Daniel's vision of Nebuchadnezzar and his empire as a mighty tree (Dan. 4:10–12, 20–27). In Psalm 104 one of the beauties of God's creation is a verdant tree where "the birds of the air have their habitation; they sing among the branches" (v. 12). The imagery here evokes other places in the OT where a verdant tree is a symbol of God's favor (see Pss. 1:3; 92:13–15; Jer. 17:7–8). In the other texts the tree is an allegory of kingdoms or empires (cf. Judg. 9:7–15), and nesting birds stand for the subjects of imperial rule. Mark's final verse has most direct contact with the allegorical usages.

It is impossible to know definitely whether there was a nonallegorical version. If there was, then the original version may be an allusion to Ps. 104:12 and the tree would evoke images of God's provident care. The allegorical usage may stem from the early church's understanding that the kingdom that Jesus came to proclaim supplants the mighty kingdoms of history. The term "dwell" (*kataskēnoun*) evokes images of the ingathering at the end time. The Markan version, along with its allegorical overtones, contains, however, a comic twist.[22] The place where the birds (i.e., nations) will gather is not a mighty tree but "the greatest of all shrubs," a subtle hint that God's kingdom is not to be like the mighty trees (i.e., empires) of old which are established through power and violence.

22. Funk, "The Looking-Glass Tree Is for the Birds."

The Seed Parables and the
Kingdom Proclamation of Jesus

It is hazardous to make statements about the kingdom proclamation of Jesus on the basis of only three parables, so what we offer are elements of such a proclamation that contribute to a synthetic presentation of the kingdom. Also, as Norman Perrin has stressed, there is no one-to-one correspondence between kingdom of God and any concept or expression of it. It is a "tensive symbol," which "can have a set of meanings that can neither be exhausted nor adequately expressed by any one referent," in contrast to a "steno symbol" which has a single referent (e.g., mathematical symbols).[23] The "seed parables" in which this symbol comes to expression use images taken from and oriented to the mystery of growth and human engagement in it. As poetic images they are able to evoke a whole network of meanings: the mystery of growth, its hidden quality, the rhythmic and unhurried pace of nature, the need to respect the times and seasons, the urgency of the harvest as well as eschatological sifting and judgment. These images point to the ways in which God's power and presence intersect with human history. Yet the ordinary process of growth is surpassed and new meanings emerge. The harvest is extraordinary, beyond all expectation and experience (4:8); the farmer seems unconcerned about the growth of the seed, and the smallest of all seeds becomes a haven for the birds of the air.

The processes of nature tell us what the kingdom of God is "like," and alteration of these same processes shatters the mold into which we try to fit the kingdom. The familiarity of the images tells us that the kingdom is near; the improbability of the images tells us that it also transcends our attempts to define it. Jesus calls his hearers to see in his ministry the inbreaking of God's presence. The ordinary world where they dwell is to be the arena of this presence, but the kingdom has its own time and its own rhythm of growth. Jesus' hearers are to find God in his word and work, but they are to look beyond what they see to what they hope for. Failure, hiddenness, and insignificance are not the final word. The kingdom parables of Jesus are not simply Jesus' teaching *about* the kingdom but they are

Perrin, *Jesus and the Language*, 30; 196–203.

his own experience of the kingdom coming to expression in image and symbol. Therefore they put us in contact not simply with Jesus the teacher but with Jesus the believer who creates a parabolic world to which he commits himself as his life and mission unfold. Therefore we are led *from* the preaching of the historical Jesus (stage one of the tradition) *to* Mark's understanding and presentation of Jesus (stage three). Hence a study of the other elements of Mark 4 is necessary.

Discipleship and the Mystery
of the Kingdom of God
(Mark 4:10–25)

In my proposed structure, the middle section of Mark 4 consists of a saying on the reason for speaking in parables (4:10–12), the allegory of the seeds (4:13–20, which is the center of the whole chapter), and the four sayings of 4:21–25. In the framing sections (4:1–9, 26–34), Jesus is established as one who discloses the kingdom in parable; the middle section deals with the effect and reception of the parables. Theologically this division serves to unite Christology (the person and work of Jesus) and discipleship (the response to Jesus' summons and actions).

The Reason for Speaking in Parables
(Mark 4:10–12)

Few sayings in the NT have received as much attention as these puzzling verses. After the text indicates that Jesus was alone, "those who were about him with the twelve" ask him about "the parables." Jesus then responds:

> To you has been given the secret [*mystērion*]
>   of the kingdom of God,
> but for those outside [*tois exō*]
>   everything is [*ginetai*, also translated
>   as "happens"] in parables;
> so that [*hina*] they may indeed see but not
>   perceive, and may indeed hear but not
>   understand;
> lest [*mēpote*] they should turn again, and be forgiven.
>   (Mark 4:11–12; v. 12 = Isa. 6:9–10)

Many problems of interpretation confront the reader. In v. 10 the disciples, who are inexplicably alone with Jesus, ask him about parables when only one has been given (4:3–9). "Those outside" are not identified. Are they the crowds of vv. 1 and 33–34? The word "secret" (*mystērion*) occurs only here in the Synoptic Gospels.[24] The quotation from Isaiah corresponds neither to the Hebrew text nor to the Greek translation (Septuagint). The deterministic theology that implies that Jesus' teaching "hardened" the outsiders does not jibe with other aspects of Mark, such as the favorable reaction of the crowds (2:13; 5:24; 6:34; 12:17), the following of those not explicitly called to be disciples (2:15; 10:52), the praise of the unknown exorcist who is an outsider (9:38–41), and the confession of the gentile centurion (15:39). The portrayal of the disciples as a privileged group of insiders in 4:11 clashes with the repeated indications that the disciples fail to understand (6:52; 7:18; 8:31–32; and esp. 8:17–21, where the disciples, like the outsiders of 4:11, have eyes that do not see and ears that do not understand). They also fail in the face of the passion of Jesus (14:50, 71).

These verses are a constant reminder that the mystery given to the disciples remains for subsequent generations. Frank Kermode may be correct in suggesting that Mark simply leaves us with an unresolved riddle and enigma.[25] At the risk of joining the ranks of the outsiders, however, I will chance some response to the questions raised by this text in terms of Mark's theology in parable.

Excursus: The Enigma of Mark 4:10–12

The most disturbing thing about Mark 4:10–12 for many scholars has been the harsh deterministic theology put on the lips of Jesus. Our purpose is not to defend the historical authenticity of the saying but to ask whether the scandal it causes may not be due to the last residue of the Enlightenment, liberal Jesus in contemporary thought. A "reasonable" Jesus who reached out to and loved all people would hardly speak in this way! If, however, the historical Jesus is seen more as a prophet grappling with the presence and power of God, such a saying is not as scandalous. Isaiah was commanded to "make the heart of this people fat, and their ears heavy, and [to] shut their eyes" (Isa. 6:10), and Jeremiah is called "to pluck up and to break down, to destroy and to overthrow" (Jer. 1:10).

The first way in which the historical Jesus has been absolved of blame for

---

24. Cf. Matt. 13:11, where the plural *mystēria* appears.
25. See the original treatment of Mark 4 in Kermode, *The Genesis of Secrecy*, 23–47.

this harsh saying is to ascribe its present deterministic thrust to a mistranslation, either of the Aramaic into Greek or of the Greek into modern languages. In favor of some Aramaic substratum is the fact that the Greek text of Mark 4:12 is closest to the Aramaic Targum (= translation) of Isaiah. Since synagogue readings were in Aramaic, Jesus would have heard and presumably cited the text in Aramaic. Jeremias proposes the following translation of the reconstructed, original text: 'To you has God given the secret of the kingdom of God; but to those who are without everything is obscure, in order that they (as it is written) may 'see and yet not see, may hear and yet not understand, unless they turn and God will forgive them.' "[26] The key points in this reconstruction are the understanding of the Markan "so that" (hina) as a code word for the fulfillment of Scripture rather than direct divine purpose, and the Markan "lest they should turn" as a mistranslation of the Aramaic dil*ma, which can also mean "unless." Jeremias also claims that the saying was originally meant to describe the reaction to Jesus' ministry and teaching as a whole and not to the parables, which for Jeremias are clear ways of proclaiming the kingdom. The problem with such a reconstruction is that while absolving the historical Jesus of a deterministic purpose, it leaves us with a picture of the Markan Jesus (also the "canonical" one) who articulates such a theology.

A reconstruction on the basis of the Aramaic Targum of Isaiah is problematic, however, since its extant text dates from the fourth or fifth century A.D. An alternate mistranslation theory is to recognize that the Greek hina during this period can mean either purpose or result, so that the blinding is the result of Jesus' parabolic teaching rather than its purpose.[27] The problem of "lest" (mēpote), however, remains unresolved by this suggestion.

The second major solution has been to accept the deterministic or predestinarian thrust of the passage but to interpret it as a saying of the early church which betrays its perspective on salvation history. This perspective is fueled by the "hardening" of the heart theology of the OT (Exod. 4:21; 8:15, 32; 9:34), which, in effect, holds that God can be rejected by human beings only because God wills such rejection. Such a perspective also fits in with the deterministic bent of apocalyptic thought where the "secrets" of history are known to God and revealed to human beings, even though the course of history is predetermined. Early Christian thinkers explained Israel's nonacceptance of Jesus as having been willed in advance (cf. Rom. 9:16–29; 10:16–21; 11:7–10; John 12:37–41; Acts 28:25–28). Mark is thus seen to be adopting this perspective and applying it to the parables of Jesus. Though Jesus spoke in parables to win over his hearers, it was in effect willed that they would not perceive or understand. The problem with such a perspective is that in Mark 12:12 the Jewish opponents

26. Jeremias, Parables, 13–18, translation from pp. 17–18.
27. See Moule, An Idiom Book of New Testament Greek, 142–46. Matthew (13:13) changes Mark's hina ("in order that") to hoti ("because"), thus making the blindness a cause of parabolic teaching rather than its consequence.

of Jesus perceive very clearly the meaning of the parable and this intensifies their opposition to Jesus.

The third major direction for a solution to this difficult saying is through redaction criticism which explains the saying as Mark's conscious purpose rather than simply as his recording of church tradition. One approach is to interpret the saying in terms of the Messianic Secret in Mark. Here the "nondisclosure" in parable is likened to those places where Jesus forbids demons to reveal his identity (1:25, 34; 3:11–12), where he prohibits publicity after miracles (1:43–45; 5:43; 7:36; 8:26), where he forbids Peter's confession to be made public (8:30; cf. 9:9), and where Jesus remains hidden (7:24; 9:30) or gives private teaching to his disciples (esp. 4:10–12, 34; 7:17–22; 13:3–37). By noting this, however, one intensifies the problem, since the meaning and function of the Messianic Secret in Mark are themselves widely debated.[28]

The Reason for Speaking in Parables in Mark's Context

The solution that I will propose has points of contact with the question of the messiahship of Jesus but embraces other aspects of Mark's theology. The first set of issues concerns the identity of the "you" to whom the mystery of the kingdom of God is given (4:11) as well as that of "those outside" for whom everything happens in parables. The second issue concerns the meaning of the terms "mystery of the kingdom of God" and "in parables." These observations will prompt some suggestions about the theological ramifications of 4:10–12.

The question in Mark 4:10 is posed by "those who were about him with the twelve," and in 4:11–12 the response is directed to them. These questioners are often identified in the light of 4:33–34, where Jesus explains the parables to his disciples in private but speaks to the crowd in parables. The "you" is therefore thought to be the disciples, while "those outside" refers to the crowd. Jesus thus speaks to the crowd in riddles, which he explains to the disciples in private. Problems, however, attend this interpretation, and a key

28. Since the foundational study of Wrede (*The Messianic Secret*), there has been a wide-ranging debate on the origin of these texts (i.e., do they represent authentic sayings of Jesus? an apologetic theology of early church? or a creation of Mark?) and on which texts should be subsumed under the aegis of the secret as well as on their theological purpose in Mark. See the essays in Tuckett, *The Messianic Secret*. See also Kingsbury, *Christology of Mark's Gospel*, 1–23; and Kilgallen, "The Messianic Secret and Mark's Purpose." S. Brown argues against interpretation of Mark 4:11 from the perspective of the secret ("The Secret of the Kingdom," 60–74).

to the proper meaning of the terms is found in the section immediately preceding chapter 4, which is Jesus' first discourse in parables (3:23).[29] The latter part of chapter 3 contains an instance of the Markan framing technique. In 3:19–20 Jesus is pressed in by crowds (as in 4:1). When his family (*hoi par' autou*) hear of this, they try to seize him, for they think he is out of his mind (3:21).[30] There follows the accusation by the scribes from Jerusalem that Jesus casts out demons by the power of Beelzebul, and Jesus responds with the parables of the divided kingdom and the strong man's house. This section then concludes with a solemn warning about sins against the Holy Spirit (3:23–30).

In 3:31 relatives of Jesus again appear. While the mother and brothers of Jesus are standing "outside" (*exō*; cf. 4:11), the crowd is sitting around him (*peri auton*; cf. 4:10). In both 4:10 and 3:31 we have the same juxtaposition of people around Jesus contrasted with outsiders. In 3:32 the crowd announces to Jesus that his mother and brothers (and sisters in some manuscripts) are outside "seeking" him—which often in Mark has pejorative connotations (1:37; 11:18; 12:12; 14:1). In response, Jesus turns to those around him (*tous peri auton*) and says, "Behold my mother, brothers and sisters! Whoever does the will of God is my brother and sister, and mother" (3:34, 35, au. trans.). Given the Markan technique of framing, one can assume that the family of 3:21 seek again to restrain him. In contrast, Jesus pronounces those around him (the crowd) to be potential family members if they do the will of God. Here the terms "those outside" and "those around him" connote the direct opposite of the common interpretation of 4:10–12. The crowds are the "insiders" who are around Jesus and receive private teaching. The intimates of Jesus are outsiders who misunderstand him. I would claim, then, that the distinction between those around Jesus and the outsiders is not between called disciples and the crowd, nor is it between Jews and Christians, but it is a distinction between those who will understand the true meaning of discipleship and those who will not. *"Inside" and "outside" are existential, religious categories, determined*

29. See esp. Marcus, "Mark 4:10–12 and Marcan Epistemology," above, n. 4.
30. The identity of *hoi par' autou* (RSV: "his friends") in Mark 3:21 is also disputed. In Koine Greek it frequently means family or relatives (see BAGD, 610) and is so interpreted by a number of scholars: e.g., Crossan, "Mark and the Relatives of Jesus"; and Kelber, *Kingdom in Mark*, 59.

by the kind of response one makes to the demands of Jesus. One of the great paradoxes in Mark is that Peter, the one first called (1:16–17) who stands at the head of the Twelve (3:16), in his final appearance in the Gospel, goes "outside," where he denies that he ever knew Jesus (14:68–71).

The second major issue concerns the meaning of the terms "mystery" and "in parables." "In parables," used frequently in Mark, is generally admitted to mean, in 4:12, "in riddles" or "enigmatic sayings" which need explanation. Also the *ginetai* ("is" or "happens") suggests that the deeds as well as the sayings of Jesus are enigmatic to outsiders. The "mystery" (RSV: "secret") of the kingdom of God does not denote, as in later Christian usage, something incomprehensible to human reason, but the once hidden, now revealed salvific plan of God now manifest in the proclamation of a rejected and crucified Messiah (1 Cor. 2:1–2, 7; Rom. 11:25; 16:25; Eph. 1:9; 3:3, 4, 9).[31] Christian preachers, among whom we should count the evangelist Mark, are to be "stewards of the mysteries of God" (1 Cor. 4:1).

I contend that the content of the "mystery of the kingdom" in Mark is that the reign or power of God is now manifest in the brokenness of Jesus on the cross, his hiddenness which is to be revealed. Faith in such a Jesus places one "around him." My main arguments are the following:

1. While the citation of Isa. 6:9–10 in Mark 4:12 gives the impression that the outsiders fail to understand *the teaching* of Jesus, citations elsewhere of this same text deal with the rejection of the *person* of Jesus and his death on the cross. Acts 28:23–31 recounts the final appearance of the historical Paul. From his Roman house arrest he testifies to the kingdom of God, which is described as teaching "about Jesus" (Acts 28:23). When this teaching is rejected, Paul then cites Isa. 6:9–10. In John 12:40, after Jesus says that he must be lifted up (i.e., crucified, 12:27–36), the crowd refuses to believe in him and the narrator cites Isa. 6:10. Therefore, in Mark 4:11–12 that which causes unbelief and is a riddle to the outsider is the cross of Christ (cf. 1 Cor. 1:23 where Paul describes the cross

---

31. For the understanding of mystery adopted here, see Boucher, *Mysterious Parable,* 56–63; R. Brown, *The Semitic Background of the Term "Mystery"*; and S. Brown, "The Secret of the Kingdom," above, n. 28.

similarly as a scandal). For the one who will be around Jesus, this is a mystery given by God.

2. Other aspects of Mark's theology support a relation between 4:10–12 and the cross of Christ. As noted, the mystery of the kingdom is given to those around Jesus, who earlier in 3:34 become the new family of Jesus because they are summoned to do the will of God. The will of God is not simply a general term in Mark for all that is commanded in the Torah and teaching of Jesus. In Gal. 1:3–4 Paul describes the will of God:

> Grace to you and peace from God the Father and our Lord Jesus Christ, who gave himself for our sins to deliver us from the present evil age, *according to the will of our God and Father.* (Italics mine)

In Mark 8:31 when Jesus first predicts his passion and death he announces that "it is necessary" (*dei*, RSV: "must") that the Son of man suffer. This phrase suggests divine necessity or God's will. When Peter rejects the necessity of suffering, Jesus rebukes him by saying, "You do not think the thoughts of God, but human thoughts" (8:33, au. trans.). Peter's "failure" is not lack of dedication or courage but an inability to see that the passion is willed by God.[32] In the Garden of Gethsemane when Jesus confronts most deeply the mystery of suffering he prays, "Abba, Father, all things are possible to thee; remove this cup from me; yet not what I will, but what thou wilt" (14:36). The will of God in the Gospel of Mark is that Jesus suffer and die. Jesus accepts this will. Those who are to be "around him" and who will become members of the family of Jesus are to do the will of God. Peter, who ends up as an "outsider," does not see suffering and death as willed by God. Such is the mystery which, when given and accepted, makes one a true disciple; when rejected, it makes one an outsider.

A few summary remarks here may prevent my exposition from becoming yet another riddle in an ever-puzzling chapter. The enigmatic saying of 4:10–12 occupies a central place in Mark 4 and in Mark's theology. It may well originate in the prophetic consciousness of Jesus, who, like the prophets of the OT (e.g., Isa. 1:2–20; 6:9–13; Jer. 1:9–10), was commissioned to proclaim conversion and judgment. The result would be that some would see but not perceive;

---

32. On the will of God in Mark, see Donahue, "A Neglected Factor."

hear but not understand. The early church probably adopted this prophetic proclamation to explain the rejection of Jesus by his own people (cf. Mark 6:1–6). Mark then incorporates the saying both in the literary structure of chapter 4 and in the theological structure of his whole Gospel. Mark offers to his community on the lips of Jesus the gospel of God (1:14) which is specified as the proclamation of the kingdom and the demand for belief and conversion (1:15). "Kingdom" is thus a code word for both the proclamation *of* Jesus and that *about* him. The mystery of the kingdom which God gave to the community in the gospel of Jesus is for Mark the scandal of the cross. Proclamation, Christology, and discipleship are thus intertwined in 4:10–12, perspectives that are fleshed out in the rest of the chapter.

The Allegory of the Seeds
(Mark 4:13–20)

Scholars often suggest that in the pre-Markan tradition this text followed immediately the parable of the Sower.[33] In its present location it is the centerpiece of chapter 4. The introductory verse (v. 13) looks in two directions.[34] "Do you not understand this parable [riddle]?" looks back to 4:10–12; "How then will you understand all the parables [riddles]?" looks forward to both chapter 4 and the rest of the Gospel. Realization that the mystery of the kingdom involves discipleship on the way of the cross is a key to all the parables of Mark's Gospel.

The explanation of the Sower in 4:13–20 has become a parade example of the use of allegory to interpret the sayings of Jesus.[35] The evidence that it springs from the early church is multiple.

"The word" used absolutely in 4:14 mirrors early Christian usage (e.g., Acts 4:4; 8:4; 1 Thess. 1:6; Gal. 6:6). Terms occur here which are not found elsewhere in the Synoptics but are frequent in other NT writings, especially Paul (e.g., "sow" [*speirein*] in the sense of "preach," 1 Cor. 9:11; "root" for inward stability, Col. 2:7; Eph. 3:17; "lure" of riches, Col. 2:8; 2 Pet. 2:13). The situation of both persecution and the danger of wealth does not reflect the ministry of Jesus but represents a more developed church setting. The tendency to turn eschatological sayings of Jesus into ethical ones also

33. See esp. Pesch, *Das Markusevangelium* 1:225–27.
34. I draw here on the insights of Gnilka, *Das Evangelium nach Markus*, 1:173.
35. The evidence is found in Jeremias, *Parables*, 77–79.

mirrors church development. Finally the parable of 4:1–9 is allegorized, with each detail achieving independent significance which is to be understood by insiders. Like allegory in general, 4:13–20 suggests a situation of tension or persecution (esp. 4:17).

In Mark's context and because of its points of contact with other parts of this Gospel, the allegory receives added significance as a key to Mark's understanding of discipleship. The different fates of the seed become images for different negative responses to Jesus and his teaching throughout the Gospel. In 4:15 the seed along the way symbolizes situations where Satan immediately snatches the word. This situation is hauntingly similar to what happens after Jesus proclaims the word (*ton logon*, used absolutely, as in 4:14) that he must suffer and die (8:31–32). In the very next phrase Peter rebukes Jesus for this saying and Jesus immediately calls Peter "Satan." In 4:17 the fate of the seed is that it has no root and when tribulation or persecution comes, they fall away (lit., "are scandalized"). In Mark, being scandalized is clearly the fate of those who were close to Jesus but who failed after a short time: the family and relatives of Jesus are initially amazed at his teaching and wisdom (6:2) only to be scandalized; the disciples, who Jesus prophesies will be scandalized when the shepherd is struck (14:27–28), flee when Jesus is arrested (14:50). In 4:19 the word is choked by the lure of riches and desire for other things. In the only "negative call narrative" in Mark, a young man refuses to follow Jesus because he had many possessions (10:22) and Jesus speaks about the difficulty the rich have entering the kingdom of God (10:23–25). The seed (word) which will bear fruit is that which is heard and accepted (4:20). This last verse functions as an example of true discipleship for the Markan community. The summons to discipleship is in the form of a call (1:16–20; 2:14–15) and its reward will be "a hundredfold" (10:30), just as the good seed bears fruit a hundredfold (4:20). The allegory of the seeds then echoes throughout the Gospel. By placing it after the revelation of the mystery of the kingdom, Mark suggests that "those who were about him with the twelve," disciples, may become themselves outsiders.

The Parabolic Sayings (Mark 4:21–25)

In this section Jesus continues his explanation to the disciples of the riddle of the kingdom (4:11–12). Since these sayings appear in the triple tradition (Mark, followed by Matthew and Luke) as well as in the double tradition (the sayings source or Q which Matthew and Luke share in common) and since three of them are in the *Gospel of Thomas*, they have a high claim to authenticity.[36] Since they also are adapted to different contexts (cf. Matt. 5:15; 10:26; 7:2; 25:29), it is almost impossible to know their original meaning and context. Mark here links four independent sayings together (4:21–22, 24–25), punctuated by his warning about hearing (4:23; cf. 4:9).

The first saying begins with the unusual phrase "Does a lamp *come in* to be put under a bushel?" (au. trans.) in place of some expected word for "lighting a lamp" (cf. Luke 8:16; Matt. 5:15; Luke 11:33).[37] The use of "come" may have a christological nuance, since the verb "to come" (*erchesthai*) is used so often of Jesus in Mark (esp. 1:14, 39; 6:1; 8:38; 10:45; 14:62). The second saying (4:22), which promises that what is hidden and secret will be made manifest, picks up other motifs of chapter 4: hidden growth which will yield a rich harvest and the secret of the kingdom of God which will be manifest. These first two sayings encourage the disciples in their mission of hearing and proclaiming the word. The second pair of sayings which also begin with a warning to hear (4:24) serve more as warnings about the dangers of discipleship. The measure the disciples give will be the measure they get. This may be an enigmatic reference to the allegory of the seeds (4:13–20), that is, that the care and zeal with which they receive the word (the measure you give) will be an index of the fruit of the harvest. The final saying, "To the one who has will more be given; and from the one who has not, even what he has will be taken away" (au. trans.), may refer to the eschatological judgment when the time for action is past (cf. the Talents, Matt. 25:14–30, which has the same motif in story form). In its present Markan context it continues the warning of 4:13 against improper hearing. It also repeats the motif of the Sower where the first, unfruitful buddings will be "taken away," while the fruitful harvest will be extravagant. For those who do not accept the word, even what they have will be lost; for those who accept, even more will

---

36. *Gospel of Thomas* 33 (= Mark 4:21–22); 5 (= Mark 4:22); 6 (= Mark 4:22).
37. The RSV's "Is a lamp brought in?" misses Mark's wordplay with its christological overtones in the frequent use of "coming" for Jesus (e.g., 1:7, 9, 14) and here for the lamp (4:21).

be given them. These four sayings, then, recapitulate motifs of 4:10–12, 13–20 and with 4:10–12 provide the frame for the allegory on the demands of discipleship.

Theology and Proclamation of the Parable Discourse

By taking over various traditions, by arranging them in a definite structure, and by locating this material in chapter 4, Mark presents major theological motifs of his Gospel. A Christology emerges that not only continues the portrait of Jesus as one who teaches with authority (1:27; cf. 4:1–2) but that also proclaims that the death and resurrection of Jesus is the mystery of the kingdom. This is present in the material that precedes and follows chapter 4. In 3:23–30 Jesus is "the stronger one" (cf. 1:7) who comes to despoil the kingdom of Satan (cf. 1:24). The kind of disbelief that attributes Jesus' power to Satan is blasphemy (3:28), the same charge that will be leveled at Jesus (14:64). In the pericope that immediately follows the parable discourse Jesus is addressed as "teacher" (4:38; cf. 4:1–2, 33–34), but his teaching is manifest in control over the chaotic power of nature (4:35–41; cf. Pss. 65:7; 104:7; 107:23–31: God has power over the raging sea and rescues those threatened by it).

In Mark 4 Jesus is the powerful one whose power will ultimately be made manifest even if it is now as hidden as the process of growth. The seed parables acquire a christological overtone and function as parables of hope for the community. Just as the seed has its own power and dynamism which is revealed at the harvest, so too does the mystery of the kingdom. The contrast between the power of Jesus which is hidden and absent on the cross and his glory when he returns (13:26–27; 14:62) is no greater than the contrast between the smallest of all the seeds and the greatest of all the shrubs. The parables of Mark 4:1–34 are metaphors of the Christology of the Gospel.

Equally important in both content and context is the theme of discipleship, which in Mark is the correlate to Christology. Discipleship permeates chapter 4 and is highlighted by the repeated demands for "hearing" (4:3, 9, 23, 24, 33).[38] In biblical thought, hearing

38. Discipleship has become a major concern in the study of Mark. See esp. Best,

(*akouō*) is intimately related to obedience (*hypakouō*), and the demands of God are expressed in the daily prayer which begins, "Hear, O Israel" (Deut. 6:4–9; 11:13–21; Num. 15:37–41; cf. Mark 12:29). In the allegory of the seeds, each unsuccessful sowing begins with a "hearing" (4:15, 16, 18), and the outsiders of 4:12 "hear but do not understand." Throughout Mark, discipleship failure is equated with improper hearing. In 7:14–17 the disciples hear the "parable" about the clean and the unclean but are without understanding (7:18; cf. 4:12). The disciples who do not understand Jesus' teaching about the bread are described as "having ears" but not hearing (8:18). Even the opponents hear the teaching of Jesus but do not let his teaching take root.

Contrariwise, in 4:20 there is a threefold progression in responding to the word—hearing, accepting, and bearing fruit—which becomes a paradigm for true discipleship. This structure corresponds to the progress of the good seed in 4:8: budding, increasing (growing), bearing fruit to a hundredfold. The calls of the disciples in Mark convey a threefold structure (1:16–20; 3:13b–19; 6:7–13).[39] They begin with a call or summons which is heard, which then issues in following or "being with" (3:14), followed by preaching, teaching, and healing (3:14–15; 6:8–13). True discipleship is then engagement with a life and following the way of Jesus which will yield a bountiful harvest. Both the parables and the middle section of Mark 4 function as warning against false discipleship—superficial hearing, manifest in an initial and rootless enthusiasm, seduction by wealth or failure in persecution. They also function to encourage the community in the face of failure and persecution (cf. 13:9–13). Growth is taking place; initial failure is not the whole picture; Jesus is powerful in word and work; he comes to rescue his community even when they are lacking in faith (4:35–41).

Eschatology or the temporality of the kingdom is a final motif of this chapter. Mark's eschatology is very much like that of Jesus, "eschatology in the process of realization" or proleptic eschatology,

---

Following Jesus; Donahue, *Theology and Setting of Discipleship;* Schweizer, "The Portrayal of the Life of Faith"; and Tannehill, "The Disciples in Mark"; idem, "The Gospel of Mark as Narrative Christology."

39. On the "three step progressions" and their importance for understanding both the structure of Mark and his theology, see Robbins, *Jesus the Teacher,* 19–48.

a combination of the "already" and the "not yet."[40] Jesus announces that the time is fulfilled and the kingdom is imminent (1:14–15), yet its full manifestation is in the future (8:30—9:1; 13:26; 14:62). The community lives between the resurrection and the parousia. The seed parables place the reader at a similar time, between planting and harvest. They also offer a message of hope because the future will be in extravagant contrast to the present. Such an eschatology may be in opposition to some in the community who see the present as the time of manifestation. The Markan Jesus predicts that some will come claiming his name and authority and will perform signs and wonders (13:6, 21–22). Even though Mark devotes a great deal of space to miracles, especially in the first seven chapters, he subordinates them to the message of the cross, perhaps in opposition to those who invoked miracle-working powers as a sign of the presence of the kingdom.[41] These parables which emphasize hiddenness and smallness are counters to such a perspective.

The discourse in parable offers manifold possibilities for proclamation as individual texts either in the context of Jesus' kingdom proclamation or that of the theology of Mark. Continuity exists between these contexts in the message of hope that the parables offer, in the stress on the contrast between appearance and reality, and in the parables as a summons to engagement with the life and teaching of Jesus. Also present is the motif of "grace." It is the power of God which gives the growth. Mark 4 offers a message of hope but without presumption, and the warnings about false or superficial hearing can speak to a church today about the dangers of "cheap grace."[42]

The miracle and the mystery of growth provide a polyvalent cluster of images, which evoke God's power and graciousness in all areas of life. In the NT itself, images of growth have already engendered theological reflection. For John (12:23–25) the death of the seed

40. This understanding of eschatology is largely dependent on Jeremias, *Parables*, esp. 48–49, 114–24, 160–80. For a summary of Jeremias's position, along with other interpretations of the eschatology of Jesus, see Perrin, *The Kingdom of God*, esp. 79–89.

41. On miracles in Mark, see esp. Achtemeier, "Toward the Isolation of Pre-Markan Miracle Catenae"; idem, "The Origin and Function of the Pre-Marcan Miracle Catenae"; and Weeden, *Mark*, esp. 55–69.

42. Cf. the description of "cheap grace" offered by Bonhoeffer, *The Cost of Discipleship*, 45–49.

followed by the bearing of much fruit becomes a symbol of the death and resurrection of Jesus as well as the gift of self in a life of discipleship which bears fruit and issues in life eternal. Paul adopts images of planting and growing for ministry in the community (1 Cor. 3:5–10), confident that "only God gives the growth" (1 Cor. 3:7). The seed that dies, only to prepare for the plant, becomes an image of the transformation hoped for in the resurrection (1 Cor. 15:35–36, 42–43). The seeds that Mark planted in 4:1–34 continue to bear fruit.

THE DRAMA OF SALVATION HISTORY
IN MARK 12

The Parable of the Wicked Tenants
(Mark 12:1–11 = Matt. 21:33–45; Luke 20:9–18)

This is the longest narrative parable in Mark and the only one in which human, dramatic actions are significant. It presents a host of exegetical problems—most basically, whether it was ever a parable of Jesus. A number of factors underscore its problematic character. It is the only parable that includes a lengthy, almost verbatim allusion to the OT (Mark 12:1 = Isa. 5:2). The treatment of the servants (vv. 2–5) is a clear recollection of the violent rejection of the OT prophets (1 Kings 18:13, 22–27; 2 Chron. 24:21; 36:15–16; Neh. 9:26; cf. Matt. 23:29–37; Luke 13:34). The image of the vineyard and the vine, so prevalent in the OT for Israel (Isa. 5:1–2; Ps. 80:8–18; Jer. 2:21; Hos. 10:1), and the giving of the vineyard "to others" after unfaithful administration, reflect an early Christian explanation for the unbelief of Israel (cf. Rom. 11:17–24). The details of the parable are not particularly credible and may function, like allegory, to illustrate a truth already known. Would, for example, the owner send his son after the previous killings, especially if he has the power indicated in v. 9? Are the tenants realistic in thinking that they will gain respect by killing the son? Also the reference to the "beloved" son of v. 6 recalls its use as a christological title in Mark 1:11 and 9:7. Many scholars hold, then, that the parable is really an allegory of the early church about the rejection of God's beloved Son by the previous administrators of the vineyard—the Jewish leaders of 11:27 and 12:12.[43]

43. See Crossan, "Parable of the Wicked Husbandmen," 461–65; (he holds that

One of the more interesting defenses of the authenticity of the parable is that of Crossan.[44] By examining the Lukan version and that of the *Gospel of Thomas* 65, Crossan proposes an earlier version which omits the allusion to Isa. 5:1, the reference to "the only" son in v. 6, the giving of the vineyard to others (v. 9b), and the appended citation of Ps. 118:22–23 in 12:10–11. In such a form we have a narrative where a vineyard owner sends different messengers to gather the fruit of his leased vineyard. At the time of payment the tenants make the momentous decision to resist and ultimately kill the son; their action is not totally irrational, since possession was determined by occupancy and the tenants may hope that the owner will give up after the death of the son. Crossan locates this parable within a group that deals with the need for decisive action in the face of a critical situation (e.g., Mark 13:33–37; Matt. 25:14–30). The point of comparison and thrust of the parable as spoken by Jesus is that the advent of the kingdom should cause us to take that kind of resolute and decisive action which the tenants showed in their mayhem and murder. By telling a story of a shocking murder, Jesus shocks his hearers out of their complacency about the advent of God's reign.

Jeremias also holds that the parable is authentic, with the exception of vv. 10–11, but finds the point of comparison in the phrase about the vineyard being given "to others."[45] The gift of the kingdom will now be given to tax collectors and sinners rather than to the previous tenants, the Jewish leaders who criticize Jesus' fellowship with outsiders. By this parable Jesus vindicates his offer of grace and mercy to the marginal and the outcast.

While I follow Crossan and Jeremias in discovering an earlier version of the parable (ending at v. 9 and omitting "beloved son"), I claim that literary analysis discloses yet another meaning to the parable which reflects an aspect of the ministry of Jesus.

The Parable as Text

In assessing a dramatic parable, one must always ask who is the major character in the parable. Though the traditional title suggests

in its pre-Markan form it was not an allegory). See also Lambrecht, *Once More Astonished*, 127–32.

44. Crossan, "Parable of the Wicked Husbandmen"; idem, *In Parables*, 86–96; 115–20.

45. Jeremias, *Parables*, 70–77.

that it is the tenants, it is not really their actions which give either unity or suspense to the narrative. A close reading of the text reveals that the story is permeated with verbs that describe the activity of the owner: he planted, cared for, and let out the vineyard (v. 1); he sent (v. 2); he sent another and another (vv. 4–5); finally he sends the son (v. 6). He disappears in vv. 7–8, where the action shifts to the tenants, but reappears in v. 9, where his actions are in the future tense. The action of the owner determines the narrative development of the parable. Had he not sent further messengers or had he punished the tenants after the first rejection, the parable would be different. The rhetorical question of v. 9, "What will the owner of the vineyard do?" is the dramatic focus of the parable.

It is also the owner who acts in a surprising manner which arrests the hearer by its strangeness. Once the tenants beat the first servant, the reader gets an intimation that they are a bad lot. The one character who remains veiled throughout the parable is the owner; so that after his apparent folly in the continual sendings and in finally sending his son, the question of v. 9 really asks the reader not only *what the owner will do but what kind of person he is.* The surprise in the parable comes not from the killing of the son, since the tenants have shown themselves capable of brutal activity, but from the sending of the son and the almost naive musings of his father, perhaps "They will respect my son" (v. 6). Locating the main thrust of the parable here is supported by Mary Ann Tolbert's observation that the meaning of a parable should be sought where the narrative shifts to dialogue.[46] Here the shift is really to a dual dialogue where the owner and the tenants are contrasted, enhanced by the rather strange order of words in v. 6 where the father sends the son and then muses about the reason for sending. The reader is made privy to the almost simultaneous thoughts of the owner and the tenants much in the same manner as an audience hears the musings of the "Fool" in Shakespeare or of the chorus in Greek tragedy. The juxtaposition of these two soliloquies with their differing hopes and radically differing fulfillments—"they will respect" and "the inheritance will be ours"—as well as the role of the owner in determining the development of the narrative provides the key to our interpretation of the parable.

46. Tolbert, *Perspectives*, 74–82.

The parable should be viewed from the horizon of OT prophecy, as described by Abraham J. Heschel. He describes prophecy as "the inspired communication of divine attitudes to the prophetic consciousness" and notes that "the divine pathos is the ground tone of all these attitudes."[47] This pathos is an instance of what for Heschel is "the mysterious paradox" of biblical faith: God is pursuing humanity which Heschel describes as "God in search of man."[48] The prophetic books refer to the long-suffering of God, who reaches out for a human response (Hos. 2:2, 14–20; Jer. 3:11–14; Ezek. 16:59–63). The historical Jesus was perceived as a prophet (Mark 6:4, 15; 8:26; cf. Luke 24:19), and in this parable Jesus brings to expression the searching God who is "merciful and gracious, slow to anger, and abounding in steadfast love and faithfulness" (Exod. 34:6; Num. 14:18; Neh. 9:16; Pss. 86:15; 103:8; 145:8).

The parable expresses Jesus' own experience of the divine pathos. It can better be titled "the Patient Vineyard Owner," with the focus on the surprising conduct of the owner who continues to send envoys and seek a response after continued rejection. In this fashion the question of v. 9 engages the hearers in the larger question of how they think of God. Rather than an attack on unbelieving Israel for rejecting him, Jesus presents God who is longing for a response. As in the OT, rejecting God's offer is, in effect, self-judgment which evokes punishment from God. The dialogue of the tenants shows that they are people who have eyes but do not see and are hard of heart. Jesus thus summons his hearers to a conversion (cf. Mark 1:15) and warns them of the consequences of rejecting God's continual summons. It summons contemporary hearers to think of themselves as the vineyard workers, confronted by a God who continually seeks them but one they can reject.

The Parable in Context

In its Markan context, by the addition of the allegorizing allusion to the vineyard of Isa. 5:1, by the explicit designation of the son as Jesus, or the beloved son, and by the addition of the saying on the rejected stone (12:10–11), the parable is a clear allegory of the rejection of Jesus by Jewish leaders, a rejection that will ironically result in Jesus being the cornerstone of a new temple not made with

47. Heschel, *The Prophets*, 223.
48. Heschel, *God in Search of Man*, 136.

hands (cf. Mark 14:62). The parable occurs in the Jerusalem section of Mark (11:1—16:8) where the opposition to Jesus first intimated in 3:6 will culminate in his death.

By parabolic action Jesus curses the fig tree so that it will never again yield fruit (11:14), as will the destroyed vineyard never yield fruit. The story of the fig tree (11:12–14, 20–21) brackets the cleansing of the temple where Jesus says the temple will become a house of prayer for all nations (11:17). After both this incident and the parable of the vineyard workers, Mark notes plans of the officials to do violence to Jesus (11:18; 12:12). Rather ironically, while the leaders are rejecting Jesus, he pronounces God's judgment over their stewardship of the temple and the "vineyard" or the people whom God has planted.

Immediately following the allegory of the vineyard workers Mark has three important pericopes which are not so much christological controversies (see 11:1—12:12) as instruction by Jesus on three cardinal points of Jewish and later Christian faith. These points are (1) the summons to render to God the things of God while recognizing the claims of Caesar (12:13–17); (2) the affirmation that God is a "god of the living" (12:18–27) from whose presence not even death can separate a person; and (3) the command to love God and neighbor (12:28–34). When the vineyard is given "to others" in 12:9, Mark had in mind the early Christian community. The instruction of 12:13–34 presents the foundation of belief for these others as they begin to spread the word about God's beloved Son who was rejected by the Jewish leadership.[49]

The Markan redaction in the case of the Wicked Tenants is similar to that in chapter 4. There we saw that Mark took an original parable, where Jesus articulated his faith in God's power to bring about a harvest beyond all reckoning, and put it in a context of teaching about Christology, the crucified Jesus as the "mystery of the kingdom," and about discipleship. In 12:1–11, which stands at the center of the Jerusalem ministry, Mark takes an original parable in which Jesus expresses his experience of God reaching out to people and turns it into a christological allegory. Here, as in chapter 4, he

49. For a detailed study of the theology of Mark 12:13–34, see Donahue, "A Neglected Factor," 570–81.

connects the teaching of Jesus with the church's proclamation of him as the crucified one and appends to this teaching on discipleship.

COMMUNITY LIFE "BETWEEN THE TIMES": THE PARABLES OF MARK 13

The final parables of Mark come at the conclusion of the eschatological discourse (13:1–37), which itself is Jesus' final testament before his passion and death.[50] The discourse begins with a prediction by Jesus that the temple will be destroyed (13:2), which precipitates a double question by the disciples: "When will this be, and what will be the sign when these things are all to be accomplished?" (13:4). In the first major section of the discourse, traditional apocalyptic motifs—wars, earthquakes, plagues, famine (13:7–8)—are taken up, ones that herald the imminent end of history. This period is to be characterized by persecution and the profanation or destruction of the temple (13:9–23), after which there will be cosmic disturbances preceding the return of the Son of man in order to gather the elect from the ends of the earth (13:24–27).

Though Mark uses traditional material here, the discourse as a whole is directed to problems alive in his community. Mark does not want his community to view the wars, civil disturbances, and persecutions that preceded the destruction of the temple in A.D. 70 as the sign of the return of Jesus, as some claimed (13:6, 21–22). As Jesus said, these things are but antecedents to the end (13:7–8), and the end will come only "after that tribulation" (13:24). Mark counters those in his community, or known by his community, who interpreted the destruction of the temple as the final days and claimed that in some way Jesus had returned—"If any one says to you, 'Look, here is the Christ!' . . . do not believe it" (13:21)—and that they possessed the power (13:22) and authority of Jesus (13:6). Mark uses the final parables to counter these claims with a proper eschatology and a perspective on life in community prior to the return of Jesus.

---

50. It is generally admitted that, more than any other section, Mark 13 reflects the actual experiences of the Markan community. The literature on it is immense. I am influenced esp. by Cousar, "Eschatology and Mark's *Theologia Crucis*"; Grayston, "The Study of Mark XIII"; Kelber, *Kingdom in Mark*, 109–28; Hooker, "Trial and Tribulation in Mark XIII"; and Pesch, *Naherwartungen*.

The Fig Tree
(Mark 13:28–29 = Matt. 24:32–33;
Luke 21:29–31)

The two parables that conclude the discourse provide a nuanced eschatological perspective. Translated literally from the Greek, the initial verse of the first of these reads, "From the fig tree learn the parable" (RSV: "learn its lesson") (13:28). Here, "parable" is used in a sense different from Mark 3:23 and 4:11 (enigmatic saying or riddle) and with the meaning "lesson" or meaning of the illustration. The illustration is the budding fig tree. In Palestine the fig tree was distinguished from the other trees in completely shedding its leaves in winter, so that its first budding is a sign of the return of summer which followed quickly upon a short spring.[51] From this the community is to learn that the events described in 13:5–27 are not themselves the end time, but the end time will follow soon. In fact, he, the Son of man (13:26), is near "at the very gates" (13:29). Mark therefore, in rejecting the false eschatological timetable of some in the community, still retains the sense of urgency and imminence of the return of Jesus. The community is to be observant and watchful.

The Doorkeeper (Mark 13:33–37)

Verses 30–32, while maintaining that the return of Jesus is imminent, reject the use of Jesus' words to identify any specific event with this return, since not even Jesus himself knew the day or the hour (13:31). The final "parable" of the Gospel (13:33–36) describes in some detail the posture of the community prior to the return of Jesus. I will argue that this is a Markan allegory about the community life between the resurrection and the parousia.

The "parable" itself through having points of contact with other "parousia" parables (e.g., the Q parable of the Talents, Matt. 25:14–30 = Luke 19:11–27) shows wide variation, and neither Matthew nor Luke recounts it in the corresponding place at the end of his eschatological discourse. Most likely the core parable was a simple exhortation to watchfulness in the face of some imminent crisis such

---

51. Jeremias, *Parables*, 120.

as the advent of the kingdom of God or the return of Jesus soon after the resurrection (cf. Mark 1:14–15; Luke 12:35–56).

By the phrasing of the introductory verse (13:33) and by the addition of important details, Mark gives a distinctive meaning to the parable. Mark begins by saying, "Take heed, watch; for you do not know when the time will come" (13:33). The first word, "take heed" (*blepete*), links this parable with the three other places in the discourse (13:5, 9, 23) where Mark warns his community to be observant. The term for "being watchful" (*agrypneite*) occurs only here in Mark in contrast to the more normal *grēgoreite* (13:34, 35, 37; 14:34, 37, 38). Literally it means "be awake" and figuratively suggests watchful care. Paul uses it to describe his apostolic care for the churches (cf. 2 Cor. 6:5; 11:27–28), and in Heb. 13:17 it describes that care which church leaders are to show the community. The Greek word for "time" in the phrase "The time will come" is *kairos*, which is used in Mark 1:15 for time as an event or occasion when one should "be converted and believe in the gospel" and in 12:2 for the time to render fruit to the absent landowner. By this introductory verse Mark thus exhorts the leaders in his community to proper conduct in the light of the imminent parousia. The following parable, which can be called "the Waiting Servants," extends this theme.

The community's life is compared to a situation where a man, later identified as the "lord of the house" (13:35), goes on a journey, a familiar metaphor for the absence of Jesus before the parousia (cf. Matt. 25:14; Luke 19:12). Only in Mark, however, does the man leave "his house" (cf. Matt. 25:14). While gone, he entrusts his authority (*exousian*, 13:34) to his servants (*doulois*). Both terms are important in Mark. Jesus' first appearance in the Gospel is as one who possesses a new teaching with authority (1:22, 27) and as Son of man who has power (*exousia*) to forgive sin (2:10).[52] When Jesus calls his disciples, he bestows power (*exousia*) on them (3:15; 6:7). The description of those waiting as servants (*douloi*) not only reflects a widely attested early Christian usage (e.g., Gal. 1:10; Phil. 1:1) but

---

52. Perrin has called attention to the parallelism that Mark creates between the community and Jesus through the use of *exousia* as well as that between the fate of John, Jesus, and the disciples (see esp. Mark 1:14–16; 6:14–29—John is handed over and killed; Mark 8:31–32; 9:31; 10:33–34—Jesus will be handed over and killed; Mark 13:9–13—Jesus' followers will be handed over and killed). See Perrin, *A Modern Pilgrimage*, esp. 78–93.

recalls Jesus' command to the disciples to be a servant of all (*pantōn doulos*, 10:44; cf. 9:35) in imitation of the Son of man who came not to be served but to serve (10:45). Power, in Mark's community, is to be expressed in service.

The short indication that the master leaves the servants with power (RSV: "in charge"), "each with his work" (*hekastō to ergon*), like many details in an allegory, has wider significance. The phrase initially suggests that there are different tasks to be performed in the community even though they all share the same power, a perspective similar to Paul's description of different gifts and different ministries all inspired "by one and the same Spirit" (1 Cor. 12:4–11; cf. Rom. 12:6–8). In the parable itself, "work" is that mission given by the absent "lord of the house"—therefore, work *of* or *from* the Lord. In Paul "the work of the Lord" is equivalent to faithful Christian existence before the return of the Lord (1 Cor. 15:58) and to missionary activity (1 Cor. 16:10). In the context of Mark 13, all these nuances are possible. The larger context is one of an exhortation to fidelity amid eschatological trials (cf. 13:13), yet this period is also to be one when the gospel will be preached to all nations (13:10). The "work" of the Markan community includes both service within the community and missionary activity.

In the allegory, household language has links with other parts of Mark. Mark manifests a number of places where significant events take place in a house: healings (1:29; 2:1–12; 5:39–43), private instruction to the disciples (7:17; 9:28; 10:10); and house is a designation for the community itself (11:17). Mark also uses household and family imagery to describe doing the will of God (in 3:31–35 those who do the will of God are Jesus' new family) and the disciples who left all to follow Jesus receive a new family along with houses (10:28–31). Since we know from other passages that the first Christian meeting places were "house churches" (1 Cor. 16:19; Col. 4:15), it is safe to assume that Mark's community was such and that 13:33–37 is an allegory of life in Mark's house churches prior to the return of Jesus.[53]

---

53. Developed in more detail in Donahue, *Theology and Setting of Discipleship*, 31–51. For a discussion of the significance of "house" in Mark, as well as for the other architectural, topographical, and geopolitical references, see Malbon, *Narrative Space and Mythic Meaning in Mark*, esp. 106–40.

The Eschatological Parables in Context

In the parable of the budding fig tree and the allegory of the waiting servants, we find points of contact with both the immediate and the larger context of Mark's theology. In the context of the eschatological discourse, these passages give a balanced eschatology. In contrast to passivity or hopelessness in the face of suffering, Mark tells his community that the end time when they will see the Son of man is as near as the summer after the budding of the fig tree. In contrast to an enthusiasm that would claim that the end time has arrived and that the Christ has returned with "signs and wonders" (13:22), Mark says that the words of Jesus cannot be invoked to determine the day or the hour of his return (13:32), and the community is to wait in faithful vigilance.

There are points of contact between chapters 4 and 13, the other major discourse of Jesus in Mark. In both chapters we have the structure of a nature parable (4:1–9; 13:28–29), followed by words of Jesus expressing a promise to the community (4:10–12; 13:30–32) and a concluding allegory on discipleship (4:13–20; 13:33–37). In both chapters also the blessings and the dangers of discipleship are underscored. The disciples who hear the word and accept it will bear great fruit (4:20), and even more will be given (4:22). Those who persevere to the end will be saved (13:13) and will be gathered to the Son of man (13:27). Yet many of those who hear the word will be unfruitful, just as there will be betrayals within the community (13:12). In the allegory of the waiting servants, even though the servants are commanded to watch, in Gethsemane they are unable to watch even one hour (14:37). Radically, however, the message of both Mark 4 and Mark 13 is one of hope. Just as there is no comparison between the three failures and the bountiful harvest, so there is no comparison between the sufferings of the end time and the return of the Son of man. Just as the farmer waits in patience while the seed grows secretly (4:26–29), patient fidelity is to characterize the community (13:13, 33–36).

The community has been summoned to believe in the good news (1:15). From a previous generation Jesus speaks to the trials of the generation that hears Mark's good news. This is a story of one who, though mighty in word and work, chose the way of powerless self-giving that others might be free (10:45). His death was not the end of the story, for he has been raised up (16:6). The community lives between the resurrection and the return of Jesus, between promise and presence. Jesus is "lord of the house" which awaits his return. The community lives therefore by hope as well as by faith. When it recounts the parables and allegories of Jesus, it shares the memories of Jesus that have been handed down. A community that can share such memories can become a community of shared hopes.

3

THE
PARABLES
OF
MATTHEW

INTRODUCTION

In contrast to Mark, Matthew has a great number of parables: four from Mark (Matthew omits the Seed Growing Secretly); nine from Q (the sayings source which he shares in common with Luke); and ten that are called M or Matthean special material.[1] Matthew's parables manifest certain common traits.[2] Many are dramatic parables where human actions and human decisions engage the hearers. Matthew loves the grand scale. Mark's shrub (Mark 4:32) becomes a tree (Matt. 13:32); the treasure and the pearl exceed all value (Matt. 13:44–46); the debt of the servant exceeds the taxes from Syria, Phoenicia, Judea, and Samaria (Matt. 18:24); ten bridesmaids are the retinue for a rich man's daughter (Matt. 25:1–13); and the talents given to the servants equal wages for thirty, sixty, or 150 years (Matt. 25:15). Matthew also loves stark contrasts and reversals. His parables contain more allegorical elements than those of Mark or Luke, and he exhibits a fondness for apocalyptic imagery to underscore the crisis occasioned by the teaching of Jesus. The stakes are heaven or hell, outer darkness, weeping and gnashing of teeth. This combination of dramatic interaction, imaginative language, and religious awe provides an entree into the theological world of Matthew.

1. Numbers are based on the list of parables in Jeremias, *Parables*, 247–48. For a more complete list which includes parabolic sayings, see Drury, *Parables*, 70–72.
2. Goulder, "Characteristics of the Parables," 52–53.

ETHICS AND DISCIPLESHIP:
MATTHEW'S REDACTION OF MARK 4

In his sermon in parable (Matt. 13:1–52), by changes in his Markan source, by the addition of his own material, and by his own placing and arrangement of material, Matthew creates a discourse twenty verses longer than Mark's and one that conveys distinctive themes of his theology.[3] While I do not undertake an exhaustive study of Matthew 13, I will call attention to major characteristics of the discourse and aspects of its theology. To anticipate my conclusions, I will suggest that, while Mark's discourse serves his Christology and the *summons to discipleship*, Matthew stresses more the *ethics of discipleship* and the relation of ethics to eschatology.

Matthew 13 is the third of the five major discourses that give the Gospel its distinctive flavor (chaps. 5—7, the Sermon on the Mount; chap. 10, the Mission Discourse; chap. 13, the Discourse in Parables; chap. 18, Instructions on Life in Community; chaps. 24—25, the Eschatological Discourse). The parable discourse follows narratives portraying the growing estrangement between Jesus and his contemporaries. While Matthew follows Mark in placing the discourse immediately *after* the saying that those who do God's will are the true family of Jesus (Matt. 12:46–50 = Mark 3:31–35), he leaves the Markan order at the conclusion of the discourse by telling the story of the rejection at Nazareth (Matt. 13:53–58 = Mark 6:1–6a).

Also, while Matthew follows Mark closely in reproducing the text of the Sower, the following section which corresponds to Mark 4:10–12 is considerably expanded by Matthew (Matt. 13:10–17). In Matthew only disciples (*mathētai*) ask the question, which is not about the meaning of the parables but about the reason for speaking in parables at all: "Why do you speak to them in parables?" (13:10). The response of Jesus is also different: "To you it has been given *to know* the secrets of the kingdom of heaven" (13:11). There is no explicit reference to "those outside," as in Mark. Matthew immediately adds Mark 4:25, "For to him who has will more be given." In 13:13 (= Mark 4:12) Matthew changes Mark's puzzling *hina*

---

3. The most important study of Matthew 13 is by Kingsbury, *Matthew 13;* cf. the summary by W. Harrington, *Parables Told by Jesus.*

("in order that") to *hoti* ("because") and adds the full quotation from Isa. 6:9–10 as a proof from Scripture to confirm the deafness and blindness of the hearers. These later changes soften the predestinarian potential of Mark's text and root the hardening effect of the parabolic discourse in the obstinacy of the hearers. In Matthew the parables clearly do not cause the division between the disciples and others but are a consequence of it, that is, Jesus turns to special instruction of the disciples because others have rejected his teaching.

After the quotation from Isaiah, Matthew then adds a blessing on the disciples which comes from Q (13:16–17 = Luke 10:23–24). In his presentation of the allegory of the seeds Matthew stresses not only hearing the word but also understanding it (13:19). He omits the parable of the Seed Growing Secretly as well as the sayings of Mark 4:21–24, even though he has these at other places in his Gospel (5:15; 7:2; 10:26). He adds the parable of the Wheat and the Tares (13:24–30), and to the parable of the Mustard Seed (13:31–32) he joins the parable of the Leaven (13:33)—which shows a Matthean penchant for a triadic grouping of parables. He then concludes this section of the discourse by showing that Jesus' discourse in parables is in fulfillment of Scripture (13:35 = Ps. 78:2).

At 13:36 there is a major shift in the discourse. Jesus leaves the crowds, enters a house, and speaks to his disciples alone. He also leaves the Markan source here, and the following material is completely from his own tradition, or due to his own composition.[4] This section contains an allegorical interpretation of the Wheat and the Tares (13:36–43), a triad of kingdom parables—the Hidden Treasure, the Pearl, and the Net (13:44–50)—and a concluding saying about a scribe trained for the kingdom of heaven who brings from his treasure what is new and what is old (13:51–52), which could well be Matthew's self-description of his literary technique.[5] The chapter ends with a formula similar to the conclusion of the other major discourses: "and when Jesus had finished these parables" (13:53; cf. 7:28; 11:1; 19:1; 26:1).

---

4. M is used to designate material in Matthew without parallels in either Mark or Q. It is virtually impossible to distinguish here actual Matthean composition from tradition. For a catalogue and commentary on this material, see Manson, *Sayings,* 149–252.

5. See Cope, *Matthew: A Scribe Trained for the Kingdom of Heaven,* esp. 11–31.

Matthean Theology in the Discourse

In his groundbreaking study of Matthew 13, Jack D. Kingsbury argued that the discourse marks a great shift in the Gospel when Jesus turns away from the crowds and toward the disciples, which is underscored by the division at 13:36. He argues that the crowd symbolizes the Judaism of Matthew's own time and its rejection of Christian claims.[6] Matthew portrays Jesus as experiencing this same rejection and turning away from his contemporaries to form a new Israel of which the historical disciples of Jesus were to be a nucleus. The Matthean church is the heir of the disciples, and the same Jesus who taught the disciples now as exalted Lord (Matt. 28:16–20) continues to instruct his church.

While Kingsbury's presentation is a model of careful research and methodological clarity, and while it has won wide acceptance, it captures only one aspect of Matthew's theology. I propose that the discourse is equally concerned with the responsibility of "Christian discipleship."[7] In fact, throughout his Gospel, Matthew uses the rejection of Jesus by his contemporaries as a warning to the disciples that they too can reject Jesus. The main thrust of the discourse deals with the ethics of discipleship, an ethics that is qualified by Matthew's eschatological vision.

The focus on the responsibility of the disciples is marked initially by the relocation of Mark 4:25 to Matt. 13:12. After the expanded version of the hardening saying in Matt. 13:11 (= Mark 4:10) which stresses the culpable responsibility of those who do not understand the parables, Matthew adds a blessing on the disciples who have seen and understood (Matt. 13:15–17). Thus the disciples become clear examples of those who "will have abundance" (13:12). He then directs the interpretation of the Sower explicitly to the disciples by the phrase "You, therefore, learn the meaning of the parable"

6. Kingsbury, *Matthew 13*, esp. 130–37.
7. For this aspect of the discourse I follow Dupont, "Le point de vue de Matthieu dans le chapitre des paraboles," 221–59. For discipleship as a major theme in Matthew, see Bornkamm, Barth, and Held, *Tradition and Interpretation in Matthew*, esp. 15–57, 95–125, 200–206; Kingsbury, *Jesus Christ in Matthew, Mark and Luke*, 85–88; idem, *Matthew as Story*, 103–19; and U. Luz, "The Disciples in the Gospel according to Matthew," 98–128.

(13:18, au. trans.) and stresses that hearing must be joined to understanding.

In 13:24 Matthew then returns to the crowds (the "them" [autois] refers to the crowds in chap. 13) and addresses three parables to them. The first, the Wheat and the Tares (13:24–30), often thought to be a variant of Mark's Seed Growing Secretly (Mark 4:26–29), allows different interpretations, depending on the context. The surprising element in the parable is that the householder allows the thorns to grow alongside the wheat. The central thrust of the parable is the contrast between the householder who waits until the harvest and the servants who are eager to root out the weeds at first sight. The parable also contains the paradox that the action of the enemy which was meant to harm the owner of the field ends up for his benefit, since the weeds can be burned for fuel (13:30).

In the kingdom proclamation of Jesus, this parable may have served as a defense of his association with sinners and his unwillingness to establish a "pure Messianic community."[8] As the Psalms of Solomon (first century B.C.) attests, the arrival of God's kingdom was to be marked by the separation of the good from the evil and the purification of the land.[9] Jesus does not deny that such a separation will take place but disassociates it from his proclamation of the kingdom. Now is the time for the offer of mercy and forgiveness to the sinner. Those who will be "blessed of my Father" (Matt. 25:34) will be known only at the final judgment.

In Matthew this parable is to be read along with the Mustard Seed (13:31–32) and the Leaven (13:33), both of which stress the hidden nature of the kingdom. All three capture the paradoxical nature of the Matthean church. The church is a corpus mixtum, a body in which the good and the bad are mixed together. Like the mustard seed, it is small and insignificant, but it will become a tree. Its growth is as imperceptible as that of the rising of leavened bread. There is an

---

8. Jeremias, Parables, 223–25.
9. See esp. Pss. Sol. 17:23. The psalmist prays that the hoped-for king, a son of David, will "expel sinners from the inheritance" and "smash the sinner's arrogance like a potter's vessel" (v. 23) so that "he shall gather together a holy people, whom he shall lead in righteousness," trans. Brock, in Sparks's The Apocryphal Old Testament, 678.

added paradox in that leaven is often a symbol of evil in biblical thought (cf. 1 Cor. 5:6–8).[10]

Therefore, in these parables, which along with the Sower are addressed to the crowds (= potential believers in Matthew's own day), Matthew explains the paradoxical nature of his church. It is no less paradoxical for him than the teaching of Jesus which was rejected but which bore great fruit, bringing forth a community that contains both the good and the bad. The future manifestation of this kingdom is hidden now under the insignificance of its present state, and even what may appear evil to outsiders conceals the mystery of God's growth.

The next major section of the parable discourse begins at 13:36 where Jesus enters a house to give private instruction to his disciples. Here the demands of discipleship are made explicit and are placed in the context of ethics qualified by eschatology, that is, conduct in the light of God's future for the world.

The instruction begins with the allegory of the Wheat and the Tares (13:36–43), couched in dualistic and apocalyptic language. The disciples (and Matthew's readers) are transported to the end of history. The Son of man will separate all causes of sin and evil; the righteous will shine like the sun, and for evildoers there will be weeping and gnashing of teeth. The allegory serves both to encourage and to warn the Matthean church. They are exhorted to patience in the face of evil and warned against precipitous judgment of evildoers. At the same time, they are assured that the just will be rewarded and the evil punished.

The next parables of this section are totally different in language and atmosphere. The reader moves away from the violent world of the final judgment to the almost idyllic atmosphere of folk tales about finding a treasure and a pearl (13:44–46).[11] These short parables admit of multiple interpretations. Traditionally they have been interpreted in terms of the "cost of discipleship"—that is, like those who sell all they have to secure their discovery, disciples are to sacrifice all to respond to the proclamation of the kingdom.[12] In the first parable, however, there is the note that it is the joy of

---

10. Funk, "Beyond Criticism in Quest of Literacy."
11. See Crossan, *Finding Is the First Act*, esp. 73–122.
12. Perkins (*Hearing*, 26–29) centers on the risk involved in the parables.

discovery which precipitates the decision to sell all (13:44).[13] The joy of receiving God's forgiveness proclaimed by Jesus releases the hearer to respond without counting the cost of the response.

The third parable in this section, the Net (13:47–50), reiterates motifs from the Wheat and the Tares. The kingdom is like a large fish net that gathers up both the good and the bad and after the large catch the good and bad are separated. The eschatological application is that such a separation will take place at the "close of the age" (cf. 13:40) when the just (righteous) will be separated from the evil and, as in 13:42, there will be weeping and gnashing of teeth.

By his arrangement and structure here Matthew makes a programmatic statement about the relation of ethics and eschatology. Both the first and the third "parable" (13:36–43, 47–50) are in reality allegories of the end time; both employ standard apocalyptic imagery and motifs: reference to the close of the age; the presence of the Son of man and angels; separation of the good and the bad; and punishment by fire.[14] In contrast the twin parables of the hidden treasure and the pearl are not allegorical; the imagery is this-worldly and the application deals with immediate activity. Therefore, by bracketing these parables by the two apocalyptic allegories Matthew shows that conduct or the ethics of response to the kingdom is qualified by eschatology. The present is not simply the time for passive waiting but is to be characterized by the joy of finding and the risk of losing all to possess a treasure. At the same time, the disciples are not to be overly concerned about apparent failure and by the presence of evil in their midst. Ultimate judgment is in the hands of God, and the end time will be the time when their hidden deeds of justice will be disclosed.

Therefore, while Mark took over the seed parables of Jesus to stress Christology and discipleship, Matthew sharpens the focus on discipleship and qualifies it by his eschatological vision. To respond to the teaching of Jesus ("God with us," Matt. 1:23; cf. 28:20) means to do the will of God (7:21). The disciples are those who not only hear but understand. Unbelief is due to the deafness of the

---

13. Crossan (*In Parables*, 38) notes the "joy and discovery" in these parables.
14. On apocalyptic imagery, see esp. J.J. Collins, *The Apocalyptic Imagination*, 1–32.

hearers but has been willed by God. The failure of the ministry of
Jesus, the insignificance of the present church, and the presence of
evil should not be a cause of scandal or discouragement. The ultimate
separation of good from evil is reserved for the end time, and the
criterion will be whether one is truly just or not. Prior to that time
the community should be more concerned with their own response
to Jesus than with separating the good from the evil. Matthew's
discourse in parable sets the tone for the interpretation of subsequent
parables where Matthew instructs his community on how they are
to live in recollection of the teaching of Jesus and on how their
present life is to be sustained by the hope of God's future.

THE JUSTICE OF THE KINGDOM
IN MATTHEW

After the parables of chapter 13, the next major parables of
Matthew are in the Sermon on the Church, or on life in community
(chap. 18), and in the teaching of Jesus between 19:1 and 20:16.
Two parables in these sections, the Unmerciful Servant (18:23–35)
and the Laborers in the Vineyard (20:1–16), reveal Matthew's
fundamental convictions in a special way.[15] These parables each deal
with Matthew's distinctive understanding of "justice" (Hebrew *ṣe-
dāqāh*; Greek, *dikaiosynē*), a concern where Matthew manifests the
profound influence of his Jewish heritage. All references to *dikaiosynē*
in Matthew are without parallels in the other Synoptics and they
give a distinct flavor to the Gospel.[16] Mark never uses the noun
"justice" and Luke uses it only once; Matthew uses it 7 times and
uses the adjective *dikaios* 17 times (contrast, Mark, 2 times; Luke,
11 times). One needs to be sensitive to the richness of Matthew's
appropriation of this important term.

Dikaiosynē is a multidimensional term which evokes a rich heritage
of associations.[17] The translations "righteousness" and "righteous,"
found in many contemporary translations (e.g., RSV), with their
overtones of moral rectitude, do not capture the richness of the
biblical terms, which convey a sense of "rightness" or what should

15. I am in debt to the interesting study of Daniel Patte for showing the relation
of chap. 18 to the material that follows (*The Gospel according to Matthew*, 244–80).
16. Bornkamm, "The Better Righteousness," in *Tradition and Interpretation in
Matthew*, 24–32; and Przybylski, *Righteousness in Matthew and His World of Thought*.
17. Donahue, "Biblical Perspectives on Justice," 68–112.

happen. Paths, for example, are called just when they do what a path should do: lead to a goal. Laws are just when they create unity and harmony within the community.[18]

In the OT, Yahweh is proclaimed as just (2 Chron. 12:6; Neh. 9:8; Pss. 7:9; 103:17; 116:5; Jer. 9:24; Dan. 9:14) and seeks justice (Isa. 5:1–7). Justice has also the overtones of saving help. God is just in coming to the rescue of the threatened community or in defending those in the community who have no one to defend them (Pss. 82:3–4; 103:6). God is also just in punishing those who turn away from the Torah or follow other gods. Justice is associated with a number of other central concepts of biblical faith, such as "just judgments" (mišpāt, Isa. 28:17–18) and "steadfast love, mercy and fidelity" (Hos. 2:19–20; cf. Matt. 23:23).

In Matthew, John prepares for the ministry of Jesus by coming in the "way of justice" (21:32; RSV: "way of righteousness"), and in his inaugural Sermon on the Mount (chaps. 5—7) Jesus praises those who hunger and thirst for justice (5:6) and who are persecuted for the sake of justice (5:10). The justice of those who would heed his words must be greater than that of the Pharisees (5:20), and the prescriptions of the law are to be observed not simply by external observance but by a renewal of mind and heart culminating in love of God and neighbor (5:21–48; 22:34–40). Matthew pictures Jesus as the Servant who proclaims justice to the nations and who will bring justice to victory (12:18–21, citing Isa. 42:1–4). The harshest criticism of the Pharisees is that they have neglected "the weightier matters of the law, justice and mercy and faith" (23:23).[19] The "gospel of the kingdom" (Matt. 4:23; 9:35; 24:14; cf. 26:13) which Jesus proclaims and enacts is the way the world is made "right," or just, before God.

In two significant parables Matthew adapts Jesus' proclamation of the justice of the kingdom to the needs of his community. Both use legal language and both have the atmosphere of a trial or hearing before a lord or judge. They both come in sections of the Gospel that deal with instruction to the disciples about life in community. In these parables—the Unmerciful Servant (Matt. 18:23–35) and the

18. Pedersen, Israel: Its Life and Culture I-II, 337–40.
19. The text here reads krisin which in the LXX translates the Hebrew mišpāt, a term often synonymous with ṣedāqāh/dikaiosynē.

Laborers in the Vineyard (Matt. 20:1–16)—Matthew's Jesus teaches his disciples that pursuit of the justice of the kingdom flows from the experience of unmerited forgiveness from God. They are to manifest it to others with the realization that God's justice is always joined with mercy and with surprising lovingkindness. In the words of Abraham J. Heschel, "God is compassion, not compromise; justice, though not inclemency."[20]

Justice, Mercy, and the Unmerciful Servant (Matt. 18:23–35)

Matthew's sermon on church order is often divided into two major sections: care for little ones (18:1–14) and care for sinners (18:15–35).[21] It begins with an address of Jesus to the disciples, and the tone of the whole chapter is set by the concern for the little ones (18:1–10), those in the Matthean community whose faith is weak (6:30; 8:26; 14:31; 16:8; 17:20, those of "little faith") or who need special care (10:42; cf. 25:40, 45, "the least").[22] While in the first part of the chapter Matthew takes over material from Mark (18:1–9 = Mark 9:33–37, 42–48) and Q (18:10–14 = Luke 15:3–7), the second part consists of material from his own tradition, M, or of his own composition. Within this larger twofold structure there is a substructure whereby the two parables (18:10–14 and 18:23–35) which conclude each section also bracket disciplinary regulations dealing with sin and conflict within the community (18:15–20).

The parable of the Lost Sheep and the parable of the Unmerciful Servant not only transmit important aspects of the teaching of Jesus but give a definite theological stamp to the Gospel of Matthew. In Matthew the Lost Sheep is clearly marked by its context, and the Lukan context is closer to the meaning of the parable in the ministry of Jesus, where he defends his ministry to the "lost" of his society: tax collectors, sinners, and those whom his contemporaries consider outside the pale of God's mercy (Luke 15:1–2).[23] Matthew's application of the parable to his community emerges from his distinctive

20. Heschel, *The Prophets*, 16.
21. Gundry, *Matthew*, 358; and Meier, *Matthew*, 199–200. For a complete discussion of the structure and content of this chapter, see Thompson, *Matthew's Advice to a Divided Community*.
22. On identity of "little ones," see Gundry, *Matthew*, 203. Little ones are "disciples who do not occupy positions of leadership in the church." Meier says they are "insignificant disciples who easily go astray" (*Matthew*, 202).
23. Jeremias, *Parables*, 38–39, 132–36; see below, pp. 147–51.

wording. In Matthew one of the sheep goes "astray" (*planēthē*, a term not usually used of wandering animals but frequently used of moral straying; cf. James 5:19–20). In 18:14 the interpretation of the parable, "It is not the will of my Father who is in heaven that one of these little ones should perish," directs the parable to leaders of Matthew's own church who are to have special care for weaker members of the community. Matthew shows here the influence of Ezek. 34:6–8, where religious leaders are criticized because God's sheep "were scattered" and "wandered over all the mountains" and "my shepherds have not searched for my sheep." The location of the parable in Matthew, immediately preceding what seems to be a rather harsh and juridical approach to failure within the community, shows that, however community discipline is to be applied, order within the community is to be measured against the claims of the weaker members for special care and assistance.

The Parable of the Unmerciful Servant (Matt. 18:23–35) as Text

The final parable of the chapter is also the first major dramatic parable in Matthew. Its context as the conclusion of the chapter marks it as the hermeneutical key to the chapter as a whole. It is introduced by a Q saying on forgiveness (Matt. 18:21–22 = Luke 17:4) taken from a collection of sayings on discipleship preserved by Luke in their more original form.[24] Three things are distinctive to Matthew's version: (1) He makes the saying a direct response to Peter's question: "Lord, how often shall my brother sin against me, and I forgive him? As many as seven times?" (Matt. 18:21). (2) He changes the numbers from the offense and the repentance (Luke 17:4, "If he sins against you seven times in the day, and turns to you seven times, and says, 'I repent,' you must forgive him") to the forgiveness. (3) He magnifies the forgiveness: "Jesus said to him, 'I do not say to you seven times, but seventy times seven' " (Matt. 18:22). Also, as we shall see, the parable itself does not really answer the question of Peter "How often?" but deals with the precondition (i.e., the quality) of forgiveness rather than with the number of times (quantity) it must be extended.

The concluding verse of the parable (18:35), "So also my heavenly

---

24. Fitzmyer, *Luke X—XXIV*, 1136–40.

Father will do to every one of you, if you do not forgive your brother from your heart," reflects Matthew's editing in the use of "heavenly Father" and sounds like a paraphrase of the petition of the Lord's Prayer, "Forgive us our debts, as we also have forgiven our debtors" (Matt. 6:12). By adding v. 35, Matthew makes the parable into a warning, which builds on the original meaning but does not exhaust it.

In approaching the dramatic parables, it is helpful to break them into scenes or acts and to study the dramatic interaction of characters in the different parts. J. Dominic Crossan proposes a helpful division to this parable by noting a threefold division in which each part is characterized by a similar structure of introductory narrative, followed by dialogue and with concluding action.[25]

> ACT ONE: The King and the Servant with the Immense Debt
>   Narrative, vv. 23–25; dialogue, v. 26; action, v. 27
> ACT TWO: The forgiven Servant and the fellow Servant with Debt
>   Narrative, v. 28; dialogue, v. 29; action, v. 30
> ACT THREE: Fellow Servants, King, First Servant and Second Servant
>   Narrative, vv. 31–32a; dialogue, vv. 32b–33; action, v. 34
> MATTHEAN EPILOGUE, v. 35

Such a division enables us to follow the double dramatic movement in the parable. In the "comic" movement the first servant moves from ill fortune to good fortune in act one only to end up in tragedy in act three.[26] The second servant moves from ill fortune to good fortune in the second and third acts. The rapid interchange and intersection of movements increases the dramatic involvement. Running throughout the parable, like a musical motif, is the constant repetition of terms for "debt" (vv. 24, 27, 30, 32, 34) as well as words for mercy and strong human emotion (vv. 26, 27, 28, 33). Critical shifts in each act take place when narrative shifts to dialogue.

The power of the parable emerges from progressive engagement with the characters. When the parable begins, our sympathies are with the first servant. The desire of the king "to settle accounts" (cf. Matt. 25:19) strikes an ominous note, as does the description of the servant as being "brought" before the king. The reason for this

25. Crossan, *In Parables*, 105–7.
26. See esp. D.O. Via, *Parables*, 137–44.

threatening situation is held in suspense until the final words of v. 24, "who owed him ten thousand talents." Since the annual income of Herod the Great was about nine hundred talents and since the taxes for Galilee and Perea were two hundred talents a year, such a debt would evoke an unbelieving gasp.[27] The inability to pay is not surprising, and the king's order of slavery for the debtor with his family suggests that he is a tyrannical gentile despot, since by Jewish law only a debtor, and not the family, could be enslaved for unpaid debts.[28] At this point the sympathy of the hearers would be toward this servant, since an unpayable debt to a heartless master is pitiable.

In v. 26 the narrative shifts to dialogue and the servant makes his plea: "Lord, have patience with me, and I will pay you everything." The shock in the first part of the parable comes in the first words of v. 27. The king, who was depicted as heartless, is rather a person who takes pity (lit., "has compassion on him") and forgives the debt. A reader does not expect one who was ready to enslave a whole family to be so moved. The surprising turn of events continues when the king does not heed the servant's request for time to pay but forgives the whole debt. The parable could have ended at this point and it would have been a good illustration of Matt. 7:7, "Ask, and it will be given you," or an example of what it means to pray for forgiveness even when burdened with the debt of sin.

The parable, however, moves forward to the second act, where the major thrust is found. In contrast to his passive earlier state when he was dragged before the king, the first servant now "goes out" and chances upon a fellow servant who owes him a hundred denarii. Since one denarius is the equivalent of a day's wage (cf. Matt. 20:2), the debt is not inconsequential. Since a talent is the equivalent of fifteen years of daily wages, the contrast between the debts of the first servant and the second servant is immense. This second servant now becomes a mirror image of the first. He too falls on his knees and makes a petition in the very same words as the first servant, "Have patience with me, and I will pay you" (v. 29). The difference is that the terms of his request could be met, since in time the debt could be repaid. At this point the story could conclude with the first servant remitting the debt or even granting the request, and the

27. Linnemann, *Jesus*, 108.
28. Jeremias, *Parables*, 211.

parable would be a good illustration of the "golden rule" (Matt. 7:12, "Whatever you wish that people should do to you, do also to them," au. trans.). The opposite occurs, and with a brutality even greater than he experienced—he seized him "by the throat"—the first servant demands payment. At this point the sympathy of the readers or hearers of the parable shifts. The person with whom we rejoiced earlier now becomes repulsive. Like the fellow servants of v. 31, we are shocked at the injustice (they are "greatly distressed").

The third act begins with the actions of these servants. They do as we would like to do and go to the king in the hope of redressing the situation. The king summons the first servant, calls him wicked, and tells him what exactly happened in the first act. He was forgiven simply because the king had mercy on him and he should have expressed this mercy to his fellow servant. In v. 34 there is a tragic irony for the first servant in that now he will have what he originally requested, time to pay his debt, only the time will be spent in prison.

Interpreting the Unmerciful Servant

Redescribing the parable helps us to realize better the narrative skill and dramatic irony that permeates the story but leaves certain unanswered questions, principally why the first servant acted as he did. The answer unlocks the religious power of the parable and its importance for understanding both the message of Jesus and the theology of Matthew.

The key is the skillful way in which the narrative juxtaposes the actions and the dialogue of the first two servants. When the first servant is brought to the king his request is in the form of a plea to have time to pay a debt that is unpayable. There is something awry in his petition. Instead of asking for mercy, he thinks that the way out of his tragic situation is to restore the order of justice, of debts to be paid and obligations met. The surprise in this part is that the king acts out of mercy, not justice. Strictly speaking, the king does not grant his request but goes beyond it by granting what the servant did not even hope to receive. His request is in the order of justice; the king operates in the order of mercy out of compassion.

The second act plays out the result of the servant's faulty understanding. When he goes out and hears the request of the second servant, he hears an echo of his own disposition. He enters again the familiar world of strict justice. The forgiveness and mercy that he received were something that simply happened to him, not something that changed his way of viewing the world. His self-understanding remains unaltered by the gift he received.[29] The statement of the "lord" in v. 33 is the moment of tragic revelation of why he acted as he did, "Should not you have had mercy on your fellow servant, as I had mercy on you?" The master says, in effect: Even given your predisposition to view the world through the eyes of strict justice, you should have seen that the mercy which was "right" in your case was also owed to your fellow servant. Paradoxically, then, mercy becomes justice and justice or "the right order" between God and humanity is maintained through mercy.[30] The Matthean addition of v. 35 stresses that forgiveness must be "from your heart." This is a warning that unless the gospel transforms the innermost dispositions of its hearers, they will act in much the same fashion as the first servant. The Jewish-Christian letter to James, with its accustomed directness, conveys a similar view: "For judgment is without mercy to one who has shown no mercy; yet mercy triumphs over judgment" (James 2:13). The parable thus conveys the precondition for a proper Christian ethic, and not simply an exhortation to forgiveness.

In the kingdom proclamation of Jesus this parable invites one to experience through narrative the challenge of Jesus' summons "to repent" or to have a change of heart (metanoia, Matt. 4:17). What is called for is a totally new way of viewing the world which shatters misunderstandings of the justice of God. Behind the God who comes to expression in the parables of Jesus is the God of Hos. 2:19 in whom are joined righteousness, justice, steadfast love (closely akin to compassion; cf. Matt. 18:27), and mercy. Behind the image of the king stands the God of Jesus who summons people to be forgiving because they have experienced forgiveness. It cautions against a legalistic or closed way of experiencing life which filters the unexpected through the narrow categories of rights and duties. In the ministry of Jesus this parable could have had a polemical thrust against religious leaders, who through the Torah and the saving act

---

29. D.O. Via, Parables, 143.
30. See esp. Linnemann, Jesus, 111–13.

of God in history have received mercy and forgiveness but would want to deny this to others.

The Parable in Context

The parable picks up motifs from earlier in the Gospel such as the petition "Forgive us our debts, as we also have forgiven our debtors" (Matt. 6:12) and the statement "If you do not forgive others their trespasses, neither will your Father forgive your trespasses" (6:15, au. trans.). It also anticipates the attack on the Pharisees in 23:23, "You have neglected the weightier matters of the law, justice and mercy and faith." Its immediate context, however, is Matthew's concern for life in community.

As noted, it concludes a chapter where the central theme is care for the little ones, and serves, with the parable of the Lost Sheep, to bracket the disciplinary regulations of 18:15–20. Here Matthew describes a quasi-legal procedure (v. 16, "evidence," "witnesses") which can result in the exclusion of someone from the community— "let him be to you as a Gentile and a tax collector" (18:17). These decisions are to be made with confidence that they will be ratified by God, who is present in the midst of the assembled community (18:18–19; cf. 16:19). Similar processes of exclusion of unrepentant members from the community are known both from Qumran and from the Pauline churches (cf. 1 Cor. 5:1–13).[31] The Matthean structure, however, puts such power in a proper context. A community that confronts the sinner and excludes the incorrigible must first realize that it too is a community of the little ones who have strayed and been found and who have been surprised by undeserved mercy. It will bear authentic witness to the teaching of Jesus only when its juridical procedures are subject to the "law of mercy."

Matthew's readers may even see a certain irony in treating the recalcitrant member of the community like "a Gentile and a tax collector"—groups which in the Gospel receive the special attention of Jesus. Though Matthew follows the Markan order of the beginning of the public ministry of Jesus, he inserts after Mark's first miracle,

31. On similar but more extensive procedures at Qumran, see the Community Rule (1QS 5:25—6:1; 6:24—7:25; 8:20—9:2). Eng. trans.: Dupont-Sommer, *The Essene Writings from Qumran*, 84–85, 87–90, 91–93; and Vermes, *The Dead Sea Scrolls in English*, 82–86.

the healing of a Jewish leper (8:1–4), the healing of the servant of a gentile centurion (8:5–13). He also places early in his Gospel the charge against Jesus that he is a friend of tax collectors and sinners (9:11; cf. Luke 15:1–2). It is when ordinary community order breaks down that the shepherd leaves the ninety-nine to seek those who have strayed.

Matthew seems to confront two distinct groups that are causing difficulty in the community.[32] One consists of "enthusiasts" who seem to reject any legal constraint and take pride in their prophecy and mighty works (7:15–23). To these Matthew affirms the enduring validity of the law (Matt. 5:17–20). At the same time, Matthew rejects a "Christian Pharisaism" which would turn the gospel into a rigid system of rights and duties, and argues that life in the church is to be under the new law of mercy and love. Mercy is not an exception to the rule of justice. A person is perfect as the heavenly Father is perfect (Matt. 5:48) when he or she relates to others with that mercy and love which he or she has received.

The Laborers in the Vineyard
(Matt. 20:1–16)

The Parable as Text

This parable takes as its field of comparison the practice of hiring day laborers for occasional work. Though a large number of characters are mentioned—the householder, five groups of laborers, and the steward—the interaction between the householder and those first hired is the key to interpreting the parable. The parable can be divided into three acts: Act One, the hirings (20:1–7); Act Two, the payments (20:8–11); and Act Three, the dialogue between the owner and the grumbling workers (20:11–15).

The first act begins with a familiar sight: day laborers waiting for work. In first-century Palestine work was scarce and poverty widespread, so a story of a householder who engages a great number of workers would be appealing. At the outset, however, there is a surprising note. The householder (and not his steward) goes out

---

32. On Matthew's battle on two fronts, see R. Brown and Meier, *Antioch and Rome*, esp. 57–72 by Meier; and Schweizer, "Observance of the Law and Charismatic Activity in Matthew."

from "early in the morning" until the eleventh hour to assemble the workers. The hearers are given a hint that their normal view of the world is to be challenged. Important to the narrative development of the parable are the different wage agreements. The first group of workers agree to the normal day's wage (v. 2); those hired in the third hour agree to "whatever is right" (v. 4; lit., "just," *dikaion*) as presumably do those hired in the sixth and the ninth hour. The first act of the parable—the different hirings by the householder—ends in v. 7 with the hiring of the eleventh-hour workers without any mention of payment. If the parable ended here, it would be an illustration of a saying such as, "The harvest is plentiful, but the laborers are few; pray therefore the Lord of the harvest to send out laborers into his harvest" (Matt. 9:37–38).

The second act (vv. 8–11) begins with a rather solemn introduction: "but [the adversative particle *de* in Greek] when evening came." Also the master who previously had personally summoned the workers now orders his steward to assemble them. The image is almost that of a trial or a hearing. The forthcoming surprise in the action of the owner is anticipated by the order of payment (v. 8). Normally those who had already worked twelve hours would be the first to receive their wages. As we stand with the workers and watch the payment, when those who are hired last receive a denarius, we begin to have the same feelings as those hired first (v. 10, they thought they would receive more). Since the householder has already emerged as both just and generous, the shock comes in v. 11 when those hired first do not receive more.

In the third act (vv. 12–15) the narrative shifts to dialogue, and the deep meaning of the parable emerges. As one might expect, those who worked all day grumble because "you have made them equal to us" (v. 12). The response of the householder begins with the somewhat ironic "friend" and comprises a threefold counter to their complaint: (*a*) I did you no injustice (v. 13); (*b*) since no injustice has occurred, "I can do with my goods as I wish" (v. 14); and (*c*) I question your attitude, "Do you begrudge my generosity?" (lit., "Is your eye evil because I am good?" v. 15). The final saying, "So the last will be first, and the first last" (v. 16), is an interpretation of the parable where Matthew adapts to this context a common saying about the eschatological reversal (cf. Luke 13:30; Matt. 19:30; Mark 10:30).

This parable is a good example of one with a central thrust but with different subthemes. Literary analysis calls into question the traditional title of "the Laborers (or Workers) in the Vineyard." The main character in the parable and the one who gives it its shape is the owner. He hires, decides the wage, directs the order of payment, and defends his action. For this reason Joachim Jeremias calls it the parable of "the Good Employer."[33] This is not totally accurate since the employer would be good had he only hired the workers or had he hired them and given those who worked all day a higher wage. The grumbling workers, while not the main characters in the parable, provide the dramatic foil for the interpretation of the parable.

If a reader too quickly identifies the owner as God and is unwilling to experience the same feelings as those who worked all day, the challenge of the parable loses its force. Hardly any parable in the Gospels seems to upset the basic structure of an orderly society as does this one. Were this parable normative for economic life, or were it implemented even in church life, chaos would result (what would happen to "merit increases"?). The constant complaint in our society about welfare is proof that popular morality operates according to the principle of "equal pay for equal work."

The potential affront caused by this parable emerges by comparing it to a rabbinic parable which, even if later than the parable of Jesus, is remarkably similar—and different.[34]

Unto what was Rabbi bar Hiya like? He was like unto a king who hired many laborers of whom one was more industrious than the others. What did the king do? He called him out and walked up and down

33. Jeremias, Parables, 136.
34. Cited in Johnston, "The Study of Rabbinic Parables," 346; and by Oesterley, The Gospel Parables, 108. Jeremias (Parables, 138) notes that the Jewish parable dates from a text of about A.D. 300 and that, even if based on early tradition, priority belongs to Jesus' version. L. Schottroff ("Human Solidarity and the Goodness of God," 138) finds the comparison with the rabbinic parable "misleading," since it simply illustrates that the rabbi who dies young is not at a disadvantage. See also Derrett, "Workers in the Vineyard: A Parable of Jesus," in Studies in the New Testament 1:48–75, esp. 50–51. In his survey, Johnston ("The Study of Rabbinic Parables," 346) notes that while Jesus' parables tend to reverse conventional values, rabbinic parables tend to reinforce them.

with him. In the evening the workmen came to be paid. He gave also a full day's pay to the man he had walked with. When the other workers saw this they complained and said: We have been working hard all day, and this one who only labored two hours receives as much wages as we do? The king answered: It is because this one has done more in two hours than you in a whole day. Likewise R. Abun, although he had studied the Torah only until the age of twenty-eight, he knew it better than a scholar or pious man who would have studied until a hundred.[35]

Like the parable of Jesus, this parable treats of payment for laborers who have worked different amounts of time and a complaint by those who have worked longest that one who did not do equal work received the same payment. As with the parable of Jesus, an application is attached (the defense of R. Abun), which might not have been the original application. Contrary to the parable of Jesus, the response to the complaining workers maintains a strict order of justice. Though working for a short time, the more skillful worker accomplishes as much as those who worked long hours. Such an interpretation resonates well with a human and popular understanding of justice.

Any interpretation of the parable of Jesus must respect the fact that in his parable the order of justice is maintained. Even the grumbling workers received what they had originally contracted, and to their complaint the owner responds, "I am doing you no wrong" (v. 13, *ouk a-dikō*, lit., "I am not acting unjustly"). Justice forms the background against which goodness can appear as true goodness. The complaint of the dissatisfied workers is, strictly speaking, "You have made them equal to us" (v. 12). They are defining their personal worth in contrast to others; they are not so much angered by what happened to them as envious of the good fortune of the other workers. They are so inclosed in their understanding of justice that it becomes a norm by which they become judges of others. They want to order the world by their norms which limit the master's freedom and exclude unexpected generosity. The final words of the owner, "Is your eye evil because I am good?" (au. trans.; cf. RSV: "Do you begrudge my generosity?"), underscores the defect in these servants. Since in Matthew "the eye is the lamp of the body" (Matt.

35. *Jerusalem Talmud, Berakoth* 2:8; *Song of Songs Rabbah* 6:2; translation as in Johnston, "The Study of Rabbinic Parables," 346.

6:22) and "if your eye causes you to sin, pluck it out" (5:29), these servants allow their attitude to "darken" their whole way of viewing the world.[36] What began as an act of goodness to them and unfolded as an act of generosity to others blinded them to the goodness of the owner and the good fortune of others.

The Parable in the Ministry of Jesus

Both Jeremias and Eta Linnemann locate this parable in Jesus' defense of his proclamation of God's love and forgiveness to outcasts and sinners.[37] The Pharisees are like the grumbling workers who have borne the heat of the day. The eleventh hour workers are those who receive from Jesus a chance to share equally in the coming kingdom. Even granting such a setting, the parable need not be seen as simply polemical. Jesus does not deny that the Pharisees have been faithful to the covenant, nor does he deny that God is just and calls for justice. In the spirit of OT prophecy, he states that justice must be seen as wedded to love and mercy (Hos. 2:19). Justice cannot be used to erect a wall between those whom God would join together. Jesus proclaims a wholehearted love of neighbor, and even of the enemy, and speaks of a Father who makes his light shine on the just and the unjust (Matt. 5:43–46). This God loves the person who is faithful throughout the day as well as the one called at the last hour. Jesus does not condemn the Pharisees but warns that a desire to live justly according to the covenant should not lead to an attitude that dictates to the covenant God how mercy and generosity should be shown. The line between following God's will and *deciding what God wills* is always thin and fragile.

The Parable in Context

The immediate context is Matthew's rewriting of the great middle section of Mark (8:27—10:45). Here Jesus begins his journey toward Jerusalem and three times predicts that he will suffer, die, and be raised up.[38] Mark integrates into this journey much of the material

---

36. D. O. Via (*Parables*, 152–54) says that since the grumbling workers were unable to accept the incalculable in human relationships they were ultimately estranged from the source of graciousness.

37. Jeremias, *Parables*, 136–39; and Linnemann, *Jesus*, 86–88.

38. Mark 8:31–32 = Matt. 16:30–33; Mark 9:30–32 = Matt. 17:22–23; Mark 10:32–34 = Matt. 20:17–19.

where Jesus instructs his disciples on the true meaning of following him. Though this section does not have the significance in Matthew that it has in Mark, Matthew follows Mark closely here and inserts his own material into the Markan structure. Between the second and third passion predictions (Matt. 17:22–23; 20:17–18) Matthew inserts his sermon on church order, with the parable of the Unmerciful Servant (chap. 18), and the parable of the Laborers in the Vineyard (20:1–16). Both contribute to Matthew's understanding of discipleship.

The parable begins and ends with sayings on the reversal whereby the first become the last and the last first (Matt. 19:30; 20:16), so the reader is prepared for reversal of expectations. In the context of teaching on discipleship, what is reversed is that those disciples who think they are "first" or greatest may have to yield to the last or least. Immediately preceding the parable is Matthew's retelling of the praise of the disciples who left all and followed Jesus and are now promised the hundredfold. In addition to this they are told that "you who have followed me will also sit on twelve thrones, judging the twelve tribes of Israel" (19:28). The "twelve" are to be the nucleus of the new eschatological people of God and to be viceregents with the Son of man in judging. One function of the parable of the Laborers in the Vineyard is to give a proper perspective to the privilege given the disciples. Though they have followed Jesus when first summoned (Matt. 4:18–22), both the call and the reward are still in the hand of the householder. The promise to the community that they will be eschatological judges should not lead them to assume this role prematurely. As the parable states, the first may be last and the last first. God's generosity is equally present to those called last.

The wider context is Jesus' command to the disciples "to seek first God's kingdom and God's justice" (6:33, au. trans.). Though Matthew is in debt to his Jewish heritage in his understanding of justice, he redefines justice in terms of God's generous and saving intervention on behalf of those whom others might see as outside the pale of God's care. God's justice is different from human justice. It forgives unpayable debts and summons the disciples to live a life of forgiveness to others as an expression of gratitude. To do otherwise is to risk the ultimate (i.e., eschatological) judgment pronounced on the unmerciful servant. God's justice is also not to be limited by human conceptions of a strict mathematical judgment where reward is in exact proportion to merit. Mercy and goodness challenge us, as in the Laborers in the Vineyard, to move beyond justice, even though they do not exist at the expense of justice. God's ways are not human ways. Those categories of worth and value which people erect to separate themselves from others are reversed in God's eyes. If divine freedom is limited by human conceptions of God's goodness, men and women may never be able to experience unmerited goodness.[39] Not to rejoice in the benefits given others is to cut ourselves off from those benefits we ourselves have received. Our eyes too become evil.

MATTHEW'S DEBATE WITH
"THE SYNAGOGUE ACROSS THE STREET"

Matthew's Gospel, though the most Jewish in flavor (e.g., 5:17–20, the enduring validity of the law) and structure (e.g., the five discourses reminiscent of collections of "five" in Jewish literature, such as the Pentateuch, the Psalms, and *1 Enoch*), contains also some of the most anti-Jewish statements of the New Testament. The polemic against the Pharisees in Matthew 23 is a caricature of what is known historically about the Pharisees, who, though teachers of the law, tended to be a group from the people, not from the elite such as the Sadducees. They were concerned that God's saving love touch all areas of life and probably shared many religious perspectives with Jesus.[40] In Matthew, however, the synagogues are now "their synagogues" (4:23; 9:35; 10:17; 12:9; 13:54) and Matthew contains the cry of the people, "His blood be on us and on our children!" (27:25), which has provided fodder for anti-Semitism down through the ages.[41]

Contemporary study of Matthew locates the violence of this polemic in the historical situation in which Matthew wrote, roughly two decades after the destruction of the temple in A.D. 70, during the reconstruction of Judaism around Pharisaic models, associated with Jamnia (or Yabneh Yam), a city on the Mediterranean where, according to Jewish tradition, Pharisaic leaders met at the end of the

39. Bultmann, *This World and the Beyond*, 178–88.
40. See the excellent discussion by Rivkin. s.v. "Pharisees," *IDBSup*, 657–63.
41. On interpretation of this saying as arising from late first-century polemics rather than from the historical Jesus, see Fitzymer, "Anti-Semitism and the Cry of 'All the People' (Mt 27:25)."

first century to determine the Jewish canon and codify oral tradition.[42] The burning issue among Jews at the end of the first century was who is true heir to the traditions of Israel. The claims of the priests and of apocalyptic groups like the Zealots lay dormant in the embers of a burned temple and city. Matthew, throughout his Gospel, attempts to claim the heritage of Israel for his own community and in so doing engages in a bitter polemic against his own coreligionists. History sadly teaches that the most bitter disputes occur among religious people claiming to be the authentic heirs and interpreters of a common tradition. Just as Matthew roots his community's origin in the call of the first disciples (4:18–22) and the mission given them (28:16–20), and just as he grounds the ethics of the community in the teaching of Jesus, so he roots his strongest anti-Pharisaic statements in the sayings of Jesus. By the standards of modern historical criticism the most bitter sayings are due to Matthew or his own tradition rather than to Jesus himself. Matthew also warns his own community against adopting those very "Pharisaical" attitudes which Jesus criticizes.[43]

The strained relation between Matthew's community and Judaism is found in a triad of parables, a familiar Matthean grouping, uttered by Jesus in controversy with Jewish leaders after his entry into Jerusalem (Matt. 21:28—22:14). Matthew follows Mark's order but adds to the Markan parable of the Wicked Tenants, which forms the centerpiece of the triad (Matt. 21:33–43), a parable from his own tradition, the Two Sons (21:28–32), and one from Q, the Marriage Feast (22:1–14 = Luke 14:16–24). Though these parables are often called the parables of "the True Israel," no such term is ever found in Matthew or in any other book of the New Testament.[44]

---

42. See the comprehensive exposition of this position by W. D. Davies, *The Setting of the Sermon on the Mount.* See also R. Brown and Meier, *Antioch and Rome,* 46–49; and Hare, *The Theme of Jewish Persecution of Christians.* Though the consolidation of Judaism after A.D. 70 is widely admitted, the "historicity" of Jamnia is debated. See Neusner, "The Formation of Rabbinic Judaism: Yabneh (Jamnia) from A.D. 70–100"; idem, *The Pharisees: Rabbinic Perspectives,* 239–46.

43. Garland (*The Intention of Matthew 23*) argues that in chap. 23 and elsewhere Matthew is concerned with those in his own community. See also Légasse, " 'L'antijudaïsme' dans l'Evangile selon Matthieu," 417–28.

44. See Dillon, "Towards a Tradition-History of the Parables of the True Israel"; and Ogawa, "Paraboles de l'Israël véritable?" The closest approximation to the term is 1 Cor. 10:18 where Paul speaks of Israel "according to the flesh" and Gal. 6:16 where he speaks of Christians, those living in the new creation, as "the Israel of God."

The Parable of the Two Sons
(Matt. 21:28–32)

The Parable as Text

This parable follows immediately the challenge to the authority of Jesus (21:23–27) and precedes the parable of the Wicked Tenants (21:33–45). In content it seems rather simple and lacks the elements of surprise and paradox we associate with other parables of Jesus.[45] A man asks his first son to work in the vineyard (v. 28). At first he refuses, but later, having repented, he goes to the vineyard. Knowing only his refusal, the father goes to the second son and asks him to go to the vineyard. He answers, "I go, sir" (*kyrie*), but does not go. Jesus then asks the question: "Which of the two did the will of his father?" The chief priests, the scribes, and the elders, caught by the parable in much the same sense that David is trapped by Nathan's parable (2 Sam. 12:5), respond that it was the first son. The parable is then followed by an application: "The tax collectors and the harlots go into the kingdom of God before you," which then recalls the ministry of John (the Baptist) who "came to you in the way of righteousness [justice], and you did not believe him, but the tax collectors and the harlots believed him; and even when you saw it, you did not afterward repent and believe him" (vv. 31–32).

Though Jeremias feels that the parable is an authentic parable of Jesus and locates it in the context of Jesus' vindication of the good news to the outcasts (i.e., his proclamation was refused by those who by profession were servants of God, but accepted by the ungodly), in its present form the parable resonates with Matthean language and concerns.[46]

The Parable in Context

I hold that the parable does not simply depict the rejection of Jewish leaders in contrast to the true sons of Matthew's community. The first key to interpretation comes from the question, "Which of

---

45. The simplicity of this parable is a bit misleading, and a few ancient manuscripts complicate the issue by reversing the order of the sons. The first son says yes but refuses to go; the second refuses but goes. Apparently this manuscript variant arose from a desire to make the parable apply to the relation of Judaism and gentile Christianity: the Jewish people answered yes but did not do God's will; the pagans who did not at first do God's will later did so. See Gundry, *Matthew*, 421–22.

46. Jeremias, *Parables*, 125; and Gundry, *Matthew*, 422.

the two did the will of his father?" The term "will of the father"
occurs always in the context of Jesus' instruction to his followers
(Matt. 6:10; 7:21; 12:50; 18:14)—with the exception of this parable
and Jesus' own prayer that he do his Father's will (26:42). In this
parable the contrast is between the son who says, "yes, sir" (kyrie),
and the one who does not say yes but actually does the father's will.
This contrast also distinguishes true and false disciples at the conclusion of the Sermon on the Mount: "Not every one who says to me,
'Lord, Lord' [kyrie], shall enter the kingdom of heaven, but the one
who does the will of my Father who is in heaven" (Matt. 7:21, au.
trans.). Matthew has his own community in mind when he recalls
the parable that speaks of the true son as the one who does the will
of the father. Authentic following of Jesus consists not in using
honorific titles but in doing the will of God (cf. 23:7–10).

A second clue to Matthew's understanding of the parable is the
addition of v. 32. This verse, which in origin may be pre-Matthean,
states that the conversion of the sinners should have been the
occasion for belief on the part of the leaders to whom the parable
was addressed. Since this did not happen during Jesus' ministry, we
would suggest that Matthew adds the reference to John here as a
subtle overture to the Jewish leaders of his own time. What makes
one a true member of the vineyard, a true son (or daughter) of the
heavenly Father, is doing God's will. This will has, from Matthew's
perspective, been revealed in the life and teaching of Jesus, which
was prepared for by the preaching of John. Despite the scandal
caused by the conversion of tax collectors and sinners, a scandal that
for the previous generation of Jewish leaders was no less shocking
than the scandal of the cross to a later generation (cf. 1 Cor. 1:23),
the Jewish leaders of Matthew's day, who like the first son initially
said, "No," now are summoned to the gospel of the kingdom.

Matthew, it is true, is in conflict with fellow Jews but does not
portray their total rejection. Matthew juxtaposes the rejection of
Jesus by Jewish leaders with warnings to his community. The rejection
of Jesus by the Jewish leaders of a past generation does not determine
the decision of subsequent Jewish people. Matthew's work serves to
encourage his own community by giving an apology for the death
of Jesus but also reaches out to the Judaism of his own day. The
"surprise" of this parable is that Matthew summons the Jewish

leaders of his day to be like the first son and to join the heirs of tax collectors and harlots—the Christian community—while warning his own community not to say "Lord" without doing the will of the Father.

Matthew's Rewriting of the Wicked Tenants
(21:33–45 = Mark 12:1–11)

Mark, as we saw, took a parable of Jesus that presented the long-suffering God reaching out in the face of continued rejection and made it into a christological allegory of the rejection of Jesus (see above, pp. 52–57). In Matthew this parable is more clearly an allegory where the christological emphasis is less pronounced, with the stress on a proper understanding of Israel's rejection of Jesus and on the need for Christian disciples to "bear fruit."

The Parable as Text

Matthew joins this parable closely to the Two Sons by the introduction: "Hear another parable" (21:33). The "man" (Mark 12:1) becomes "a householder" (cf. 13:27, the Wheat and the Tares; 20:1, the Laborers in the Vineyard). A more significant change comes in 21:34, where the "season of fruit(s)" draws near, and the householder sends his servants to get his "fruit(s)." The rather awkward "fruits" is a literal translation of the Greek *karpon/ous*. As I will indicate shortly, "fruits" in Matthew stands for "good works," so that the allegorical thrust of this verse is evident. Therefore Matthew's rewriting of the request for "some of the fruit" (Mark 12:2) to "his fruit," though a violation of economic realism, makes sense if the householder is God asking for complete allegiance.

Matthew reduces the Markan sending of servants to two sendings (21:35–36), corresponding perhaps to the distinction between the former and latter prophets.[47] Matthew evokes here that strain in Judaism which sees an unconverted people rejecting the prophets: "From the day that your fathers came out of the land of Egypt to this day, I have persistently sent all my servants the prophets to them, day after day; yet they did not listen to me" (Jer. 7:25–26).

---

47. Jeremias, *Parables*, 72. In Jewish tradition, Joshua to 2 Kings are the former prophets, while Isaiah to Malachi are the latter prophets.

In 21:39 Matthew says that the son (Jesus) is cast out of the vineyard and then killed, which is a more accurate description of Jesus' crucifixion outside the city (cf. John 19:17; Heb. 13:12). In 21:40–41 Matthew makes Mark's rhetorical question (12:9) into an actual dialogue where the sentence of judgment is clearly pronounced by the Jewish leaders on themselves (cf. 21:31). Matthew's principal theological emphasis arises from his rewriting of the Markan transfer of the vineyard "to others" (Mark 12:9) to "the kingdom of God will be taken from you and given to *a nation producing the fruits of it*" (21:43). The focus shifts from the succession of Christians ("the others") to the heritage of Israel, to the challenge facing the Christian community to be a nation which will "produce fruit." Matthew concludes with the statement that the leaders did not attempt to arrest Jesus, because they feared he was a prophet (21:46). From this survey of the Matthean changes of his Markan source, two motifs emerge of special import to Matthew's theology: the significance of fruit and the understanding of prophecy.

The Parable in Context

In Matthew and in other NT texts, "fruit" is a metaphor for repentance, conversion, and actions that manifest such conversion.[48] John proclaims to the Pharisees and the Sadducees, "Bear fruit that befits repentance" (Matt. 3:8), and says that every tree "that does not bear good fruit is cut down and thrown into the fire" (3:10). In a crucial section at the conclusion of the Sermon on the Mount when he is contrasting true and false discipleship Jesus says:

> Beware of false prophets, who come to you in sheep's clothing, but inwardly are ravenous wolves. You will know them by their *fruits*. Are grapes gathered from thorns, or figs from thistles? So, every sound tree bears good *fruit*, but the bad tree bears evil *fruit*. A sound tree cannot bear evil *fruit*, nor can a bad tree bear good *fruit*. Every tree that does not bear good *fruit* is cut down and thrown into the fire. Thus you will know them by their *fruits*. (Matt. 7:15–20)

Fruit in Matthew clearly functions as a metaphor for true conver-

---

48. Cf. John 15:2, 4, 5, 8, 16; Rom. 6:22; 7:4–5; Gal. 5:22–23 (the fruit of the Spirit); Phil. 1:11; 4:17; Col. 1:6, 10; James 3:17–18; Heb. 12:11. In stressing "fruit," Matthew expands on Isa. 5:1–7. The metaphorical use of fruit for moral disposition is also frequent in the OT, esp. in the wisdom literature. Cf. Prov. 11:30–31; Job 22:21 (LXX); Sir. 1:16–18; 6:18–19 (LXX); 37:22–23. See also *1 Enoch* 10:16–19.

sion. The "fruits" that the householder sought was conversion in response to the proclamation of John and the teaching of Jesus. For this reason the original tenants of the vineyard are destroyed and the vineyard given to "a nation producing fruits."

While admitting that the previous tenants did not bear fruit, Matthew does not dwell on the rejection of the Jews but uses it as a warning to his own community. Writing after the period when the temple and the city are destroyed, and when his own community is the nation (with the overtone of "gentile," the object of the mission in Matt. 28:16–20), Matthew simultaneously warns his community that their status as tenants of God's vineyard should not be a source of presumption. True discipleship consists neither in election, nor in proper affirmations about God (cf. 21:30; 7:21), nor in mighty works (7:22), but in having fruit when the critical time (kairos, 21:34) comes.

The second major emphasis arises from locating Jesus at the end of a line of prophetic messengers (21:35, 36, 46). In Matthew a prophet is one who summons to repentance and conversion, especially John the Baptist (3:1–4; 11:9; 14:5; 21:26). Events are seen as true manifestations of God's will when they are in fulfillment of prophecy (2:17, 23; 3:3; 4:14; 8:17; 12:17; 13:35; 26:56; 27:9). Jesus comes to fulfill the law and the prophets (5:17), and the fate of the prophets from earliest times is to suffer persecution and rejection:

"Men persecuted the prophets" (5:12).

Jesus is a rejected prophet (13:57).

People hold John to be a prophet, but Herod puts him to death (14:5–9).

John was not believed (21:32).

There was bitter denunciation of the Pharisees as sons of those who murdered the prophets (23:29–32).

With this "prophetic Christology" Matthew links closely the career and the fate of John and Jesus (cf. 21:26 and 21:46) and joins their fate to that of the OT prophets. An apology is thus given for the scandal of the cross in terms of the fate of others who proclaimed God's will.

In the final verse (21:46), "But when they tried to arrest him, they feared the multitudes [lit., "crowds," *ochloi*], because they held him to be a prophet," Matthew separates the religious leaders who want to arrest Jesus and the people who hold him to be a prophet (which Matthew adds to his Markan source). Here he continues the motif that what is important is not whether one belongs to a distinct religious group or not but how one responds to Jesus. Again the rejection of the Jews is not total. The crowds are the ancestors of those in Matthew's day who are being summoned to hear again the message of Jesus.[49]

The Marriage Feast (Matt. 22:1–14)

This parable, which in Matthew is joined to the story of the guest without the proper wedding garment, from a tradition-history perspective, is one of the more complicated in the synoptic tradition.[50] It is found in Luke 14:16–24 in a form that reflects Luke's composition and theology (see below, pp. 140–146) as well as in the *Gospel of Thomas* 64 in the following form:

> Jesus said, "A man had received visitors. And when he had prepared the dinner, he sent his servant to invite the guests. He went to the first one and said to him, 'My master invites you.' He said, 'I have claims against some merchants. They are coming to me this evening. I must go and give them my orders. I ask to be excused from the dinner.' He went to another and said to him, 'My master has invited you.' He said to him, 'I have just bought a house and am required for the day. I shall not have any spare time.' He went to another and said to him, 'My master invites you.' He said to him, 'My friend is going to get married, and I am to prepare the banquet. I shall not be able to come. I ask to be excused from the dinner.' He went to another and said to him, 'My master invites you.' He said to him, 'I have just bought a farm, and I am on my way to collect the rent. I shall not be able to come. I ask to be excused.' The servant returned and said to his master, 'Those whom you invited to the dinner have asked to be excused.' The master said to his servant, 'Go outside to the streets and bring back those whom

---

49. Gundry (*Matthew*, 65): "Matthew regularly uses the crowds (usually in the plural) to represent the masses in the church, professing disciples, both true and false—the result of extensive evangelism among the Gentiles." While I agree with Gundry's equation of the crowds with disciples in Matthew's community, I argue that community continues a mission to the Jews. See Donahue, "The 'Parable' of the Sheep and the Goats," esp. 14–16.

50. See esp. Funk, *Language, Hermeneutic*, 163–98; and Crossan, *In Parables*, 69–73.

you happen to meet, so that they may dine.' Businessmen and merchants will not enter the Places of My Father."[51]

In all three versions a man prepares a feast to which guests had been invited earlier. When the announcement is given that the feast is about to begin, the invited guests offer different excuses. The one who was to give the feast then substitutes for the invited guests people chosen at random.

Within this basic framework are significant differences. Matthew enhances the occasion by calling it a marriage feast for the king's son and describes the elaborate preparations (22:2–4). The excuses are not quoted but condensed to a one-sentence narrative, and the appended narrative (vv. 11–14), as I will indicate below, reflects distinct Matthean concerns. The version in the *Gospel of Thomas* and that in Luke are similar since both describe the occasion as a banquet (not a wedding feast), and the excuses are similar, even though *Thomas* contains four rather than three excuses. Though less allegorical than Matthew or Luke, *Thomas* betrays its own distinctive theological concerns. The "application" in the *Gospel of Thomas*, "Businessmen and merchants will not enter," reflects the gnostic rejection of worldly activity, and the change of the excuse from the marriage of the one invited to the hosting of a marriage feast may reflect gnostic rejection of marriage.[52]

While reconstruction of the original text and meaning of the parable may be impossible, tentative conclusions may be made about its growth. Despite their differences, Matthew and Luke most likely received this parable as part of the sayings collection, Q, which they share in common. The urgency of the invitation and the theme of exclusion are frequent in Q and, if Gerd Theissen is correct in attributing Q to the "itinerant radicals" of the Jesus movement, as early as Q the parable may well have moved in the direction of an

---

51. Trans. Lambdin, in Robinson, *The Nag Hammadi Library in English*, 125.

52. The relation of the parables of the *Gospel of Thomas* to those of the synoptic tradition is a subject of considerable debate, as is the dating and theological perspective of the work. See the survey of opinions in Perrin, *Rediscovering the Teaching of Jesus*, 253–54; and esp. Montefiore, "A Comparison of the Parables of the Gospel according to Thomas and of the Synoptic Gospels," in *Thomas and the Evangelists*, 4–78. For recent attempts to date Thomas very early (first century A.D.) and to argue that it is not gnostic but "on the ambiguous borderline between Gnostic and Catholic Christianity," see Crossan, *Four Other Gospels*, 34; and S. Davies, *The Gospel of Thomas and Christian Wisdom*.

allegory of the rejection of Jesus' message by his contemporaries and their substitution by the Jesus movement.[53] Matthew and Luke share this perspective. Jeremias offers perhaps the best suggestion of the meaning of the original parable in the ministry of Jesus.[54] He sees a double focus: (*a*) the vindication of Jesus' offer of forgiveness to tax collectors and sinners after the invited guests (the Jewish leaders) refused, and (*b*) a warning that it may be too late—failure to act when the decisive moment comes (the announcement that the feast is near) brings exclusion from the banquet. Most subsequent interpretations, such as that of Rudolf Bultmann (that the parable warns the complacent to be ready for the call of God) are variants on this second focus.[55]

The Parable as Text and Context in Matthew

Matthew's version is most allegorical. The host is a king (cf. 18:23; 25:34, 40), and the feast is a feast for his son. When the second invitation is sent, there are three sendings and three refusals. The violent treatment of the servants is similar to that of the servants in the previous parable (Matt. 22:6; cf. 21:35–36). The reaction of the king in v. 7—destroying and burning the city—is a prediction of the destruction of the city, dependent on Isa. 5:24–25, where destruction by fire is a sign of God's judgment. The theme of the good and the bad recalls Matthew's understanding of the church as a mixed body (13:24–27, 47–50), and the appended parable of the wedding garment, as I will show, refers to the demands of Christian discipleship.

The meaning of this parable emerges from the salvation-history perspective provided by its position. In the first parable of the triad the refusal to respond begins with a rejection of John; in the second it is the historical ministry of Jesus which is rejected; in this parable the invitation that is rejected is that of the risen and returning Jesus which is made through the preaching of Christian missionaries (the servants of v. 6). The setting is before the final consummation which, in other biblical and extrabiblical literature, is symbolized by the images of the wedding feast (Isa. 62:1–5; Rev. 19:1–6) and the

53. Theissen, *Sociology of Early Palestinian Christianity*, esp. 8–16.
54. Jeremias, *Parables*, 67–69, 176–80.
55. Bultmann, *This World and the Beyond*, 143–54, esp. 152–54.

banquet (Isa. 25:6–8; *2 Apoc. Bar.* 29:4–8; *1 Enoch* 62:14). Through this allegory Matthew encourages his church in the face of failure of missionary activity. God continues to send messengers to those who were invited earlier, but these are rejected (cf. 23:34–39). Persecution has been predicted by Jesus, but so too has the judgment on the persecutors. While this may not strike one as a particularly irenic world view, it is very much part of the apocalyptic mind-set that influenced both Jewish and Christian writers of the period.

The appended narrative of 22:11–14 picks up on the theme of the good and the bad. It too is an allegory, perhaps from Matthew's tradition but reworked by him. It does not fit too easily with the previous parable. How would the poor guests brought en masse from the thoroughfares without previous invitation be expected to have proper garments? The treatment of the host seems unfair. As in many allegories, it is the inconsistency which shows that we are dealing with a story behind a story. The key to the meaning is the reference to the forgotten wedding garment (*endyma gamou*), which is from the same root as the word for putting on clothes (*endyein*). In the Pauline literature the image of "putting on" is used frequently for assuming a definite way of life. Paul tells the Romans to "put on the Lord Jesus" (Rom. 13:14), and to the Galatians he writes, "For as many of you as were baptized into Christ have put on Christ" (*enedysasthe*, lit., "worn Christ like a garment," Gal. 3:27). The community at Colossae is exhorted: "Put on then, as God's chosen ones, holy and beloved, compassion, kindness, lowliness, meekness, and patience" (3:12; cf. Eph. 4:24, put on a new person). Therefore the wedding garment stands for Christian life and those qualities which are to characterize those invited to the banquet after others refuse.[56]

The situation in this parable is similar to that envisioned in the apocalyptic scenario with which Matthew concludes the pre-passion part of Jesus' ministry (25:31–46). Here people will be judged on

---

56. Gundry (*Matthew*, 439) says the wedding garment symbolizes "evidential works of righteousness." The use of "attendants" (*diakonoi*, 22:13) who are to bind the guests without the garment and to cast them into outer darkness supports an early church setting, since it is used elsewhere for ministries or church office (cf. Phil. 1:1; Col. 4:7; 1 Tim. 3:8, 12). Matthew's *diakonoi* here may refer to "the twelve" who were promised earlier (Matt. 19:28) a role in the eschatological judgment of the twelve tribes of Israel.

the charity and mercy extended toward those in need. Prior to the judgment the church will be composed of good and bad. It is not the task of church leaders to separate the good from the bad but to proclaim the gospel to all. Those who respond to the invitation, however, must have something to bring to the judgment other than having said, "Yes, Lord." They must be properly clothed with the deeds of Christian discipleship.

This collocation of the Wedding Garment with the Marriage Feast shows the same double focus we saw in the preceding parable. The claims of "the synagogue across the street" are rejected. They answered yes but did not do God's will, they did not produce fruits worthy of repentance. The community of Matthew, however, which have been taught radical observance of the law (5:17–48) by Jesus, a new prophet, cannot claim election or membership in a community as their surety for salvation. The parables of Jesus when originally uttered summoned his hearers to critical decision. These same parables, when applied allegorically by Matthew to his church, are not to be read with complacency on the assumption that they deal with the rejection of Jewish leaders. Today they summon Christians who are the heirs of Matthew, not merely to respond with promises of labor in the vineyard, but to bear fruit and to "put on Christ" by deeds of justice and charity.

THE ESCHATOLOGICAL CRISIS AND
THE PARABLES OF MATTHEW 24 AND 25

Like all the evangelists, Matthew concludes the public ministry of Jesus with a farewell speech of Jesus to chosen disciples. Though Matthew follows his Markan source in locating the discourse after Jesus leaves Jerusalem, never again to enter it except for his trial, passion, and death, Matthew considerably alters both the thrust and the content of the discourse. Matthew prefaces the discourse with a long and bitter denunciation of "the scribes and the Pharisees" (chap. 23), undoubtedly reflecting a continuing polemic against the Judaism of his time. Two charges weigh most heavily against the Jewish leaders: they "have neglected the weightier matters of the law, justice and mercy and faith" (23:23), and they persecute "prophets and wise men and scribes" whom Jesus sends to them (23:32–36). This discourse then concludes with the lament of Jesus over Jerusalem:

"How often would I have gathered your children together as a hen gathers her brood under her wings, and you would not!" and the prediction that "your house [i.e., temple] is forsaken and desolate" (23:37–38). By locating this attack on the scribes and the Pharisees *before* the eschatological discourse, Matthew clearly indicates that the rejection of Jesus by his contemporaries and Jesus' judgment against them have taken place prior to the final discourse. The Jesus of Matthew has already predicted the destruction of the city and the temple (21:43; 22:7; 23:37–38). The final discourse then functions in Matthew, much more than in Mark, as teaching and exhortation *to the community* as it lives between the resurrection and the return of Jesus.[57]

Though the final discourse is considerably longer in Matthew (97 verses) than in Mark (37 verses), in that section of the discourse (24:1–36) where he is following Mark, Matthew abbreviates his source. The expansion occurs mainly in 24:37—25:46 through addition of material from Q and his special source. Here the distinctive Matthean perspectives on ethics and eschatology emerge, and I will concentrate on this portion of the discourse.

Key phrases and motifs, resonating throughout this section, convey its distinctive flavor:

"Watch therefore" (24:42; 25:13)

Unexpected returns or arrivals (24:37, 42–44, 50; 25:10, 19)

Delays in arrival (24:48; 25:5, 19)

The coming of the Son of man (24:27, 30, 37, 44; 25:31)

Praises of faithful servants: "blessed" (24:46); "Well done, good and faithful servant" (25:21, 23); "blessed of my Father" (25:34)

The use of "Lord" (25:11, 24, 37, 44)

Exclusions from the presence of the returning Lord (24:51; 25:10, 30, 46)

The discourse evokes an atmosphere of tension and expectation; likewise the time prior to the return is a challenge to responsibility, a time for decisions that will influence the hearers' ultimate fate.

After three short parables or similitudes which stress the need for

---

57. On setting and theology of Matthew's eschatological discourse, see S. Brown, "The Matthean Apocalypse"; Burnett, *The Testament of Jesus-Sophia;* and Lambrecht, *Once More Astonished,* 146–235.

watchfulness—the comparison with the days of Noah (24:37–39), the men in the field and the women at the mill (24:40–41), and the householder and the thief (24:42–44)—Matthew adds three longer parables (24:45—25:30) which complement this exhortation to vigilance with illustrations of responsible action. To watch means active and laborious service and not simply inactivity or passivity in the face of the imminent end. These three parables along with the final grand scenario of judgment (25:31–46) provide distinctive insights into Matthew's Gospel in parable.

The Faithful and Wise Servant
(Matt. 24:45–51)

The Parable as Text

The first in the triad of narrative parables with which Matthew concludes his Gospel is taken from Q. Luke locates it in the travel narrative of Jesus' journey to Jerusalem where he instructs the disciples on proper Christian conduct prior to the end time (Luke 12:42–46). In Luke the thrust is more ethical than eschatological. Matthew's parable begins with a rhetorical question: "Who then is the faithful and wise servant . . . ?" which sets the tone for the following parables and summons the readers or hearers to answer this question in their lives. In the parable it is evident who is the wise and faithful servant; the question to the hearers is: "Will you be such also?"

The narrative structure is concise and simple. A master or householder departs and leaves a "servant" (Luke has "steward") in charge of proper food distribution to his household (24:45). The following verses describe two ways of fulfilling the charge. In the first the master returns and finds the servant doing as he was charged (24:46). Such a servant is "blessed," a term in Matthew that suggests divine approval rather than simple human happiness (*makarios*; cf. 5:1–11; 11:6; 13:16; 16:17; 24:46). He is then set over all the possessions of the master and is not simply in charge of food distribution. The description of the second servant is more elaborate. We are given access to his interior musings (he "says to himself," v. 48) over the delay of the master. He begins to beat his fellow servants, and to dissipate his trust and the master's resources. His joy is cut short by the unexpected return of the master, who punishes him severely and puts him out of the household (vv. 50–51).

In its more simple form, which may go back to the historical Jesus, the parable reflects a pattern where a person goes on a journey and leaves servants with a commission. Upon returning and finding that the commission has been observed or misused, he rewards one servant and punishes the others. Such a structure is at the basis of the waiting and watching parables (e.g., Mark 13:33–37), and its most developed form is the parable of the Talents (Matt. 25:14–30). Jeremias suggests that the setting for such parables in the life of Jesus was his attack on Jewish leaders.[58] From the OT, Jesus' hearers would have been familiar with the image of religious officials as servants. Jesus compares them to those unfaithful servants and warns them that the time of reckoning is near, which will reveal whether they have been faithful to the trust. The advent of the kingdom which has begun in the ministry of Jesus is a time of conversion (*metanoia*), and even if the kingdom has not been fully revealed, those who resist its message will be in danger of exclusion from its benefits.

As in other instances (e.g., the Lost Sheep, Matt. 18:10–14), parables that were originally directed to opponents now are directed to inner church concerns.[59] A number of elements in this parable reflect such concerns which may also have existed in Matthew's community. The explicit description of the servant as "faithful" and "wise" is unusual in the parables of Jesus where the moral dispositions of characters are deduced from their actions. The term "faithful" (*pistos*) in the sense of "reliable" rather than "believing" is a quality often found as a requisite for leadership in the early church (1 Cor. 4:17; Col. 1:7; Eph. 6:21; Titus 1:9), and Paul uses the imagery of stewardship in a sense that is similar to the perspective of this parable: "This is how one should regard us, as servants of Christ and stewards of the mysteries of God. Moreover it is required of stewards that they be found trustworthy [*pistos*]" (1 Cor. 4:1–2).

The situation over which the servant is given direction is the distribution of food (*trophē*). Two things come to mind. First, conduct at communal meals and the problem of the distribution of food were

58. Jeremias, *Parables*, 166.
59. Ibid., 33–66.

clear areas of dispute in the early church (Acts 6:1–3; 1 Cor. 11:17–22). Second, food and "eating" can serve as metaphors for teaching and learning (1 Cor. 3:2; John 6:25–33), and *trophē* can be used for "spiritual nourishment" (Heb. 5:12–14, in a warning to teachers in the community). The association of the second servant with the "drunken" (*methyontōn*) reflects a problem with drunkenness seen elsewhere. Paul exhorts the community not to associate with a fellow member who is a drunkard (1 Cor. 5:11) and says that drunkards will not "inherit the kingdom of God" (1 Cor. 6:10, a perspective very similar to exclusion of the unfaithful servant in Matt. 24:51); and drunkenness was one of the abuses of the communal meals at Corinth (1 Cor. 11:21). In the Pastorals the bishop "as God's steward" should not be a drunkard (Titus 1:7; cf. 1 Tim. 3:3, 8), and in contrast to the steward who beats his fellow servants, early church leaders are exhorted in 1 Pet. 5:3 not to be domineering. The unfaithful steward in Matt. 24:48–50 is a parade example of unfaithful leadership in the community.

Such a perspective helps in understanding the final verse of the parable which has always provided a problem for translation and exegesis. The problem is that the Greek word for the punishment of the servant (*dichotomēsei*), which literally means "cut in two" (English, "dichotomize"), while reflecting the horrible Persian punishment of dismemberment, seems especially harsh on the lips of Jesus. It also makes little sense when in the next verse the servant is sent off to be with hypocrites where there will be weeping and gnashing of teeth—a strange image if one part of his body is severed from the other. Several solutions have been proposed from metaphorical exaggeration to a suggestion that it is a mistranslation of an Aramaic phrase meaning "to punish with many blows."[60] The solution that best fits the context is that proposed by Eduard Schweizer.[61] The phrase is said to refer to "cutting off" from the community and is similar to the language of exclusion found at Qumran and to the practice attested in passages such as Matt. 18:17 and 1 Cor. 6:7–13 (see above, pp. 78–79).

Matthew thus turns an original parable of Jesus into an allegory about the irresponsible action of church leaders prior to the parousia.

---

60. Marshall, *Luke*, 543, apropos of Luke 12:46.
61. Schweizer, *Matthew*, 463.

They abuse their charge to administer the goods of the community properly by faithful oversight of its material and spiritual sustenance, and they tyrannize members of the community as if they were slaves.[62] Such conduct blinds them to the eschatological summons of the risen and coming Jesus. By locating such an allegory here, Matthew turns away from interest in the events that will accompany Jesus' return (24:1–36) to clear instructions for church leaders as they await the return of Jesus. He joins ethics to eschatology and provides a key for interpreting the two subsequent parables.

The Parable of the Ten Maidens
(Matt. 25:1–13)

The second of Matthew's three parables on vigilance before the return of Jesus has divided commentators. The major area of debate is whether it truly represents Palestinian wedding customs. If the details are unrealistic, then the parable is understood as an allegory of the early church's expectation of the returning Lord.[63]

The Parable as Text

It begins as a kingdom parable where the coming of the kingdom is compared not simply to the ten maidens but to the whole situation. The characterization of the maidens as "wise" and "foolish" is unusual in the parables of Jesus but characteristic of Matthew in this section; it also links this parable to the previous one. The delay of the bridegroom recalls also the delay of the master's return in the preceding parable. The first major problem of interpretation arises with the apparent point of the parable in 25:13, "Watch therefore, for you know neither the day nor the hour." Yet in the parable all the bridesmaids sleep; none are "watching" when the cry is heard, "Behold, the bridegroom!"

The drama of the parable comes in the contrast of the action of the two groups. This begins in v. 3 when the foolish "took no oil with them." The delay of the bridegroom creates an expectation in the readers that the maidens still have time to make up for their lack

---

62. Meier, *Matthew*, 293.
63. See Jeremias, *Parables*, 171–75 (originally a parable of Jesus); followed by Lambrecht, *Once More Astonished*, 146–63; Linnemann, *Jesus*, 126 (a certain creation of the early church); and Perkins, *Hearing*, 104 (a prime example of early Christian allegorical preaching).

of foresight. Instead, they sleep; when the bridegroom's arrival is announced, they try to remedy the situation, first by asking for oil from the "wise" maidens, then by seeking to buy oil. Their "foolishness" meets with a double refusal: the other maidens do not share their oil and the "Lord" does not open the door to the wedding feast.

Joachim Jeremias and Dan O. Via, who hold that this pericope may be a parable and not an allegory, propose different interpretations. For Jeremias the parable illustrates the theme of Jesus' teaching "it may be too late" and is directed at Jewish leaders who are delaying in responding to the kingdom proclamation of Jesus.[64] Via calls it a "tragic parable" in which the central thrust is the failure of the foolish maidens to take adequate preparations to pursue their intention. They illustrate that when a critical situation is not responsibly met, "the opportunity for further action may be cut off."[65] On a theological level the important element of the parable is the time of waiting. The maidens should have used this time to prepare; "the present is not a time which is to be exhausted by straining to realize the future. There is time and room to live *now*."[66] If the time before the end of history is seen simply as gift and not also as responsibility for and to the future, human existence may be lost.

The Parable in Context

The test of whether a text is an allegory is twofold: (a) whether the details are unrealistic, and (b) whether some of these same details admit of other explanations. Jeremias argues that the parable is realistic, even though his closest parallels are twentieth-century Middle Eastern customs, since there is very little secure data on first-century Palestinian wedding customs.[67] The details of the parable, however, conflict with the meager information given in two other places in Matthew. In the Marriage Feast (Matt. 22:1–2) the guests are invited *to the home* of the bridegroom, where weddings were celebrated, and in the parabolic saying of Matt. 9:15 (= Mark 2:19; Luke 5:34) the groom is accompanied by male attendants, the "sons

64. Jeremias, *Parables*, 174–75.
65. D. O. Via, *Parables*, 125.
66. Ibid., 128.
67. Jeremias, *Parables*, 172–73.

of the bridegroom."[68] The long delay, the midnight arrival, and the supposition that the shops would have been open for the sleeping maidens to buy oil (cf. Luke 11:5–8) are unrealistic. The arrival in the middle of the night (25:6) reflects the expectation of Jesus' return like a thief in the night (Matt. 24:43) or in the middle of the night (Mark 13:35). The "cry" and the summons "to meet" (eis apantēsin) the bridegroom use eschatological imagery similar to 1 Thess. 4:16–17: "For the Lord (ho kyrios; cf. Matt. 25:11) himself will descend from heaven with a cry of command. . . . Then we who are alive . . . shall be caught up . . . to meet (eis apantēsin) the Lord in the air."

The details, however, do make sense when the text is read as an allegory of the delay of the parousia in Matthew's community.[69] Of initial interest is that of all the parables dealing with watching or waiting servants this alone has female protagonists.[70] Despite some titles of the parable as "the Ten Bridesmaids," they are never so called, nor is the bride mentioned.[71] Rather, those who await the return of the groom (nymphios) are called explicitly "virgins" (parthenoi). In 1 Corinthians, Paul discusses virginity in an eschatological context. Life is qualified by an awareness that the time is short (1 Cor. 7:25–31). Virginity is recommended because the unmarried man or woman is concerned for the things "of the Lord" rather than for the spouse. Matthew's language here reflects the same thought world (cf. Matt. 19:10–12). The five virgins who are prepared for the return are symbols of eschatological existence and proper Christian discipleship during delay of the parousia.[72] Attention to the other allegorical details supports this perspective.[73]

Crucial to the allegory is the stress on oil and burning lamps. The maidens are excluded not because they slept but because their lamps were not lit. In his exhortations to discipleship in 5:14–16 the

<hr>

68. Posner, "Marriage Ceremony," EncJud 11:1032–42.
69. In addition to Linnemann and Perkins (see above, n. 63), I am in debt to Donfried, "The Allegory of the Ten Virgins."
70. Ford, "The Parable of the Foolish Scholars," 107.
71. The Greek terms for "bridesmaids" (nympheutria and nymphagōgos) are never used.
72. Gundry, Matthew, 498–99.
73. Though I argue that the text is allegorical, it is not an allegory of Christ and his bride, the church, as is found in 2 Cor. 11:2; Eph. 5:23–33, and in later theology. Some manuscripts, apparently aware of this problem, add "and the bride" in 25:1. See Manson, Sayings, 243–44; and Batey, New Testament Nuptial Imagery, 45–47.

Matthean Jesus exhorts his disciples, "Let your light shine before men and women that they may see your good works and give glory to your father in heaven" (au. trans.). Matthew says that "the righteous will shine like the sun in the kingdom of their Father" (13:43). "Light" (as in Mark 4:21 and Luke 11:33) is a symbol of good deeds or proper moral disposition. In the *Midrash Rabbah* to Numbers, the commentator notes that "mingled with oil" (7:19) means that the study of the Torah should be mingled with good deeds.[74]

The division of the women into five wise and five foolish and the exclusion of the latter reflect Matthew's view that the parousia will be a time that discloses and separates the good and the bad in the community (cf. 13:36–43; 25:31–46). The cry of the women, "Lord, lord," and their subsequent exclusion recall the conclusion of the Sermon on the Mount. After the denunciation of those who do not bear fruit (7:15–18; see above, pp. 90–91), Jesus says, "Not every one who says to me, 'Lord, Lord,' shall enter the kingdom of heaven, but the one who does the will of my Father who is in heaven" (au. trans.). Those who prophesied or cast out demons in the name of Jesus but did not obey God's will will hear from Jesus the condemnation "I never knew you; depart from me, you evildoers" (7:21–23). Both the plea of the maidens, "Lord, lord," and the seemingly harsh exclusion of them, "I do not know you," in Matt. 25:11–12 reflect exactly the language and the situation of 7:21–23.

Therefore in this allegory Matthew summons his community to responsible discipleship in the face of the delay of the parousia. While the return of Jesus has been delayed, it is no less certain and its advent will be no less threatening. Matthew retains the critical urgency which was associated with the early Christian hope of the parousia without retaining its temporal immediacy. Discipleship is not passive waiting for the end time. Like the maidens, the Christians may know what is needed—oil, good deeds—but they may lose the opportunity for proper action. This is an eschatological ethic for Matthew, not simply an interim ethic. Vigilance is not simply waiting for the future but active engagement in the present which will

74. *Num R.* xiii.15, 16, cited by Donfried, "The Allegory of the Ten Virgins," 427. See also Manson (*Sayings*, 244) for Jewish texts where the lamp and oil are symbols of the law.

determine the shape of the future. In Pauline terms the Christian is "to ransom the time" (Col. 4:5, au. trans.).

Matthew's addition to the parable (25:13) is in harmony with its allegorical meaning. "Watching" is not simply being awake at the time of the return of Jesus, nor is it speculation about the time and hour; it is preparation in the present. Unlike the servants of the previous parable who abused the time of waiting and patently violated the master's trust, the maidens fail by inactivity. In older theological language we might say that Matthew rejects both sins of commission and sins of omission. Presumption about a gracious future is as dangerous as misuse of the present. Passivity in the face of the eschaton is as evil as reveling in its delay.

The Parable of the Talents
(Matt. 25:14–30 = Luke 19:11–27)

The Parable as Text

This is one of the longest and most complicated of Matthew's parables. It apparently caused problems in the tradition prior to Matthew. The appended interpretation, "For to every one who has will more be given, and he will have abundance; but from him who has not, even what he has will be taken away" (Matt. 25:29), is a doublet (found both in the Markan tradition [Mark 4:25 = Matt. 13:12; Luke 8:18] and in Q [Matt. 25:29; Luke 19:26]) which is most likely an authentic saying of Jesus, originally perhaps free floating but attached by Q to this parable. As an independent saying it reflects proverbial wisdom (e.g., the rich get richer and the poor get poorer). Though it seems to capture the surface meaning of the parable, it does not exhaust the parable's meaning either as a text or in the context of Matthew's theology.

Since both Matthew and Luke share this parable, it is attributed to Q, but the path from the versions in these Gospels to the original is difficult to follow.[75] Luke combines it with another parable about the man who goes away to claim his throne (Luke 19:11–12, 27) and edits it in terms of his perspective on the delay of the parousia (Luke 19:11, "He proceeded to tell a parable, because he was near

75. For the growth of the parable, see Fitzmyer, *Luke X—XXIV*, 1228–33; Jeremias, *Parables*, 58–63; and Lambrecht, *Once More Astonished*, 167–87.

to Jerusalem, and because they supposed that the kingdom of God was to appear immediately").

The parable is a dramatic one in which the dialogue and the interaction of the characters are important. The traditional title of "the Talents" does not capture the meaning. The main character is the first actor introduced, the person (anthrōpos) who departs and entrusts his "property" to others (hyparchonta, the same word used of the "possessions" entrusted to the unfaithful steward in 24:47). The reader is thus alerted to the possibility that here too the issue will be faithful maintenance of a trust. The distribution of the property is unequal, but each servant receives specific talents—five, two, or one—"according to his ability" (v. 15). The narrative then moves quickly. The five talent servant immediately trades and doubles his talents, as does the two talent servant. The one talent servant goes, digs a hole in the ground, and hides the one talent. The text states that "after a long time" the master (or lord, kyrios) returns and settles accounts (the same phrase used in 18:23, with overtones of a juridical inquiry). The five talent man states quickly, "I have made five talents more," and the two talent man reports a profit of two talents. Both receive the same accolade: "Well done, good and faithful servant [pistos]; you have been faithful over a little, I will set you over much; enter into the joy of your master" (vv. 21, 23).

If the parable concluded at this point or if the one talent man had made another talent, the parable would be an interesting counterpart to the parable of the "unfaithful steward" of 24:49–50. Both parables would be simply illustrations of infidelity or fidelity in maintenance of a trust. But the mood of the parable shifts in 25:24 with the arrival of the one talent man. This section begins with almost the same words as the encounters with the other two servants, almost lulling the reader into an expectation that a similar favorable encounter will take place. Since the dialogue between the master and this servant is the most extensive and most interesting of the three, the central thrust of the parable is to be sought here.

The shock to our sensibilities is the apparent harsh treatment of the third servant. When he is summoned to give account, he states that he knew the master to be a "hard" man and that he was afraid. In a poignant phrase, he describes what he thought was prudent action, hiding the talent, and then almost proudly he says to the master, "Here you have what is yours." The master, however, calls him "wicked and slothful" (ponēre kai oknēre), takes his talent and gives it to the ten talent man and, as he did with the unfaithful servant of 24:50, casts him outside, where there will be weeping and gnashing of teeth. The rapidity with which the master's reaction and actions are described suggests the shattering of the world of the third servant—it falls apart immediately.

This is the section of the parable that causes shock and surprise. In the earlier parable of infidelity the fault of the servant was clear; he beat his fellow servants and spent his time with drunkards. The third servant here reflects only a timid prudence. Given the uncertain economic and political environment in which most people lived in first-century Palestine, it is quite likely that the original hearers would have identified with this third servant. The apocryphal Gospel of the Nazoreans softens this shock of the parable, since in its version the servant who is punished wastes the master's money with "harlots and flute players," while the one who hid the talents is only rebuked.[76] Behind the excuses of the third servant, however, lies a "fatal flaw" which challenges the readers to see things from the side of the master, even in the face of a harsh judgment.[77] In his excuse the third servant says that the master was a hard man, "reaping where you did not sow, and gathering where you did not winnow" (v. 24).[78] When the master castigates the servant prior to executing the judgment he accepts the characterization, "I reap where I have not sowed, and gather where I have not winnowed" (a saying that may evoke Matt. 12:30 = Luke 11:23, "He who does not gather with me scatters"). In a legal context (25:14) this serves almost as the charge on which the third servant is convicted, since, knowing this, he should have invested the money.

The defect of the third servant emerges from his characterization of the master which in his response the master does not accept. The servant calls the master "hard." There is nothing in the parable to justify this charge; in fact, to entrust even one talent—the wage of

76. Text in Funk, New Gospel Parallels, 139.
77. D. O. Via, Parables, 119.
78. Gundry (Matthew, 507) notes two metaphors here, agricultural (reap/sow) and mercantile (gather/winnow). Fitzmyer (Luke X—XXIV, 1237) argues that these are metaphors of exploitation. Interestingly, the moral shock of this parable (i.e., the approval of usury) is rarely raised in discussing this parable; contrast Luke 16:1–8.

an ordinary worker for fifteen years—to someone else shows considerable magnanimity. Also the third servant states that his motivation for hiding the talent was that he "feared" (*phobētheis*); it was timidity that spelled his downfall, which was not warranted by anything known directly about the master. John Meier comments, "Out of fear of failure, he has refused even to try to succeed."[79]

The third talent man resembles other characters in Matthean parables. Like the unmerciful servant of 18:23–35, who thought in terms of strict justice and could not recognize unmerited forgiveness, this servant works out of an incorrect understanding of the master. He thought him hard, even though he himself had been treated generously. He thought of himself as victim and created a world in which, with tragic irony, he became victim.[80] Like those who labored the whole day in the vineyard (20:1–15), he seems to know what the master should or should not do and lets his attitude be governed by his misperceptions. Both of these are called "evil" (*ponēros*, 18:32; 20:15), as is the servant in this parable. T. W. Manson has described well such an attitude in commenting that it is not the task of men and women to sit in judgment on God but to do their best in the situation in which they find themselves.[81]

The Parable in Context

While it is impossible to reconstruct the original form of the parable and thus determine exactly Matthew's redaction, general aspects of the parable as well as a number of specific phrases have a decidedly Matthean flavor. Also its location as the conclusion to a triad of parables that deal with responsibility in the face of absent masters is due to Matthew's composition and gives an added meaning to the parable.

We have already noted that the phrase "his possessions" links this parable with the first in the triad (24:47). The description of the events in grand scale, with talents (cf. 18:24) in place of pounds, or some lesser sum, is Matthean. The repetition of key phrases and the parallelism of vv. 19–24 are reminiscent of places where the same techniques are used (18:23–30; 20:1–13). The description of the proper conduct of the first two servants may be a Matthean play on

79. Meier, *Matthew*, 300.
80. D. O. Via, *Parables*, 118–19.
81. Manson, *Sayings*, 247.

words. They are described as being "faithful over a little" (*epi oliga es pistos*), which is hardly accurate, since a talent is scarcely "a little." In Matthew, however, one of the interesting descriptions of disciples is those of "little faith" (*oligopistoi*, lit., "little faithful," 6:30; 8:26; 14:31; 16:8; cf. 17:20). This attitude is precipitated by anxiety (6:25), by fear (8:26), by doubt (14:31), and by lack of trust (16:8). The fondness for wordplay both in the NT and in the environment out of which Matthew comes suggests that Matthew sees the first two servants as symbols of faithful discipleship even when confronted by a demanding master. This is in contrast to the paralyzing fear of the third servant. The description of the servant as "slothful" (*oknēre*) supports this view. The term is used by Paul (Rom. 12:11) in an exhortation "not to be indolent when earnestness is needed."[82] In Prov. 6:6–11 there is a sardonic satire on the person who is so slothful or indolent that "poverty will come upon you like a vagabond, and want like an armed man" (v. 11).

Matthew places this parable as the conclusion of a triad of parables that affirm both the delay of the parousia and its certainty and that describe proper action in the interim period. This parable is closest to the first, since both servants are severely punished and both act in ways that are seen as evil. But like the maidens, the third servant is punished for presumptuous inactivity. The time before the return of Jesus is, for Matthew, a time that must be used responsibly. The end of history will be a revelation of who has used the time well. For Matthew, eschatology has a revelatory or disclosive function. Prior to the end time, his church is a mixed body where the good and the bad will grow together (13:24–30, 36–43). In these parables Matthew warns against those attitudes which will bring about exclusion from God's kingdom. In the following scene of cosmic judgment with which he concludes the public ministry of Jesus, not only will attitudes be revealed but Matthew will describe those actions which will determine exclusion or inclusion in the kingdom.

The Sheep and the Goats
(Matt. 25:31–46)

The final section of Jesus' farewell discourse in Matthew is a scene of power and grandeur. Though it is often called a parable, the

---

82. Translation as in BAGD, 563.

comparison of the separation of the nations with the division of the sheep and the goats (25:32) constitutes the formal parabolic section.[83] In form it is similar to the "parables" or similitudes of Enoch which vividly depict heavenly scenes of final judgment (1 Enoch 39–71), and Bultmann called it an "apocalyptic prediction" rather than a parable.[84] Nonetheless, it has many of the characteristics of the Gospel parables with its vivid and realistic dialogue between the king and those judged and in the surprising questions "Lord, when did we see thee?" The multiple interpretations of this passage offer testimony that it leaves the mind in sufficient doubt about its meaning. More accurately it can be called an "apocalyptic parable" and should be interpreted from the horizon of apocalyptic.

The classic or universalistic interpretation of this passage emerges immediately.[85] When the Son of man comes, he will judge all peoples and the criterion of judgment will be works of charity and mercy shown toward the marginal, the poor, and the suffering of the world. Jesus identifies himself with these so that whatever is done to them is done to Jesus: "As you did to the least of my brothers and sisters you have done to me" (v. 40, au. trans.; cf. v. 45).[86] People will be called "just" and "blessed" on the basis of actions done simply for any person in need. This understanding has been underscored by contemporary theologies of liberation. The praxis of justice, seen as concern for the marginal in society, rather than cult or creed, constitutes true religion, which is not limited to those who confess Jesus as "Lord."[87]

83. The secondary literature on this pericope is extensive. For a detailed study, see Donahue, "The 'Parable' of the Sheep and the Goats," esp. n. 11 for bibliography. Portions of this article are used with permission of the editor of *Theological Studies*.

84. Bultmann, *Synoptic Tradition*, 120–23.

85. On a "classic," see Tracy, *The Analogical Imagination*, esp. 99–153. He states, "What we mean in naming certain texts, events, images, rituals, symbols and persons 'classics' is that here we recognize nothing less than a disclosure of a reality we cannot but name truth" (108).

86. This text provides an instance where sex-inclusive translation is demanded. Virtually all translations render *tōn adelphōn mou tōn elachistōn* as "least of my brothers," or "brethren." Schüssler Fiorenza has argued convincingly (*In Memory of Her*, 44–45) that, when using the masculine plural grammatically in words such as "brethren" (*adelphoi*) and "saints" (*hagioi*), the NT writers obviously included women, since they were writing to communities composed of men and women. In Matt. 25:31–46 whether one accepts the classic interpretation that the "brethren" are all the needy or the modified missionary interpretation (which I will propose), the more accurate translation is "least of my brothers and sisters," since both the needy and the missionaries comprise men and women.

87. For a survey, see Bussmann, *Who Do You Say?* 82–85.

Serious objections have been raised against the classic interpretation. (1) In the NT, *adelphos* ("brother"), when not describing a
physical relationship, is used almost exclusively for a compatriot or
coreligionist, a usage that early Christianity takes over from Judaism.[88]
There is no clear instance where an unconverted Gentile is spoken
of as a brother. (2) In Matthew it is used extensively to describe the
social relationships that should exist between those who respond to
the gospel of the kingdom (5:22–24; 7:3–5; 18:15, 21, 35) or as a
reference to disciples (12:49–50; 28:10). (3) Matthew uses the term
"little ones" for the vulnerable members of the Christian community
(10:42; 11:11; 18:6, 10, 14), so that the least of the brethren of
Jesus would be Christians most in need. (4) The identification of the
Son of man with the least is to be interpreted in the light of sayings
such as "He who receives you receives me" (Matt. 10:40), which
come at the end of the Mission Discourse in Matthew and are said
to reproduce the rabbinic *šālîᵃḥ* motif where the sender is present in
the messenger. It is thus the disciples who "re-present" Jesus here.
(5) The passage comes at the end of a discourse delivered to disciples
and is preceded by three parables on proper discipleship.

On the basis of such observations Lamar Cope has argued strongly
that the "least" of the brothers and sisters of Jesus are Christian
missionaries, not simply the needy, and that pagan nations will be
judged on how they received these missionaries.[89] The ethics of the
parable is "a churchly, sectarian one" and the text *"cannot* provide
a legitimate basis for Christian concern for the poor and the needy
of the world."[90] His interpretation has been accepted even by people
committed to the engagement of the churches in the ministry of
social justice but who feel that it must be grounded on passages
other than this.[91]

Jan Lambrecht suggested a way out of the dilemma of the
"universalist" versus the "missionary" interpretation by proposing
that Jesus told a parable of the final judgment where God, not himself
as king or exalted Son of man, is the shepherd who separates the

---

88. Von Soden, "adelphos," *TDNT* 1:144–46.
89. Cope, "Matthew XXV: 31–46, 'The Sheep and the Goats' Reinterpreted."
90. Ibid., 44.
91. E.g., Thompson, "An Historical Perspective on the Gospel of Matthew";
Thompson and LaVerdiere, "New Testament Communities in Transition: A Study of
Matthew and Luke." The text has also become a battleground between liberals and
conservatives over service to all the poor or primary concern for fellow Christians.
See Sider, "A Plea for Conservative Radicals and Radical Conservatives."

sheep from the goats.[92] All people will be judged on whether they fulfilled the love command by engaging in active care for the neighbor most in need. As in Matthew's version, the criterion of judgment will be the treatment of the "least," but these least are not called "my brothers [and sisters]." Thus the "universalistic" reading comes from Jesus. Matthew, according to Lambrecht, turns the "least" into the "least of the brothers and sisters" of Jesus and directs the parable to his own community.

Egon Brandenburger reverses this view completely, arguing that Matthew takes over an original passage about the judgment which the returning Son of man will exercise and adds to it a short comparison of the king dividing humanity as a shepherd separates the sheep and the goats (25:31–32).[93] Its pre-Matthean form, which does not go back to the historical Jesus, grew out of the mission theology of early Jewish Christianity, and Matthew makes it into an apocalyptic scene of the judgment of the whole world by the royal Messiah.

Since separation of tradition and redaction is so problematic here and since the Sheep and the Goats has so many elements that are "Matthean," I will not attempt to describe a possible form or setting in the ministry of Jesus but rather attend to its meaning and context in Matthew. While I follow the general thrust of Cope's position, I reject his "sectarian" interpretation. I argue that the parable as presented by Matthew brings together many important themes from his Gospel and remains a rich source for Christian social ethics.

The Parable as Text

Unlike the three preceding parables which stress primarily waiting for the parousia, this parable transports the readers to the moment of the coming of the Son of man in glory (v. 31). The assembling of the nations and the separation of the sheep and the goats take place rapidly (vv. 32–33). As in the parable of the Rich Man and Lazarus in Luke 16:19–31 the time for conversion and change is past; what has been done on earth determines eternal destiny. Now is the time only to recognize the judgment, not to avoid it. The dialogue of the

92. Lambrecht, *Once More Astonished*, 196–235, esp. 211–20.
93. Brandenburger, *Das Recht des Weltenrichters*. Though I do not follow his division of tradition and redaction, his work is rich in theological insights about the parable.

king with those on the right and on the left is constructed in two parallel and similar columns. The king addresses a group as either blessed or cursed and announces their fates—enter into the kingdom or depart from me. In a series of rhythmic statements he affirms why each group is blessed or cursed in terms of a definite need which was met or not met by each group: I was hungry and you gave me food; thirsty and you gave me drink; a stranger and you welcomed me (lit., showed hospitality); naked and you clothed me; sick and you visited me; in prison and you came to see me (vv. 35–36, 42–43).

The "surprise" in the parable arises in the question of the "blessed" which unfolds with an equal rhythm. These verses are carefully constructed with the division of the six works of charity by three questions: "When [pote] did we see thee?" (vv. 37b, 38b, 39). Both the just and the unjust seem to know what concrete acts are demanded, so the parable is not simply an exhortation to the specific deeds mentioned. What distinguished them is to whom these acts were shown. The reason the first group is blessed and the second cursed is given in the double answer of the king: "As you did it to one of the least of these my brethren, you did it to me" (v. 40) and "Truly, I say to you, as you did it not to one of the least of these, you did it not to me" (v. 45).

The radical shock is that the presence of Jesus was hidden in the sick, the hungry, the thirsty, the naked, and the imprisoned. They are not only the "brothers" of Jesus; Jesus is identified with them. The "just" are not just because they acted out of conscious christological motivation, but simply because they cared for the "least." The answer to their question "When did we see thee?" is implicitly, When we saw the least. But "seeing" itself was not enough. It was "seeing" translated into effective care which made the first group blessed; "seeing" alone brought condemnation to the second group.

Though its rhythmic structure and repetition of key phrases confer a unified impact on the parable, certain elements suggest composition. There is a concentration of different christological descriptions: Son of man (v. 31); the King (vv. 34, 40); Lord (vv. 37, 44—which links this parable strongly with the three preceding ones; cf. 24:48; 25:11, 20, 24), and implicitly Son of God, since the King calls the just "blessed of my Father" (v. 34). Though the nations (ethnē in the

neuter) are assembled in v. 32a, the king separates "them" (*autous,*
the masculine plural). Despite the parallels between the questions of
the blessed and the cursed, the latter's dialogue is shortened to one
instance of "When did we see thee?" and their lack of action is
summed up in the term "and did not minister to thee" (v. 44). The
phrase "least of these, my brethren" in the first part is condensed
simply to "least of these" in the second part.

These aspects of the text as well as the presence of some distinctive
Matthean phrases (e.g., "throne of glory," cf. 19:28; a fondness for
tote [then]; the use of "all the nations" [*panta ta ethnē*], cf. 6:32;
24:14; 28:19) indicate considerable Matthean composition, whatever
the exact form of the tradition. After examining three aspects of
Matthew's composition that enrich our understanding—*(a)* its literary
context, *(b)* its christological focus, and *(c)* its ethical perspective—I
will then return to the question of "the least of the brothers and
sisters" of Jesus.

The Literary Context

This parable concludes a long discourse *to the disciples* which begins
in 24:1. In form it is an "apocalyptic testament" (like the *Testaments
of the Twelve Patriarchs*) where a departing figure speaks of future
dangers facing his disciples and exhorts them to fidelity. While the
first half of the discourse treats of the nature and time of the parousia,
the second half (from 24:37—25:46) is concerned with proper conduct prior to the return of Jesus. The fates of the different characters
in these parables are warnings to the disciples about how they are
to act during the time remaining, and the fate of those judged in
25:31–46 has a similar function. The whole discourse proposes an
eschatological ethics for those called to be disciples of Jesus.

The parable of the Sheep and the Goats not only concludes the
apocalyptic testament of chapters 24—25, it has literary contacts with
other parts of Matthew. Most important is its relation to the Great
Commission of Matt. 28:16–20. Here the historical career of Jesus
concludes. In language reminiscent of the son of man of Dan. 7:13–
14, who receives "dominion and glory and kingdom," Jesus who
was humiliated in his cross now possesses all power and authority.[94]

94. The implicit use of Dan. 7:13–14 relates the scene to Matt. 25:31–33 where
Jesus is the enthroned Son of man; see Perkins, *Resurrection,* 133.

He then commissions his disciples to "make disciples of all nations," baptizing and teaching them to observe "all that I have commanded you." Then, just as he was God-with-them during his historical life (Matt. 1:23), Jesus promises to be with the disciples until "the close of the age" (*synteleia tou aiōnos*). Matthew has no ascension narrative; for him, Jesus is to be found in disciples as they go forth in mission to the nations.

This final scene of the Gospel provides an arch spanning the ending of the historical career of Jesus and the ending of history itself. In the salvation-history perspective of this pericope, the end will come only *after* the gospel has been proclaimed to all the nations.[95] The assembly of all the nations at the beginning of the Sheep and the Goats as well as the presence of Jesus in the least looks to the end of history promised in 28:16–20. In the period between the resurrection and the parousia the church is to be a community that "makes disciples" by teaching all nations to observe the teaching of Jesus.[96] In Matthew's perspective, all the nations will have heard the call to be disciples and will have been confronted with what Jesus did and taught as this is embodied in the life of the missionary disciples. The situation envisioned in 25:31–46 presupposes 28:16–20. All nations have heard the preaching of the gospel, and when they reject it, as they might reject a witness in a court of law, they are subject to judgment.

The Theological Context:
Christology in Matt. 25:31–46

Examination of Matt. 25:31–46 as a "parable" that is to be interpreted from the horizon of apocalyptic and of its contacts with other places in the Gospel reveals a scene when the mission to all the peoples of the world is complete and the parousia of the Son of man is at hand. But the dominant use of this pericope for Christian ethics as well as the disputed questions of who is judged and who are the least has overshadowed its christological importance. If the

95. Gundry, *Matthew*, 513–14.
96. There has been a lively debate on whether *ethnē* means "Gentiles" (excluding Jews) or "nations" (comprising all people). See Hare and Harrington, "Make Disciples of All the Gentiles (Mt. 28:19)" (for "Gentile"); and Meier, "Nations or Gentiles in Matt. 28:19?" 94–102 (all peoples). I follow Meier; see also Donahue, "The 'Parable' of the Sheep and the Goats," 14–17.

passage is to continue to be a vital source for Christian ethics, examination of the Christology is essential.

The Son of man enthroned in glory. The parable describes the arrival of the Son of man enthroned in glory, who is also a king, the shepherd of his people who addresses the just as blessed of "my Father," and who is called *kyrios* by those he will judge. Matthew thus offers a tableau of major christological themes, which have resonated throughout the Gospel.[97] Jesus is the Son of David (1:1), the royal Messiah, who was proclaimed king at his birth and whom gentile wise men came to worship (2:1–12), yet he is the *basileus praus* (the humble king, 21:5; cf. Zech. 9:9) who dies on a cross. He is also the Son of God who has his origin in God (1:20), is proclaimed as such at his baptism (3:17), and proves himself in confrontation with evil to be the faithful son (4:1–11). He speaks of God as his Father and is the Son to whom the Father has delivered all things and who reveals the Father to others, especially "to babes" (11:25–27). Though Matthew offers a rich christological tableau which stresses the majesty of Jesus, the exalted Son of man is also the hidden and suffering Son of man who gave his life for others and who was rejected by his people.

The presence of the king/Son of man who was hidden in the suffering community, yet who is the exalted judge of evildoers, represents an integration of major motifs from Matthew's heritage. Matthew integrates a Christology of Jesus as the Suffering Servant of Isaiah (esp. Isa. 52:13—53:12) as well as the Suffering Just One (Wisd. of Sol. 2:12–24; 5:1–23). In the baptism, the passion predictions, and the account of the passion Matthew appropriates the Servant Christology but develops it in a manner that is unique to his theology.

In 12:17–21, Matthew has the longest "fulfillment" quotation of his Gospel, a citation of the first Servant Song of Isa. 42:1–4. This citation comes at a significant place in the structure of the Gospel. After the missionary discourse to the disciples (chap. 10) Matthew portrays Jesus as the "ideal missionary," preaching, teaching, and healing throughout Galilee (chaps. 11—12). The "fulfillment" quo-

97. On Matthew's Christology, see Kingsbury, *Matthew: Structure, Christology, Kingdom,* 40–127; idem, *Jesus Christ in Matthew, Mark and Luke,* 73–85.

tation interprets this as an instance of the servant who will "proclaim justice to the Gentiles" (or nations) and who will not "break a bruised reed or quench a smoldering wick, till he brings justice to victory; and in his name will the Gentiles hope" (12:18–20). In one sense the application of this passage to Jesus is inappropriate, since in chapters 10—13 Jesus has not worked among the Gentiles, but in Galilee, and earlier had charged his disciples, "Go nowhere among the Gentiles" (10:5). Why, then, does Matthew cite here a text that stresses that justice will be proclaimed to the Gentiles and that the Gentiles will hope in the name of the Servant? The answer seems to be that Jesus anticipates that mission which the church will undertake. In the final commission (28:19–20) when the disciples are "sent forth" to all nations Jesus promises to be with them. He is to be with them as the "servant" who will proclaim justice to the nations in the form of the proclamation of the kingdom and its enactment through works of healing and mercy as well as through the suffering and rejection they will meet in their mission (Matt. 10:17–18). The community is to be a community in mission which proclaims justice to the nations in the midst of suffering and persecution. The Son of man hidden in the least of the brethren is also the Servant who will bring God's justice to victory and in whom the nations can hope.

The Son of man as king. In the parable of the Sheep and the Goats the Son of man is also king, which, as noted above, has led some commentators to postulate two layers of tradition here. From the viewpoint of the final redaction, however, the important point is Matthew's use of the royal motifs here.

Though the description of Jesus as king is muted in the synoptic tradition and generally limited to the passion narrative (e.g., Matt. 27:11, 29, 37, 42), Matthew makes most use of the motif. The child who is born is "king of the Jews" (2:2) and seen by Herod as a rival to the throne (2:13–14). A major part of the infancy narrative is concerned to show the Davidic descent of Jesus (1:1, 20), and, unlike Mark who is most reserved about any public description of Jesus as Son of David, Matthew pictures Jesus often as the healing Son of David.[98] The expression "Have mercy on me, Son of David" (9:27; 15:22; 20:30–31) is almost a prayer in Matthew.

98. Duling, "The Therapeutic Son of David."

In Israel's history there is a parallelism between the historical king and the attributes of God.[99] God is a God of justice who is concerned for the poor and the marginal in the land, and this mandate is given to the king.[100] When Israel no longer had historical kings much of the royal ideology was transferred to the messianic king or to eschatological saving figures. The hoped-for Son of David in the *Psalms of Solomon* will restore justice to the land.[101] In *1 Enoch* the Son of man and the Elect One, though they are not called kings, are associated with the "throne of glory" (*1 Enoch* 61:8; 62:2, 5) and they exercise domination over earthly kings and participate in judgment, a royal function.

Aspects of the ancient royal ideology influence the Matthean presentation of Jesus. Jesus announces the kingdom (4:17; cf. 10:7), and his ministry is the "gospel of the kingdom"—an expression used only by Matthew (4:23; 9:35; 24:14; cf. 26:13; 13:9). He proclaims God's will for the people and takes the side of the poor and the marginal. In the Sheep and the Goats the juxtaposition of king and Son of man represents a melding of descriptions that have been held apart in the historical ministry of Jesus. As Son of man, Jesus is the one who suffered and was exalted; as king, he is the eschatological Messiah who will execute judgment and vindicate those who were defenseless.

The Ethical Perspective

Justice and mercy. Significant, then, is the description twice in the parable (vv. 37, 46) of the blessed as *dikaioi*. Their justice gives them a share in royal dominion, the *basileia* prepared for them (25:34). As noted (see above, pp. 70–72), justice is a central motif in Matthew. It comprises both the demand that God's will be followed and God's saving help for the marginal by which the world is made "right." Both John and Jesus proclaim justice, and the disciples are to embody a "better righteousness." Equally central to Matthew is *eleos* (mercy

---

99. Brandenburger, *Das Recht des Weltenrichters*, 43–51; and Ringgren, *Israelite Religion*, 5–9, 34–39, 57–88.
100. See Isa. 30:18; 61:8; Pss. 11:7; 33:5; 37:28; 99:4 (on a God of justice); Exod. 22:21–27; Deut. 15:1–11 (on concern for the marginal); Isa. 9:6–7; 11:3–5; Jer. 22:15–17; Ps. 82:1–5 (on the duty of a king to uphold justice).
101. *Pss. Sol.* 17:26–42.

or lovingkindness).[102] In the Beatitudes which inaugurate the first
major discourse they are side by side: those who hunger and thirst
for justice will be filled; the merciful shall obtain mercy (5:6–7).
Their location here at the conclusion of the final discourse of Jesus
provides an overarching structure to the whole Gospel.

The frequent translation of *eleos* as "mercy," which suggests
forbearance from inflicting harm or forgiveness of wrong, conceals
its dynamic character. The biblical terms *ḥesed* and *eleos* primarily
describe an action rather than an attitude; saving help, rather than
passive forbearance.[103] Matthew invokes the saying of Hos. 6:6, "I
desire mercy, and not sacrifice," to interpret both the call of Levi
(9:13) and the plucking of grain on the Sabbath (12:7). Both
association with marginal groups and violation of the Sabbath are
examples of deeds of lovingkindness that transcend legalism. Those
who seek healing from Jesus cry out, "Have mercy on me, Son of
David" (9:27; 15:22; [17:15]; 20:30, 31). Concrete actions of
lovingkindness to those in need constitute the mercy which God
desires.

Now I will attempt to weave some of these threads together. In
the story of the last judgment we have a juridical situation in which
one group are called just (*dikaioi*, 25:37, 46) because they have
performed acts of mercy and lovingkindness to those in need and
therefore inherit the kingdom prepared from the foundation of the
world; the other group are cursed because they neglected these
deeds. As mentioned earlier, the horizon of this scene is apocalyptic.
One critical aspect of apocalyptic thought is that the scenes of
judgment disclose the transcendent values that should have been
operative prior to the judgment. Apocalyptic is a view of history and
human life from God's side. It also offers a solution to the problem
of theodicy, that is, why do evil people flourish and why do the
innocent suffer? Apocalyptic affirms that the sufferings and injustice
which mar this world will be bearable because the order of justice
will be restored. Sin and evil will be unmasked and goodness
rewarded. Simply put, the world will be made "right" again.

Matthew adopts this perspective, since the parable of the Sheep
and the Goats reveals the actions that should have been normative

102. Gundry, *Matthew*, 70–71.
103. R. Bultmann, "eleos," *TDNT* 2:479.

in the world. Matthew also modifies the apocalyptic perspective. First by his double repetition of the deeds done or not done, he calls attention to the norms by which people will be judged rather than to detailed descriptions of the judgment. For Matthew, the world will be made right when acts of mercy and lovingkindness are shown to those most in need. He modifies apocalyptic also by his perspective on salvation history. The end time has been inaugurated by the ministry, death and resurrection of Jesus, and its benefits have already begun with Jesus, who expresses the higher form of justice in concrete deeds of love. So too after the historical ministry of Jesus when the Son of man is hidden in the least of his brothers and sisters the true order of justice is maintained when those acts of mercy and loving-kindness characterize the life of discipleship.

The Least of the Brothers and Sisters of the Son of Man

Now I can address the question most debated: whether "the least of the brothers and sisters" of the Son of man are all the needy or Christian disciples. The position I propose is that "the least of my brothers and sisters" refers primarily to Christian disciples or missionaries, which for Matthew are virtually the same, but that this does not make the pericope into a sectarian ethic where the disciples can simply look forward to the punishment of those who do not welcome them or respond to their needs. Such an interpretation would leave the passage with little relevance for contemporary ethics or homiletics. My claim is that a proper understanding of the "least" as disciples is more faithful to the text and offers a deeper challenge to contemporary Christians than either the sectarian interpretation or the summons to universal benevolence implicit in the understanding of "the least" simply as any needy person.

The Matthean church is a community in mission until the end of the age. In addition to teaching what Jesus taught, this mission is to take place through witness. Matthew highlights the motif of witness early in his Gospel when, after the Beatitudes, he adds a series of sayings on the disciples as salt of the earth and light of the world (5:13–16), which circulated independently and are found in different forms in Mark and Q.[104] The first saying, "You are the salt of the

---

104. Fitzmyer, *Luke I—IX*, 717–20; and Gundry, *Matthew*, 75–78.

earth," has no direct correspondence but appears in Mark 9:50 as "Salt is good; but if the salt has lost its saltness, how will you season it?" (followed by Luke 14:34). Here it serves as a warning to disciples against scandal and halfhearted discipleship (Mark 9:42–50). The second saying, "You are the light of the world," appears in both Mark (4:21 = Luke 8:16) and Q (Luke 11:33) in the form of a parable about not lighting a lamp and then hiding it, but rather placing it where it may be seen. Matthew radically reinterprets these sayings in the following manner: First, he adds the emphatic "you are" (5:13, 14) before each saying which, along with the frequent use of "your" (your lamp, your good deeds, your Father in heaven, v. 16), stresses the personal and positive quality of discipleship rather than its dangers, as in Mark and Q.[105] Second, he makes the witness motif explicit by adding the sentence "Let your light so shine before others (RSV: "men"), that they may see your good works and give glory to your Father who is in heaven" (5:16). This latter phrase reflects the vocation of Israel, the covenant people in Isa. 42:6, to be "a light to the nations." Third, and finally, Matthew locates these sayings after those beatitudes which bless the disciples when they are persecuted (5:11–12), so that in their mission and witness "those persecuted by the world are nevertheless the world's salvation."[106]

This perspective is undergirded by the two explicit uses of *martyrion* in Matt. 10:18 and 24:14. Both appear in persecution sayings. The first is in the context of the mission discourse of Matthew 10, where, after predicting rejection of their message, Jesus tells the disciples that they will be delivered up to councils, synagogues, governors, and kings, "to bear witness before them and to the nations" (10:18, au. trans.). The second instance comes in Matthew's own eschatological discourse (24:9–14) where he edits those sections of Mark 13:9–13 which he had not previously transferred to 10:17–21. Matthew changes the sequence of the eschatological events as found in Mark. In Mark, testimony before governors and kings is part of the sequence of persecutions that will precede the end. In Matt. 24:10–12 the persecution will be followed by apostasy and betrayal, and "love will grow cold" (v. 12). Following Mark, Matthew (24:13) says that the one who endures to the end will be saved and adds (v. 14), "This gospel of the kingdom will be preached throughout the

105. Gundry, *Matthew*, 77.
106. Meier, *Matthew*, 43.

whole world, as a witness (RSV: "testimony") to all nations; and then the end will come." In this fashion Matthew brings the eschatological discourse of chapter 24 into close connection with the mission discourse of chapter 10. During both the earthly career of Jesus (the setting of chap. 10) and the period prior to the final coming (the setting of chap. 24) a life of discipleship is to be one of continued witness in the face of persecution. This is also the exact sequence found in the Great Commission (28:18–20): the consummation of the age will come at the end of the mission.

The Matthean church is to be a community in mission that will bear witness to the "gospel of the kingdom" in the awareness that they will face rejection and persecution. The identity of the least of the brothers and sisters of Jesus in Matt. 25:31–46 and their specific sufferings are to be interpreted from this perspective. The sufferings borne by the least of the brothers and sisters of Jesus are apostolic sufferings borne in proclaiming the gospel. Such a perspective is found also in the letters of Paul.

Paul's reference to his apostolic sufferings comes mainly in the hardship lists (*Peristasiskatalogen*) of 1 Cor. 4:9–13; 2 Cor. 4:8–9; 6:4–5; 11:23–29; 12:10.[107] All the sufferings of "the least of the brothers and sisters" in Matt. 25:34–36 are mentioned by Paul— hunger (1 Cor. 4:11), thirst (1 Cor. 4:11; 2 Cor. 11:27), living as a stranger or an itinerant (1 Cor. 4:11, "homeless"), nakedness (1 Cor. 4:11; 2 Cor. 11:27), sickness (Matt. 25:36, *ēsthenēsa*; cf. 1 Cor. 4:10, "We are weak," *astheneis*), imprisonment (2 Cor. 11:23; Philem. 9). Such lists are well known in the philosophical and ethical treatises of many of Paul's contemporaries, especially Epictetus, and in the literature of apocalyptic Judaism.[108] Though Paul may be influenced by the form of these lists, they function differently. In Hellenism they show either the courage that the philosopher exhibits in surmounting such difficulties or the inability of worldly cares to impinge on philosophic equilibrium.[109] In Paul, however, they indicate either that "the transcendent power belongs to God" (2 Cor. 4:7) or that "power is made perfect in weakness" (2 Cor. 12:9). These apostolic

107. For a discussion of these catalogues, see Furnish, *II Corinthians*, 280–83, 354–55, 535–39.
108. Ibid., 281–82.
109. Ibid., 282, 354–55.

sufferings conceal the power of Christ which is at work in the one who proclaims the gospel. This is exactly the same function of the list of sufferings in the parable of the Sheep and the Goats. The exalted Son of man is hidden in the presence of those who are undergoing the same sufferings that Paul undergoes in his mission to the nations.

Therefore, I claim that the brothers and sisters of the Son of man in Matt. 25:31–46 are not simply passive victims of pagan rejection but rather are a church in mission which through its teaching and way of life gives witness to Jesus. In such preaching the disciple is not above the teacher (Matt. 10:24) nor the servant above the master. Just as Jesus was the lowly one, meek and humble, who suffered rejection and persecution, so too will his community. The community through its witness is not simply to indict an evil world. It is to be a light so that humanity will give glory to God.

Matthew's Parable as a Challenge to Contemporary Ethics

As I remarked earlier, this text has become a classic for persons concerned about the effects of injustice and poverty on wide segments of the human family. To challenge its generalized use is, for many, tantamount to abrogating the claim of the gospel. In advocating a position that the "least of the brothers and sisters of Jesus" are not principally all the poor and needy, but the church in mission, we do not have to forsake the claims that this passage makes on contemporary church and society. Four considerations are important.

1. The apocalyptic horizon of the parables of Matthew 24—25 is a caution against abandoning apocalyptic as a resource for contemporary social ethics. New Testament apocalyptic has always been somewhat of an embarrassment for social ethics, since it seems to be opposed to concern for the world. It is often demythologized or simply ignored as part of an outmoded world view. Apocalyptic and eschatology have also spawned the idea of an "interim ethic"—that the teaching of Jesus and of much of Paul was so influenced by the prospect of the imminent end of the world that it has little relevance for the long course of history.[110] Much contemporary use of the Bible

---

110. The term "interim ethic" is associated with Schweitzer, *The Quest of the Historical Jesus*, 354.

for social ethics simply ignores this material and prefers to center on the historical career of Jesus, especially his liberating praxis and radical love. At the risk of oversimplifying a complex hermeneutical issue, I would simply follow Adela Collins in noting that apocalyptic reminds us that the love command must always be complemented by the call for justice.[111]

Reflection on justice from its apocalyptic horizon led Ernst Käsemann to state that God's aim in the New Testament is not the salvation of the individual but the justification of the world.[112] Apocalyptic literature arises generally among people who are themselves suffering or oppressed, and its images of the destruction of evil and new creation remind us that evil is not to be lord of human life and that God's will is that justice be victorious.[113] Apocalyptic affirms that life must be shaped not simply by its present evil but by its future promises.

2. The Sheep and the Goats in Matthew as an apocalyptic parable reveals to Matthew's community the criteria by which all people are to be judged and the norms by which they, like those on the right, can be called just (*dikaioi*). The Son of man will return as king and restore the order of justice. Treatment of the least, whom I have argued are Christians in mission and witness to the world, becomes the occasion by which the true meaning of justice is revealed. The parable reveals that justice is constituted by acts of lovingkindness and mercy to those in need; the world will be made "right" or "just" when the way the least are treated becomes the norm of action. What is done positively *for* them is not to be limited *to* them. What is proposed is not a "sectarian ethic" where Christians are to revel in the punishment of their oppressors. Rather, it is an ethics of faithful witness where the Christian, like Jesus in the proclamation of the gospel of the kingdom, becomes the locus for the disclosure of God's will for all peoples.

3. The ethic proposed is a Christian ethic—an ethics of discipleship. It draws its strength not simply from a humanitarian compassion for those in need but from a sense that, like the first disciples, Christians

111. A. Y. Collins, *The Apocalypse*, x.
112. Quoted from a lecture delivered by Ernst Käsemann (in Koch, *Rediscovery of Apocalyptic*, 77).
113. J. J. Collins, *The Apocalyptic Imagination*, 214–15.

are to hear again the call "Follow me" and are to be caught up in the mission of Jesus. I have stressed the literary context of this passage at the conclusion of the eschatological discourse and its implications for discipleship. The parable of the Sheep and the Goats contains also the final words of Jesus before the passion, when the Son of man will be delivered up to be crucified (Matt. 26:2). The one who will come in glory and grant a kingdom to the just will also suffer, die, and be raised up. An ethics of discipleship involves deep engagement with the mystery of the cross, which for Matthew, in common with other early Christian perspectives, is a life given in ransom for others.[114] The service to others which the king/Son of man demands in the parable is a service which he has not only proclaimed but embodied.[115] Jesus' gift of his life for others is also paradoxically the victory over death at the very moment when death seems itself sovereign.

4. From the perspective of Christians who retell this parable today, the sufferings borne by the least of the brothers and sisters of the Son of man summon the church to be an authentic and faithful witness of the gospel and serve as a warning against what Dietrich Bonhoeffer called "cheap grace," grace without conversion and engagement in the scandal of the cross.[116] Christian churches cannot preach acts of lovingkindness to the hungry, the thirsty, the imprisoned, and the naked unless they too are churches in mission which bear these same sufferings. No gospel is harsher than Matthew on an ethics of words without deeds. No gospel is more eloquent on the dialectic of concealment and revelation, of weakness and power. The ethics that the church proposes to the nations must be an ethics to which the church gives living witness in the midst of the nations.

The parable of the Sheep and the Goats, the final parable uttered by the earthly Jesus in the Gospel of Matthew, provides in the form of an apocalyptic revelation an integration of Christology, discipleship, and ethics. It provides the hermeneutical key to Matthew's Gospel in parable.

114. Matt. 20:28 = Mark 10:45; see also 1 Cor. 1:30; Rom. 3:24–25; 8:23; 1 Pet. 2:21–25.
115. Brandenburger, *Das Recht des Weltenrichters*, 131.
116. Bonhoeffer, *The Cost of Discipleship*, 45–47.

4

THE
PARABLES
OF
LUKE

INTRODUCTION

Among the Synoptic Gospels, Luke contains the most extensive collection of parables, including those which have become classic representatives of Jesus' teaching: the Good Samaritan, the Prodigal Son, and the Pharisee and the Tax Collector, for example. With Luke we enter a world different from that of Matthew and Mark. The drama in Luke's parables arises less from the mystery of nature or the threat of judgment than from the mystery of human interaction. For Luke, the human condition is a stage on which appear memorable characters: the churlish older brother (15:25–32), the crafty steward (16:1–8), or the persistent widow (18:1–8). Luke invites us into this world by the frequent use of soliloquy (e.g., 12:19; 15:17; 16:3; 18:4–5) where we are made privy to the inner musings of the characters. Luke eschews allegory and expresses realistic sympathy for the dilemmas of ordinary human existence. His memorable characters offer paradigms of discipleship for daily Christian existence.

With the exception of the Two Debtors (7:41–43), the parables exclusive to Luke occur in the travel narrative (9:51—19:27), the great central section of the Gospel where Luke from 9:51 to 18:14 abandons his Markan source and incorporates only Q material or material from his own tradition, L. Though general agreement exists on the importance of this section, little consensus exists on either its structure or unifying theological perspective. The section is influenced by the Markan motif of "the way" (Mark 8:27; 9:33; 10:32; cf.

Luke 9:3, 57), with its double nuance of the way to Jerusalem and the way of discipleship (Luke 20:21; Acts 9:2), but is less tightly organized than Mark's. Though there are indications of movement throughout the section (9:57; 10:1, 17, 38; 11:1; 13:30; 14:1, 25), attempts to map the journey are fruitless. Jerusalem is the clear goal (9:51; 13:22, 33; 17:11; 18:35; 19:1, 11), but movement toward it lacks Mark's clear articulation. While the Markan Jesus instructs his disciples primarily on the necessity and theology of the cross, the Lukan Jesus offers a developed ethics of discipleship. Much of the Q material that Matthew contains in his Sermon on the Mount, Luke includes in the travel narrative rather than in the Sermon on the Plain.[1]

Different proposals vie to find unity in this section, such as the suggestion that the Lukan Jesus here offers a commentary on the Book of Deuteronomy[2] or that Luke presents an elaborate chiastic structure where the central section is surrounded by parallel incidents.[3] While individual groupings of material within the larger section show clear artistry (see below, pp. 138, 173), no proposed structure has carried the day.

Though there is no single unifying theological motif, the section offers a cameo of the major theological themes of Luke-Acts.[4] Some of these are:

- The importance of Jerusalem as the goal of Jesus' "taking up" (*analēmpsis*, 9:51; cf. Acts 1:10) as well as the place from which God's saving action begins (1:5–13; 24:47; Acts 1:8–9)
- Concern for non-Jews as shown in the positive view of the Samaritans (10:29–37; 17:16; Acts 8:25)
- Stress on the offer of mercy to sinners (15:1–2; Acts 2:38; 10:43)
- Concern for outcasts and those on the margin of society (14:13, 21; 15:1–2; 17:11–19; 18:1–14; Acts 3:1–10; 8:25)
- Strong emphasis on prayer (10:2; 11:13; 18:1–14; Acts 1:14; 2:42)

---

1. Lambrecht, *The Sermon on the Mount*, 35–39.
2. See Evans, "Central Section," esp. 42–49; and Cave, "Lazarus and the Lukan Deuteronomy."
3. Talbert, *Literary Patterns, Theological Themes, and the Genre of Luke-Acts*, 51–56.
4. See Fitzmyer (*Luke I—IX*, 143–270) for an excellent "Sketch of Lucan Theology"; and also below, chap. 5, n. 36.

• Teaching on the danger of wealth and the proper use of possessions (12:13–21, 33–34; 16:1–13, 19–31; 19:1–10; Acts 2:43–45; 4:32–33; 5:1–10).

Therefore, whatever the organizing principle of the travel narrative, Luke clearly wants to portray Jesus as teaching his disciples that way of discipleship which they themselves are to follow as they spread the gospel to the ends of the earth (Acts 1:8; cf. Luke 24:47).

In engaging Luke's "Gospel in parable," I will concentrate on the parables from the travel narrative. Also, since Luke tends to treat similar motifs in different places, I will subsume related material under what seems to be the major statement of a theme. The method can be broadly called "redactional-thematic," with an emphasis on the immediate and the broader context of a given theme or motif.

LUKE'S THEOLOGICAL PROGRAM:
THE GOOD SAMARITAN IN CONTEXT

At the beginning of the travel narrative Jesus sets his face toward Jerusalem and dispatches his disciples as an advance party who are quickly rejected by the Samaritans (9:51–56). Jesus rejects their suggestion of violent reprisal and then spells out the radical demands of discipleship (9:57–62), prior to a unit of material that deals with the sending and the return of the Seventy (10:1–20). Jesus then prays in thanksgiving for God's revelation and privately blesses the disciples (10:21–24). The abrupt question of the lawyer in 10:25 ("And behold, a lawyer stood up") interrupts the somewhat serene atmosphere of the preceding verses and seems relatively unrelated to the previous material. My contention is that after the missionary charges of 9:51–10:20 which inaugurate the "way to Jerusalem," Luke from 10:21 to 11:4 creates a "theological arch" depicting the essential qualities of discipleship—a theme which determines the shape of the whole "travel narrative" (9:51—19:27).

The Lawyer's Question (10:25–28)

The dialogue about the greatest commandment appears in all three Synoptic Gospels (Mark 12:28–34 = Matt. 22:34–40) but in different contexts. In Mark and Matthew it occurs as part of the Jerusalem ministry where Jesus' conflict with Jewish leaders grows increasingly bitter; it concludes a triad of incidents in which Jewish leaders try to trap Jesus (Mark 12:13–34 = Matt. 22:15–40), and in both is followed by polemical statements against Jewish leaders. In Luke not only is the dialogue between Jesus and the lawyer more irenic but the actual conversation is significantly altered. Whereas in Mark the question is "Which commandment is the first of all?" (Mark 12:28) and in Matthew "Which is the great commandment?" (Matt. 22:36), the lawyer in Luke asks what he must do to inherit "eternal life" (Luke 10:25). This reflects Luke's more positive estimation of Judaism and its institutions and his understanding that the law was to bring the fullness of life. Also in Luke it is not Jesus who articulates the command but the lawyer himself, and, in contrast to Mark and Matthew, there is no reference to a "first" or "second" command (see below, pp. 136–37).

The irenic tone of the dialogue changes in 10:29 when the lawyer tries to "justify himself" by posing the counterquestion "Who is my neighbor?" This question is not facetious, since the scribes debated whether the neighbor of Lev. 19:18 included Gentiles and Samaritans.[5] Jesus does not answer the question but rather tells the parable of the Good Samaritan. Whereas the lawyer asks, "Who is my neighbor?" the parable says rather what it means to be a neighbor (10:36). (Compare Matt. 18:23–35, where Peter asks how often he must forgive, while the parable deals with the experience of forgiveness as a presupposition to forgiveness.) The lawyer, who perhaps wonders whether the Samaritan is the neighbor whom he must love, now finds that the Samaritan is the one who teaches the true meaning of the law of love of neighbor.

The Good Samaritan (Luke 10:29–37)

The Parable as Text

The parable narrates the chance intersection of various personal histories. Though compact, it moves forward rapidly by engaging the reader in a series of dramatic tensions. The description of the traveler simply as *anthrōpos tis* (someone, a certain person) involves the reader as do the medieval Everyman plays. Even today the road from

5. Jeremias, *Parables*, 202–3; and Bailey, *Through Peasant Eyes*, 39–40.

Jerusalem to Jericho traverses lonely and difficult terrain and in antiquity was proverbial as a haven for bands of robbers.[6] The fate of the unaccompanied traveler is almost anticipated; he is beaten, robbed, and left for dead. Lying there naked, the injured man is without the signs of either nationality or social status—both of which are indicated by clothing, especially in first-century Judea. He is simply a person in need, whose only claim is his need. With their gaze still fixed on Everyman the attention of the audience is turned to the chance presence (v. 31) of other travelers, not just any wayfarers but members of the religious establishment, who would be expected to assist an injured person. The first major shock of the parable comes when they simply gaze upon the injured man and pass by on the other side.

At this point the narrative potential of the story is manifold. After the two Jewish religious leaders, it could portray the arrival of Roman officials, Jewish laypeople, or the return of the robbers. As J. Dominic Crossan has brilliantly noted, if the main thrust of the parable was simply an illustration of love of neighbor or even a diatribe against heartless religious leaders, the offer of aid by a Jewish layperson would be sufficient.[7] The major shock comes when it is the Samaritan who stops. Centuries of pious reflection have dulled our sensibilities to the hatred that existed between Jews and Samaritans. After the Babylonian exile the Samaritans had opposed the restoration of Jerusalem and in the second century B.C., had helped the Syrian rulers in their wars against the Jews. In Sirach (50:25–26), about 200 B.C., the Samaritans are called "no nation," and in 128 B.C. the Jewish high priest burned the Samaritan temple on Mt. Gerizim.[8] In the early first century A.D. the Samaritans scattered the bones of a corpse in the temple during Passover, defiling the temple and preventing the celebration of the feast.[9] In John 8:48 the Jews assume that Jesus is a Samaritan and demon possessed (cf. John 4:7–10), and, in the mission charge in Matthew, Jesus tells the disciples to

6. Strabo (Geography 16.2.41) notes that Pompey had to wipe out "strongholds of brigands" near Jericho; cited in Bailey, Through Peasant Eyes, 41.
7. Crossan, "Parable and Example in the Teaching of Jesus," 294–95; idem, Dark Interval, 104–8.
8. R. Brown, John I—XII, 170; and Bailey, Through Peasant Eyes, 47–48.
9. Josephus, Jewish Antiquities 18.2.2 (29–30). Eng. trans. L. H. Feldman, Josephus: Jewish Antiquities, LCL 9:25–27.

avoid Samaritan territory (Matt. 10:5; cf. Luke 9:51–55). The shock of the parable is that the one who stops, who paradoxically fulfills the law, is the enemy and religious apostate. This shock challenges the hearers' understanding of God and whom God approves; it shatters a narrow interpretation of the law and unmasks the hatreds and divisions which often become institutionalized by religious strife. This parabolic paradox is parallel to the kingdom proclamation of Jesus and to his offer of God's mercy to sinners and outcasts.

While the challenge to join "good" to "Samaritan" is the central thrust of the parable, the other narrative details of the parable enrich its meanings and applications. While one is tempted to view the priest and the Levite as callous clerics, perhaps overly taken up with the "business" of religion, the parable provides an excuse for their action. The injured man is, to all external appearances, dead. He is described as "half dead" and never speaks or moves in the narrative. If the priest and the Levite were journeying to Jericho, a priestly city, for some stated religious rite (e.g., to offer a daily sacrifice), contact with a corpse would have made them ritually unclean (Lev. 21:1–2), which may explain why they not only do not stop but deliberately go to the other side of the road.[10] They are caught in a moral dilemma—to observe the torah on uncleanness or the torah on love of neighbor. The Samaritan, who is both a layperson and an outsider, embodies the true interpretation of the law. This is also ironic since one of the major disputes between Jews and Samaritans was over the observance of the laws of the first five books of Moses.

In the text there is a further hint—perhaps added by Luke since it is so much a part of his theology—of why the characters act as they do. In describing the travelers, the Greek text creates a rhythmic cadence, like the tolling of a distant bell. A priest was going down, and "when he sees" (kai idōn), he passed by on the other side (antiparēlthen); a Levite came to the same place and "when he sees" (kai idōn), he passed by on the other side (antiparēlthen). The repetition of seeing and bypassing prepares us for the arrival of the Samaritan, who is initially described in the same way. He is "making his way" and "when he sees" (kai idōn)—at this point we expect a repetition

10. Bailey, *Through Peasant Eyes*, 44–46; and Derrett, *Law*, 212–17. For an opposing view that a priest must attend to an unburied corpse, see E. Feldman, *Biblical and Post-Biblical Defilement and Mourning*, 60–62.

of "passing by" (*antiparēlthen*).[11] Instead, the rhythm is broken·by the explosive verb *esplanchnisthē* ("he had compassion"). Each of the travelers "sees"; the Samaritan "sees and has compassion." Compassion is the bridge between simply looking on injured and half-dead fellow human beings and entering their world with saving care.

This same juxtaposition of seeing and compassion occurs elsewhere. In Luke 7:13 Jesus sees (*kai idōn*) the woman who is burying her son, has compassion (*esplanchnisthē*) on her, and then restores her son. In 15:20 the father sees the returning son, has compassion (*esplanchnisthē*), and welcomes him home. In one of the hymns of the infancy narrative—an overture to the major theological themes of the Gospel—Zechariah praises John, who will "go before the Lord to prepare his ways, to give knowledge of salvation to his people in the forgiveness of their sins, through the tender mercy [or compassion, *splanchna eleous*] of our God, when the day [i.e., the coming of Jesus] shall dawn upon us from on high" (1:76–78). The compassion of God stands behind the coming of Jesus, just as in Exod. 3:7–8 the Lord comes to the aid of the suffering people of Israel, after seeing their affliction, hearing their cries, and knowing their sufferings. Compassion is that divine quality which, when present in human beings, enables them to share deeply in the sufferings and needs of others and enables them to move from one world to the other: from the world of helper to the one needing help; from the world of the innocent to that of the sinner. Under Luke's tutelage the parable becomes *a paradigm of the compassionate vision* which is the presupposition for ethical action.

The other actions of the Samaritan enrich our reading of the parable. Though the pouring of oil and wine on the wounds may reflect first-century medicinal customs, oil and wine are also the elements of the daily temple sacrifice (see Lev. 23:13; cf. Rev. 6:6).[12] This should be connected with the admission of the lawyer in 10:37 that the neighbor is "the one who showed mercy [*eleos*]," which is an allusion to Hos. 6:6, "I desire mercy [*eleos*] and not sacrifice" (LXX; cf. Matt. 9:13; 12:7). Here and especially in Isa. 58:5–9 true religious observance consists of deeds of mercy and lovingkindness.

---

11. I have literally translated the aorist participles here as historical presents to capture the vivid style of the narrative.
12. Derrett, *Law*, 220.

Ironically then, the Samaritan who was doubly unclean, because of his apostate status and potential contact with a corpse, offers the true sacrifice, and, though a member of a religious group that did not recognize the prophets—the Samaritans recognized only the five books of Moses—he embodies the prophetic call to true religion.

The final action of the Samaritan when he brings the injured man to the inn is more than a narrative epilogue or an added indication of the excess of charity in a person we have come to admire. He takes care of him, stays the night, in perhaps a hostile environment, then pays the innkeeper two denarii (= two normal days' wages), and enters into a contract to pay for other bills the injured man might incur. As a paradigm for compassionate entry into the world of an injured brother or sister, this final action is indispensable. According to the law of the time, a person with an unpaid debt could be enslaved until the debt was paid (cf. Matt. 18:23–35). Since the injured man was robbed and stripped—deprived of all resources— he could have been at the mercy of the innkeeper, a profession that had a bad reputation in antiquity for dishonesty and violence. The Samaritan assures the injured man's freedom and independence. The parable here addresses its subsequent use in Christian ethics. It is not enough simply to enter the world of the neighbor with care and compassion; one must enter and leave it in such a way that the neighbor is given freedom along with the very help that is offered.

Though the action of the Samaritan is at the center of the parable, as polyvalent, it invites us to identify with the other characters. The parable, as Robert Funk has noted, also calls on its readers to identify with the victim in the ditch. He writes:

> The future which the parable discloses is the future of every hearer who grasps and is grasped by his position in the ditch. . . . The poor traveler is literally the victim of a ruthless robber. So were the poor, the lame, the blind, and others whom Jesus drew to his side. In fact, one has to understand himself as the victim in order to be eligible.[13]

Patristic allegory, though fanciful in detail, was perhaps not too far afield when it identified the Samaritan with Christ coming to the aid

---

13. See Funk, "The Old Testament in Parable: The Good Samaritan," in *Language, Hermeneutic*, 214. See also his essays in *Parables and Presence*: "The Good Samaritan as Metaphor," 29–34; and "Parable, Paradox, and Power: The Prodigal Samaritan," 55–65.

of wounded humanity.[14] More existentially I suggest that identification with the victim relativizes our notions of how we can receive the graciousness of God. It often comes from those least expected, from the outcast. It often comes amid powerlessness. If the injured man was a Jew, his first contact with Samaritans may have been when he awoke in the inn. His brush with death could have opened his own vision of who is neighbor and where goodness can be found.

As text, then, this parable is a "classic," that is, "any text, event or person which unites particularity of origin and expression with a disclosure of meaning and truth, available in principle to all human beings."[15] It challenges us to move beyond our social and religious constructs of good and evil; it subverts our tendency to divide the world into insiders and outsiders. It makes us realize that goodness may be found precisely in those we most often call evil or enemy. Is not one of the most fundamental root metaphors of our contemporary political and social life the "evil communist"—a view often fostered, rather than challenged, by established religion? The parable summons us to a solidarity with suffering men and women and tells us that such solidarity can come only when we acquire hearts of flesh and a compassionate vision. To fulfill the command to love God and neighbor, one must often become the Samaritan, the outsider taking a risk in a hostile world.

Martha and Mary (Luke 10:38–42) as a "Parabolic Narrative"

Luke's application of the Good Samaritan to the way of Christian discipleship can be observed from his joining the parable to the "parabolic narrative" of Martha and Mary (10:38–42) and from the changes made in the introductory material (10:25–28).

Though Jesus' relationship to Martha and Mary is part of the tradition taken over by both John (11:1–40; cf. 12:2, "Martha served") and Luke, this narrative betrays distinct Lukan characteristics. Very important, it is an instance of Luke's practice of juxtaposing two narratives where a woman or a man is the principal protagonist

---

14. See the interpretation of Augustine (*Quaestiones Evangeliorum* 2.19) in Dodd, *Parables*, 1–2.

15. Tracy, "Theological Classics in Contemporary Theology," 349. Tracy (*Analogical Imagination*, 139 n. 34) relies heavily on Kermode, *The Classic*.

in each narrative: annunciation to Zechariah and to Mary (1:8–23, 26–38); hymn of praise of Mary (1:46–55) and of Zechariah (1:67–79); centurion of Capernaum and widow at Nain (7:1–17)—along with the twin parables of 13:18–21; 15:4–10; and 18:1–14.[16] Martha is introduced by the same formula *gynē tis* (a certain woman) as the wayfarer of 10:29 *anthrōpos tis* (a certain man). Luke uses this formula frequently in parables to underscore their paradigmatic or illustrative nature.[17] Clearly he wants us to read Martha and Mary as a parable and in relation to the Good Samaritan.

This narrative shares many characteristics with the Lukan parables. It is realistic and human, with dramatic interaction. It contains a surprising twist when, instead of praising the hospitality of Martha (cf. 7:44–46), Jesus praises the inactivity of Mary. It challenges us to identify with the different characters, often evoking the feeling that Martha is unfairly criticized. It ends with an enigmatic saying of Jesus (Luke 10:42) which has caused more than sufficient doubt to commentators over the centuries.

The narrative begins with Jesus and the disciples "on the way"—with overtones of "the way" of discipleship.[18] After they enter a village, Martha receives Jesus into her house, clearly exercising a leadership role. The next verse, however, turns immediately to Mary, whose description would surprise the audience. She "sat at the Lord's feet" and "listened to his word" (10:39, au. trans.). While for modern readers "sitting at the feet" may evoke only rapt attention to Jesus, it is also a technical term for discipleship (see Acts 22:3, where Paul sits at the feet of Gamaliel). "Listening to the word" is also an important Lukan motif. Luke acknowledges his debt to the "ministers of the word" (*hypēretai tou logou*) who have preserved early Christian traditions (Luke 1:2); his redaction of the allegory of the seeds stresses the need to hold the word fast in an honest and good heart (8:15; cf. Mark 4:20); in Acts, hearing the word is a prerequisite to conversion and faith (2:22; 4:4); and the Seven are chosen so that

16. See Flender (*St. Luke*, 9–10) for a complete list of such parallels. For the balancing of male and female language in the OT, see Isa. 45:10; 49:23; 51:2; Ps. 123:2, as noted in Trible, *God and the Rhetoric of Sexuality*, 59 n. 52.

17. Sellin, "Lukas als Gleichniserzähler."

18. Even though the noun *hodos* does not appear here, the verb *poreuesthai* (lit., "walk"; cf. RSV: "went on their way") is used with overtones of a way of life or "conducting oneself" (see *1 Enoch* 99:10, "to walk in the paths of justice"; cf. Luke 1:6; Acts 9:31; 14:16).

the Twelve can dedicate themselves to the ministry of the word and prayer (Acts 6:4). Mary is thus pictured as a disciple who during Jesus' ministry embodies that response which is to characterize the nascent church.

In contrast to Mary's silent sitting, Martha is "distracted with much serving" (*diakonian*). She then "goes" to Jesus (the Greek verb *ephistēmi* has overtones of "confront") and says, "Do you not care that my sister has left me to serve alone?" (v. 40). At this point, having just been given in the Samaritan an example of active concern for another, readers might expect Jesus to urge Mary to help her sister. The answer comes as a surprise. Jesus first describes Martha as "anxious and troubled [*merimnas kai thorubazē*] about many things." Anxiety is one of the things that inhibits the growth of the word (Luke 8:14); in other NT passages it almost always has a negative connotation, suggesting a lack of trust in God's power or presence (Matt. 6:25–34; Luke 12:11, 22, 25). Jesus then adds that "Mary has chosen the good portion, which shall not be taken away from her" (v. 42). Jesus thus seems to rebuke Martha's anxiety and defends Mary's inactivity.[19] Though in the history of interpretation this passage has often been used to exalt the contemplative life over the active, the Lukan context precludes such an interpretation.

The Good Samaritan and Martha and Mary
in the Context of Luke 10

To find Luke's understanding we must return to his redaction of the Great Commandment in 10:25–28. Whereas Mark (12:28–31, followed by Matt. 24:34–40) speaks of the first commandment, love of God, and the second commandment, love of neighbor, in the Lukan formulation (10:27) there is *a single commandment* with a double focus. The parable of the Good Samaritan with its exhortation to do mercy to the neighbor and the story of Martha and Mary with its praise of the one who sits and listens to the Lord form a twofold parabolic illustration of the single command. In both, an outsider (Samaritan or woman) is chosen to shock the hearers and allow them to see discipleship in a new light. To love God with whole heart and mind and the neighbor as one's self demands both compassionate and effective entry into the world of the neighbor as

19. For discussion of the complicated textual tradition and problems of interpretation of 10:41–42, see Fitzmyer, *Luke X—XXIV*, 893–94; and Marshall, *Luke*, 452–54.

well as undistracted attentiveness to the word of the Lord. Far from exalting one mode of discipleship above the other, the two narratives say that one cannot authentically exist without the other.

This juxtaposition fits in with another important theme which Luke shares with the OT and with other parts of the NT—the necessity of combining hearing of the word with doing. In Deut. 28:13–14 the Lord commands the people to obey and do his commands (cf. Deut. 4:5–6), and an oracle of the Lord in Ezek. 33:31–32 castigates those who "hear what you say . . . but will not do it." Paul, in countering an exclusive notion of the law, says that "it is not the hearers of the law who are righteous before God, but the doers of the law who will be justified" (Rom. 2:13), and James exhorts his community to be "doers of the word, and not hearers only, deceiving yourselves" (1:22). The Q parable of the person building on rock rather than sand is an illustration of hearing and doing the words of Jesus (Luke 6:47–49 = Matt 7:24–27). Clearly, then, there is a widely based tradition, going back to Jesus, which describes authentic religion as "hearing and doing."

Luke both appropriates and accentuates this tradition. In his interpretation of the Sower he stresses those who hear the word and bring forth fruit (8:15) and Luke's version of the saying on the true family of Jesus describes the mother and brothers of Jesus not as those who do the will of God (cf. Mark 3:35; Matt. 12:50), but as those "who *hear* the word of God and *do* it" (8:21). Again, in a saying only in Luke, Jesus praises not simply his natural mother but those who hear the word of God and keep it (11:28). Finally, the unfaithful servant in Luke is the one who knows the master's will but does not do it (12:47). The word "do" appears frequently in the Good Samaritan. The lawyer asks what he must "do" to inherit eternal life and is then commanded to "do" the command he articulates (10:28). The Good Samaritan is the one who "does" mercy to the injured man, while presumably the priest and the Levite who hear the law do not "do" it. Conversely, Mary is the one who "keeps listening" (10:39, the imperfect tense [*ēkouen*] here suggests continuous action), while the "doing" of Martha is rejected. Each parabolic narrative portrays the danger of separating "doing" and "hearing"; taken together, they offer an inseparable vignette of the way of discipleship.

Luke composes the material immediately preceding and following the Good Samaritan/Martha and Mary complex in such a way that a concentric structure emerges which highlights the important motifs.

A 10:21–22: After the return of the Seventy, who anticipate the active missionary work of the early church, Jesus rejoices in the Holy Spirit, and *prays* to his Father, the Lord of heaven.

   B 10:23–24: He is *alone with his disciples* and blesses them.

      C 10:25–29: The lawyer's questions evoke a twofold parabolic illustration of love

of neighbor and of God $\begin{cases} C^1 \text{ Good Samaritan (10:30–37)} \\ C^2 \text{ Martha and Mary (10:38–42)} \end{cases}$

   B′ 11:1: Jesus is *alone with his disciples.*

A′ 11:2–4: Jesus *prays* and teaches his disciples to pray.

Luke, more than any other evangelist, portrays Jesus at prayer (see below, pp. 191–93). But the solemn way in which Luke surrounds the Great Commandment by twice portraying Jesus praying and teaching others to pray suggests that here Luke portrays Jesus himself as one who "hears" and "does." Like Jesus, the disciple is to live in the presence of God and manifest this presence to others.

Luke thus constructs a solemn introduction to the whole travel narrative. The way to eternal life leads through imitation of Jesus, the one who lived in the presence of God and came to seek and to save the lost (Luke 19:10). Following Jesus on the way involves compassion for the suffering neighbor and attention to the word of God. In choosing "outsiders" to illustrate true discipleship, Luke suggests that those most busy with religion are often least able to embody its true value. Perhaps one of the reasons that generations of Christians have found the parable of the Good Samaritan so consoling to narrate and so impossible to imitate is that they are too busy being Samaritans to listen to the word with silent attentiveness; nor do they experience that freedom possessed by the outsider who has so little to lose that only eternal life can be found.

Excursus: Martha and Mary and
the Ministry of Women

   Recently Elisabeth Schüssler Fiorenza has argued that in the Martha and Mary pericope the role of Martha as *diakonos* is downplayed and the silent

Mary is exalted.[20] She denies that Martha is literally preparing a meal and argues that *diakonia* (10:40) is a veiled reference to the eucharistic leadership of women. From analogy with Acts 6:1–6 she also argues that the *diakonia* of Martha should comprise both eucharistic table service and missionary proclamation, which the Seven perform after their appointment in Acts. After locating Luke's version of Jesus' relationship with Martha and Mary in the same milieu as the Pastorals where the active role of women is being suppressed, she then concludes: "Luke 10:38–42 pits the apostolic women of the Jesus movement against each other and appeals to a revelatory word of the resurrected Lord in order to restrict women's ministry and authority."[21]

While her thoughtful study demands a fuller engagement than the present context and space allow, in addition to considerations offered above on the context and parabolic nature of the narrative, I note the following problems. First, her position makes it difficult to explain the literary setting of the pericope. Second, though *diakonos/ia* is used for different "ministries" in the early church, its original meaning of "(table) service" is prior and gives rise to the applied meaning. In the Gospels, the latter dominates (cf. Mark 1:31 = Luke 4:39; Mark 10:45; Luke 12:37; 17:8; 22:26–27). In John 12:2, a scene that may be based on the same tradition as Luke 10:38–42, Jesus is with Lazarus, Martha, and Mary. The text reads: "They made him a supper; Martha served [*diakonei*]." Third, since in Luke, Jesus is among the disciples as "one who serves" (*ho diakonōn*, 22:27) his response to Mary in 10:41–42 should not be made into a depreciation of this ministry. Fourth, there are problems with the suggested ecclesial setting. For Luke the most important ministry is that of the word, and in saying that Mary's portion "shall not be taken away from her," Luke may actually be defending the right of women to this ministry.

In an investigation of the evidence, independent of that of Schüssler Fiorenza, E. Jane Via, after extensive discussion of "the word" in Luke, concludes that Luke subordinates the meal aspect of the Eucharist to hearing the word. She then states: "In hearing the word lies the ultimately life-giving nourishment for which the human soul longs. And it is proper and acceptable for women to leave the preparation of the meal in order to hear the word. Women are fully enfranchised in both and participate fully as disciples."[22] I follow her exposition and still argue that Luke does not exalt one form of discipleship over the other here, nor does he put down the ministry of Martha. The shock of the rebuke to Martha is, rather, part of the literary strategy of the parable to bring the hearers to a new vision of reality. Luke is less interested in "ministry" understood as office or role than in discipleship expressed in attention to God's word and response to the suffering neighbor.

20. Schüssler Fiorenza, "A Feminist Critical Interpretation for Liberation: Martha and Mary: Luke 10:38–42."
21. Ibid., 32.
22. E. Jane Via, "Women, the Discipleship of Service," 58–59.

TABLE FELLOWSHIP WITH THE MARGINAL
AND LUKE'S GOSPEL IN PARABLE

The Parable of the Great Supper
(Luke 14:16–24)

More than any other Gospel, Luke stresses both Jesus' table fellowship with sinners and others on the margin of society (e.g., 5:29; 7:33–34, 36–50; 15:1) and meals as a setting for Jesus' teaching (5:31–39; 7:36–50; 10:38–42; 11:37–52; 14:1–24; 22:14–38; 24:20–49).[23] Within chapters 14—16 is a significant collection of parables given in the context of Jesus' table talk or evoked by his table fellowship. Though much of the material here is either Q or L (i.e., material taken from Luke's special source), the arrangement is clearly due to the evangelist. In 14:1 Jesus dines at the house of a ruler (cf. 7:36; 11:37) which provides the context for the sayings on "banquet etiquette" of 14:7–14 (cf. Prov. 23:1–12; Sir. 31:12—32:13) and the parable of the Great Supper in 14:16–24.[24] The five major parables of chapters 15—16 (15:3–7, 8–10, 11–32; 16:1–13, 19–31) are narrated without an explicit change of context from 15:2: "This man receives sinners and eats with them." While Luke here may be imitating the ancient literary convention of "symposium" or banquet conversation, the polyvalent symbol of "sitting at table" with its evocation of both the eucharistic meal and the eschatological banquet (cf. 13:29; 22:29–30) provides an added dimension for understanding these parables.

The Parable as Text

In discussing Matthew's version of the Marriage Feast, I suggested that Matthew, Luke, and the *Gospel of Thomas* offer variants of an original parable. The original text is virtually impossible to reconstruct, so that exact delineation of Luke's editorial work is not possible. Nonetheless, his hand is evident in a number of ways. Luke locates the parable following the instructions of Jesus on whom to invite to a banquet (14:12–14) with the promise that those who invite the marginal will be repaid at the resurrection of the just. More important,

---

23. See Navone (*Themes of St. Luke*, 11–37) on the "banquet theme" in Luke.
24. See Ringe (*Jesus, Liberation, and the Biblical Jubilee*, 54–60) on Lukan "banquet etiquette."

the parable is precipitated by a statement of one of the guests at the banquet (14:15; cf. 14:1): "Blessed is the one who shall eat bread in the kingdom of God!" (au. trans.). This shifts the focus away from the guests who refuse the invitation, as in Matthew and the *Gospel of Thomas*, to those who actually attend the banquet. In the parable itself, in contrast to Matthew, and perhaps the earlier Q version, Luke devotes a good deal of space to the excuses (vv. 18–20), describes in detail the substitute guests as "the poor and maimed and blind and lame" (v. 21), and, when there is still room, adds a third invitation to those from the highways and hedges (v. 23). Unlike Matt. 22:5–6, Luke contains no mention of the violent treatment of the messengers or of the punishment of the guests who refused. Three major emphases thus emerge from the text of Luke: *(a)* the excuses, *(b)* the substitute guests, and *(c)* the third invitation.

The Parable in the Context of
Luke's Theology

The Excuses

The first group that were invited offered three excuses:
I have bought a field and I must go out and see it (14:18).
I have bought five yoke of oxen and I go to examine them (14:19).
I have married a wife and therefore cannot come (14:20).

While some commentators attempt to see historical plausibility in these excuses and while the *Gospel of Thomas* interprets them as immersion in the corrupting influences of the world—"tradesmen and merchants shall not enter the places of my Father"—in Luke they may best be explained in reference to the OT.[25]

In Deuteronomy (20:5–7; cf. 24:5) buying a house, planting a vineyard, and betrothal excuse a person from answering the muster for the "holy war." These were invoked as late as 1 Macc. 3:56 when Judas Maccabeus exempts from the muster "those who were building houses, or were betrothed, or were planting vineyards." The *Mishnah* (*Sotah* 8:1–7) elaborates the excuses (8:2) but adds a

25. On the historical plausibility, see Bailey, *Through Peasant Eyes*, 94–95; and Jeremias, *Parables*, 172–80. On the influence of the OT, see Ballard, "Reasons for Refusing the Great Supper"; and Derrett, *Law*, 126–55.

distinction between "a battle waged of free choice" and a battle "in a religious cause" when all must go forth, "even the bridegroom out of his chamber and the bride out of her bridechamber" (8:7).[26] The *Mishnah* is similar to Luke in depicting an occasion when the excuses of Deuteronomy do not apply.

A complex of motifs in the OT and in later Jewish literature (e.g., the Pseudepigrapha) also serve as a backdrop to this pericope.[27] The eschatological age or the final intervention of God in history to save the people and restore health and wholeness is inaugurated by violence. The victory is often followed by a banquet at which God or the messiah is the host (Isa. 25:6–8; Rev. 3:20–21; 19:9). Luke is both influenced by this ideology and modifies it. Since the end time has been inaugurated in the ministry of Jesus, his teaching is to be received with the same urgency as the summons to the holy war; it is so radical that it brooks no excuse, not even the excuses allowed by divine law in a critical situation, such as the holy war, to protect home and family. Luke underscores this urgency following the Great Supper (14:25–35) at which Jesus warns would-be disciples to think carefully about the demands of discipleship with the ominous conclusion that "whoever of you does not renounce all that he has cannot be my disciple" (14:33). As an important modification of this motif, in line with his stress on peace and nonviolence (2:14; 10:5; 12:50–51 [cf. Matt. 10:39]; 19:38; 22:50–51), Luke omits those violent elements (cf. Matt. 22:7) normally associated with the eschatological banquet.[28]

The Substitute Guests

The second major Lukan thrust is the identification of the substitute guests as the poor, the crippled, the blind, and the lame. Jesus begins his public ministry by announcing the good news to the poor (cf. Isa. 61:1), and they are blessed in the Sermon on the Plain (6:20). In 7:18–23, Luke takes over from Q (cf. Matt. 11:2–6) the reply of Jesus to John that he will recognize the presence of "the coming one" when

26. Danby, *The Mishnah*, 302–3.
27. Isa. 25:6–8; 55:1–2; 65:13–14; *1 Enoch* 62:14; *2 Apoc. Bar.* 29:4; Revelation 20—21.
28. On Luke and violence, see Ford, *My Enemy Is My Guest*, 102–5 (on the great supper); Fitzmyer, *Luke I—IX*, 224–25 (on peace).

the blind receive their sight, the lame walk, lepers are cleansed, and the deaf hear, the dead are raised up, the poor have good news preached to them. (7:22)

These benefits all occur in the ministry of Jesus, and these groups are to be invited to the banquet in 14:13; they are the substitute guests in 14:21.

Luke locates the substitute guests and the parable as a whole in the context of sayings dealing with the eschatological banquet. Immediately preceding the banquet discourse, Luke explicitly mentions the eschatological banquet when people "will come from east and west, and from north and south, and *sit at table* in the kingdom of God" (13:29 = Matt. 8:11–12). After the Sabbath healing during a meal (14:1–6) and after the teaching on "banquet etiquette" (14:7–13), Jesus says that those who invite the poor, the maimed, the lame, and the blind will be repaid "at the resurrection of the just" (14:14). The parable itself is introduced only in Luke by the statement of a dinner guest: "Blessed is the one who shall eat bread in the kingdom of God" (14:15, au trans.). Luke returns to this theme in his version of the Last Supper where Jesus says to his disciples, "I assign to you, as my Father assigned to me, a kingdom, that you may eat and drink at my table in my kingdom and sit on the thrones judging the twelve tribes of Israel" (22:29–30). Though Luke takes this saying over from Q (cf. Matt. 19:28), only in the Lukan version is there reference to "eating and drinking at my table"—which brings it in close relation to 13:29.

The anticipated eschatological banquet has a counterpart in the actions of the earthly and risen Jesus. I noted earlier (see above, pp. 140–42) the importance both of Jesus' table fellowship with the marginal and of meals as a setting for Jesus' teaching. Along with this, only in Luke, among the Synoptics, does the risen Jesus eat with the disciples, and during these meals he both explains the meaning of his death and commissions them to be witnesses to all the nations (24:28–49). I would suggest, therefore, that Luke creates a three-level correspondence between the meals of the earthly Jesus, the presence of the risen Jesus in the Lord's Supper, and the eschatological banquet. Jesus inaugurated the new age by his proclamation of the good news to the poor (Luke 4:18) and celebrated its advent by banquets with the outcast. The conduct of Jesus at meals and his "table talk" are to be normative when early Christians celebrate the Lord's Supper. In recollection of Jesus and in anticipation of sitting at table in the kingdom of God, they are to invite and welcome the marginal to their midst.[29]

The substitute guests have an added importance. Both early Christianity (Luke 22:28–30; cf. 1 Cor. 11:26) and the Qumran community saw their meals as an anticipation of the eschatological banquet. Qumran stressed that the community was to be free of any ritual or moral impurity as it prepared for the final holy war between good and evil which was to usher in this banquet. Among those not eligible for full participation in the life of the community, and therefore the meals, were the "lame, the blind, the crippled" or the afflicted (1QM 7:4–6), or "the paralyzed, the lame, the blind, or deaf" (1QSa 2:6–10). Such physical defects caused ritual uncleanness. The Cornelius story in Acts 10 and the charge against Peter in Acts 11:3 show that eating with persons considered ritually unclean was a concern to the early church (cf. Gal. 2:12).

Recent NT studies, following upon the anthropological research of Mary Douglas, have shed light on the symbolic importance of ritual impurity.[30] A community concerned with bodily integrity and ritual taboos is also concerned to keep its membership—the social body— free of impurity and outside influence. It erects social barriers that correspond to the ritual barriers.

In the banquet discourse of Luke 14 Jesus shatters such boundaries. It begins with Jesus not only healing a man with dropsy but doing so on the Sabbath (14:1). Jesus then criticizes taking positions of honor, which cement social barriers, and urges that the hosts invite the unclean (14:7–14). The parable of the Great Supper is an image of the kind of banquet the community is to hold when it celebrates its eschatological meal. In line with the eschatological shift throughout the Gospel and the Lukan stress on the demands of "daily" Christian living, Luke in effect de-apocalypticizes the eschatological banquet.[31]

29. This is an aspect of the more pervasive NT motif of welcome and hospitality to be shown to strangers. See esp. Koenig, *New Testament Hospitality*, 85–123 (on Luke).

30. Douglas, *Purity and Danger*; idem, *Natural Symbols*. For NT appropriation, see Malina, *Christian Origins and Cultural Anthropology*; and Neyrey, "The Idea of Purity in Mark's Gospel."

31. The classic exposition of Luke's move away from strong concern for the imminence of the parousia to the demands of Christian life is Conzelmann's *St. Luke*. For a clear exposition and critique, see Fitzmyer, *Luke I—IX*, 231–35.

It has begun in the ministry of Jesus, and its ethos is to be lived out in the meals of the community. The table fellowship of Luke's church as it makes its way "to the end of the earth" (Luke 24:47; Acts 1:8) is to include those normally excluded by both social status and ritual law.

The Third Invitation

Unique to Luke's version of the parable is a third invitation after the substitute guests have arrived. Though Luke, like Matthew, allegorizes the parable in the direction of salvation history—the invitation rejected by the Jews has now been given to the community—he has his own particular schema. The first invitation refers to the offer of grace made by Jesus to all his contemporaries, and especially to the Pharisees (14:1). The substitute guests who gathered from the streets and lanes of the city stand for those groups of the "lost" to whom Jesus reached out in a special way in his ministry. The Lukan community which contains a number of people of higher social and economic strata is reminded of its origin (cf. 1 Cor. 1:26–29).[32] It stems from Jesus' call to sinners, and its forebears are the lowly of the earth.

Those gathered from along the highways and hedges, presumably outside the city, are those who respond to the Christian mission. Luke's two-volume work has a definite missionary thrust, with the urgency to spread the good news from Jerusalem to the end of the earth (Acts 1:8). The mandate to the servants to "compel people to come in"—which sadly in the history of the church has been used to justify both forced conversion and forced adherence to church doctrine—underscores this eschatological urgency.[33] Since the advent of Jesus, the kingdom of God is preached and everyone enters it violently (16:16). The language of "compelling" people to violent entry is metaphoric for the urgency and wrenching quality of the demands of the gospel, a motif that Luke develops in the following verses (14:25–34).[34]

In sum, Luke takes over an original parable about the refusal of

32. For a discussion of the economic and social level of Luke's community, see Karris, "Poor and Rich," 112–24, esp. 124.
33. Norwood, "'Compel Them to Come In.'"
34. Fitzmyer (*Luke X—XXIV*, 1057) interprets "compel" (*anankason*) as "urge by convincing speech" (cf. Mark 6:45; Matt. 14:22).

an invitation and the substitution of uninvited guests. Perhaps as early as the Q version used by Matthew and Luke, it became an allegory of salvation history—the uninvited Gentiles substitute for those contemporaries of Jesus who refused his invitation. Luke extends this dimension by adding a second command to go out to the highways and hedges to bring people to the banquet (14:23). The description of the substitute guests as the poor, the maimed, the blind, and the lame gives the parable its distinctive character. Far from allowing the community to be complacent in its election after the refusal of the invited guests, Luke makes the parable into an exhortation for the community to become inclusive. Just as in the parable of the Good Samaritan the outsider is the one who fulfills the law, so the outsider must be present when the community gathers to celebrate its supper. Between recollection and anticipation the Lukan community is to show by its table fellowship with the marginal and uninvited that they hear and follow the words of Jesus.

Contemporary proclamation should be attuned to this dimension of the parable. This parable summons all Christians to remember their roots. They are the heirs of the poor, the lame, the maimed, and the blind, physically powerless and socially shunned (cf. 1 Cor. 1:26–31). Contemporary Christian bodies have also erected barriers between "clean and unclean," perhaps different from those of the first century but no less exclusive. There is often little urgency to enlarge the community by the addition of unacceptable outsiders. Within Christian communities, some of the most violent disputes continue to rage over inclusiveness, often centered on the celebration of the Lord's Supper. Yet when Luke's Jesus told a parable about eating bread in the kingdom of God, he shattered his hearers' expectations of who would be the proper table companions. Can his parabolic word continue to challenge our expectations?

A "GOSPEL WITHIN A GOSPEL":
THE PARABLES OF LUKE 15

Chapter 15 of Luke combines three parables, two from his special source, L (15:8–10, 11–32), and a third from Q (15:4–7), found also in Matthew in a different context and with a different thrust. The chapter presents those parables which Joachim Jeremias states "contain the Good News itself" and has been called the heart of the third Gospel.[35] It offers also a collage of Lukan themes: the coming of the Son of man to seek and save the lost (cf. Luke 19:10); Jesus' defense of the weak or marginal; and the offer of God's mercy in Jesus along with the joy which the coming of Christ brings.[36]

The Lost Sheep and the Lost Coin
(Luke 15:1–10)

Luke creates a panoramic setting for the three parables. "All" the tax collectors and sinners are drawing near, with the Pharisees and the scribes arrayed against them (15:1). The grumbling of the Pharisees recalls a similar scene in 5:30 where they grumble, "Why do you eat and drink with tax collectors and sinners?" But in 15:2 both the intensive form of the verb and the use of it in the imperfect tense ("kept grumbling aloud": *diegongyzon* rather than simple *egongyzon*; cf. 19:7) heighten the opposition to Jesus' action, and the charge against him is not simply eating with outcasts (cf. Gal. 2:12–13) but "hosting" or "receiving them" with overtones of religious acceptance (cf. Rom. 16:2; Phil. 2:29).[37]

These parables have a similar structure and development.[38] Something of value is lost—the word "lost" appears five times in the seven verses. The one who loses it expends unusual effort in finding it, and the finding is an occasion of joy, expressed in a celebration with neighbors and friends. The parables also provide an instance of the juxtaposition of stories with male and female protagonists (cf. 13:18–21; 18:1–14).

The Lost Sheep appears in Matthew 18, in the *Gospel of Thomas* 107, and in another gnostic work, the *Gospel of Truth*. Though commentators generally admit that Luke is the version closest to the Q original, every version reflects its literary context. In Matthew, it is an exhortation to seek out the "little ones" in the community. In the *Gospel of Thomas*, though it is a kingdom parable, it is also rationalized. The lost sheep is the "biggest one," and when the shepherd finds it he says, "I love you more than the ninety-nine,"

---

35. Jeremias, *Parables*, 124; and Ramaroson, "Le coeur du troisième évangile: Lc 15."
36. On joy in Luke, see Navone, *Themes of St. Luke*, 70–87.
37. On the verb "receive" (*prosdechomai* and its cognates), see Marshall, *Luke*, 599.
38. Bailey, *Poet*, 144–46, 156.

perhaps a veiled allusion to claims to election of the community behind the *Gospel of Thomas*. In the *Gospel of Truth*, the shepherd is explicitly identified with "the beloved son" (cf. John 10:1–18).[39] Luke's context of a defense of Jesus' acceptance of the outcast most likely reflects the original setting of the parable.

Luke's version is the most dramatic and the most picturesque. Particular to Luke is that the shepherd has "lost" the sheep and that the sheep is "in the wilderness," normally a place of threat and danger. While Luke and the *Gospel of Thomas* note that the shepherd seeks the sheep "until he finds it" (contrast Matt. 18:13, "if he finds it"), only Luke mentions that when it is found, the shepherd "lays it on his shoulders."[40] Luke underscores the personal engagement of the shepherd and heightens the contrast between losing and the joy of finding by a repetition of terms for losing (vv. 4, 6) and rejoicing (vv. 5, 6), and only Luke has the summons of friends to a celebration with the explicit call "I have found my sheep which was lost" (cf. 15:9, "I have found the coin which was lost," au. trans.).

The introductory verse of the Lost Sheep carries a special force. From the introduction we know that the parable is addressed to Pharisees and scribes. In the parable the word "shepherd" is not used but implied. The introductory question, "What man of you, having a hundred sheep . . . ?" (v. 4), would shock those to whom the parable is directed and amuse the audience. Tending sheep was one of the occupations avoided by observant Jews, as was tax collecting; it was also of a considerably lower social class than a scribe.[41] By saying "Which of you?" the parable "orients by disorienting" (Paul Ricoeur, see above, pp. 15–16). Subtly it jolts the Pharisees and the scribes out of their accustomed roles and piety and opens them to the parable. The image of the shepherd would also evoke Ezekiel 34, where religious leaders are criticized because God's sheep "were scattered" and "wandered over all the mountains" and

39. Fitzmyer, *Luke X—XXIV*, 1074, discussing the *Gospel of Truth* 31:35—32:9.
40. Marshall (*Luke*, 601) says this detail illustrates the care and joy of the shepherd. Fitzmyer (*Luke X—XXIV*, 1077) calls attention to the *kriophoros*, a figure of a god or demigod with a sheep on his shoulders, known throughout the Mediterranean world. Perhaps Luke added this detail with Hellenistic readers in mind. See also Derrett, "Fresh Light on the Lost Sheep and the Lost Coin," in *Studies in the New Testament*, 3:59–84, esp. 72–75.
41. Jeremias, *Parables*, 132; for more detail, see Donahue, "Tax Collectors and Sinners."

"my shepherds have not searched for my sheep" (34:6–8). Since in
Ezekiel and in other places in the OT, God seeks and cares for the
straying sheep, readers are to see in the parable an allusion to God's
action made present in the ministry of Jesus to the marginal.

The Lost Coin (15:8–10) is similar in structure and meaning to
the Lost Sheep (15:4–7). The introductory verse, "Or what woman
[*tis gynē*] . . . ?" also orients by disorienting. As with the shepherd,
Jesus chooses a protagonist from a group that suffered religious and
social discrimination in first-century society. Though there are important places in the OT where God's action is described in feminine
imagery, they are far from dominant.[42] To compare God to a woman
would shock and surprise the audience and challenge their fundamental image of God. The hearers are now challenged to see the
searching woman as a metaphor for God's searching love, which
paves the way for a new way of thinking about how God acts toward
the sinner and the outcast. God seeks them out and rejoices more
over finding them than over the presence of the righteous. The
inclusion of the woman as the protagonist here also reflects Luke's
interest in the gifts and roles of women in the community.[43]

Though the Lost Coin is similar to the Lost Sheep, it has some
significant differences. The loss of one drachma out of ten would be
considerably more serious than one sheep out of a hundred, so there
is an intensification within the two parables. The search of the woman
described in three actions—"light a lamp," "sweep the house," and
"seek diligently" (v. 8)—enhances the urgency of the search. The
finding and the invitation to the friends are described in virtually the
same language as in the Lost Sheep (vv. 9–10; cf. vv. 5–7). In both
parables these verses constitute almost half the text.

These short parables offer different shades of meaning. First,
concern for the lost emerges from the context. Just as the shepherd
and the woman expend much effort for the lost, so Jesus turns to
tax collectors and sinners. Though Luke omits the Markan saying of
10:45 that "the Son of man came not to be served but to serve, and
to give his life as a ransom for many," the coming of the Son of man

---

42. See Bird, "Images of Women in the Old Testament," 41–88; Trible, *God and
the Rhetoric of Sexuality*, esp. 1–59. Some of the important passages are Deut. 32:18;
Isa. 42:14; 49:13–15; 66:7–9, 13; Jer. 31:20; Hos. 11:1–4.

43. D'Angelo, "Images of Jesus and the Christian Call in the Gospels of Luke and
John."

for the sake of others emerges in the conclusion of the Zacchaeus story: "For the Son of man came to seek and to save the lost" (19:10). This saying constitutes an aphoristic commentary on these parables as well as on the entire Gospel.

Surprise, extravagance, and joy characterize these parables. As noted, the choice of the main characters causes shock and surprise. Their actions are also out of the ordinary. It is surprising that the shepherd would "leave" the ninety-nine on the hills and perhaps equally surprising that both the shepherd and the woman would entertain "friends and neighbors." The cost of the celebration may have been more than the value of the lost sheep or the lost coin. As metaphors of divine action, these parables upset the way we normally think of God and shatter the barriers to God's mercy and love erected often by religious observance itself.

Words for joy resound throughout these parables. The shepherd lays the sheep on his shoulders, "rejoicing," and summons others to rejoice with him, as does the woman. The applications of each parable (vv. 7, 10; cf. 15:32), which are highlighted by Luke's redaction, speak of a joy in heaven corresponding to the earthly joy. Joy is one of the salient characteristics of Luke.[44] The birth of John will bring "joy and gladness" to Elizabeth and Zechariah and the multitude will "rejoice" (1:14); Mary "rejoices" in "God my Savior" (1:47); Jesus' birth is proclaimed as "good news of a great joy" (2:10). Only in Luke, Jesus tells his disciples to "rejoice" because their names are written in heaven and he himself "rejoiced in the spirit" (10:20–21). Only Luke records the healing of the crippled woman on the Sabbath when the crowd "rejoiced at all the glorious things that were done by him" (13:17). After Jesus' ascension the disciples returned to Jerusalem "with great joy" (24:52). Luke describes meals of the early community as celebrated with joy (Acts 2:46). This stress on joy is undoubtedly connected with Luke's constant emphasis on the *bona messianica*—the benefits of the messianic age have begun in Jesus. (Compare Paul's superscription to his letters where he wishes the communities "grace and peace.") In the parables of Luke 15, joy has an added dimension. While "joy before the Lord" or "rejoicing in the Lord" is a frequent biblical motif, the strong statements that

44. See above, n. 36.

there will be "more joy in heaven" or "joy before the angels of God" have virtually no parallels.[45] In somewhat shocking anthropomorphic language Luke describes God as rejoicing over finding what has been lost.

These parables do not simply provide a defense of Jesus' fellowship with outcasts; they speak more of the joy of finding and of being found. Applications of these parables which stress the need for repentance are really in tension with the parabolic narrative. Neither the sheep nor the coin "repents." The one who is seeking provides all the dramatic action in the parable. The readers are summoned to rejoice with the one who finds and are invited to a joyous feast. Luke does not present simple paradigms of repentance but parables which open the possibility of conversion. Readers must hear the teaching of Jesus as the good news, not simply good advice, that he came "to seek and to save" the lost. The initiative has been taken by God through Jesus. "Conversion" or change of heart (*metanoia*) is not a condition but a consequence of God's love. As T. W. Manson noted, "The characteristic feature of these two parables is not so much the joy over the repentant sinner as the Divine Love that goes out to seek the sinner before he repents."[46] Here is an important instance where by metaphor and image the parables convey the presuppositions to ethics (the joyful experience of being found) rather than ethical precepts (the need to repent).

The Parable of the Prodigal Son
(Luke 15:11–32)

The Parable as Text

No section of the NT has received as much attention and extravagant praise as this parable. It has been called, perhaps somewhat over-enthusiastically, "the greatest short story ever told" (F. Sommer) and "the greatest of all Jesus' parables" (J. E. Compton).[47] Its drama has enchanted believer and nonbeliever. It has been a subject for

---

45. Some examples of joy before or in the Lord are Pss. 5:11; 16:11; 20:5; 21:1; 33:1; 43:4; 51:8; cf. Ps. 96:11, "Let the heavens be glad"; 104:31, "May the Lord rejoice in his works."
46. Manson, *Sayings*, 284 (cited in Bailey, *Poet*, 154).
47. Sommer, *The World's Greatest Short Story*; and Compton, "The Prodigal's Brother."

great painters (Dürer, Rembrandt), dramatists (Tudor dramatists, Gascoigne), choreographers (Balanchine), musicians (Prokofiev, Britten), novelists (Gide), and philosophers (Nietzsche).[48] A variety of approaches—existentialist, Jungian, Freudian, structuralist—have vied to enrich its meaning.[49] Like the Good Samaritan, it too is a classic.[50]

Though the traditional title "The Prodigal Son" dates back to the patristic period, more recent discussions question its aptness. German Bibles and scholars generally name it *Der verlorene Sohn* ("the Lost Son"). Jeremias has called it the parable of the father's love. Eduard Schweizer named it the parable of "the powerless almighty Father."[51] Crucial questions remain: Whose story is it? What is the central thrust of the parable? What character shapes the narrative? Attention to the dramatic structure and interaction of the characters provides some clues.

The parable falls neatly into three acts or sections: (1) the departure and fall of the younger son (15:11–19); (2) his return and welcome by the father (15:20–24); and (3) the father and the older brother (15:25–32). Each act begins with the naming of an important person in the drama: "A man had two sons" (15:11); "And he [the younger son] arose" (15:20); "Now the elder son was in the field" (15:25).

The initial task is to identify the main character. Though the two sons evoke the most emotional response—sympathy for the first and anger at the second—and though the first has given the parable its title and provided fodder in many sermons for vivid depiction of the ravages of sin, it is chiefly the father who gives shape to the drama. Though his personality is not developed, according to the literary conventions of the time, at each point from the granting of the initial son's request to the "going out" to the elder brother, the father's actions allow the narrative to unfold and provide its crucial turning points. His discourse (vv. 22, 27, 31) provides the interpretive keys to the parable. One is tempted to say that the parable is "the father's story." Who the father is, however, and how he acts are also dependent on how the sons act, and the drama arises from observing

48. References are taken from Fitzmyer, *Luke X—XXIV*, 1083.
49. For a literary and existentialist reading, see Jones, *Art and Truth*, 167–205; D. O. Via, *Parables*, 162–76; and articles by Via (Jungian), Tolbert (psychoanalytic), and Scott (structuralist) in *Semeia* 9 (1977).
50. See above, n. 15.
51. Jeremias, *Parables*, 128; and Schweizer, *Luke*, 246.

not only what the father does but what the sons will do. The text engages us primarily at the point of dialogue between the father and the sons, so that the dynamics of human relationships provide the field of comparison for the parable.

Act One: The Fall of the Younger Son (15:11–19)

The first act depicts the tragic fall of the younger son. It begins with what might have been an ordinary request at that time. Since roughly four million Jewish people in the first century lived in the Hellenistic diaspora from Persia to Rome while approximately one-half million lived in Palestine, and since the agrarian economy of Palestine was precarious, younger sons often emigrated.[52] The request of the younger son should not be considered as rebellion or a desire for unwarranted freedom. But his fate is quickly drawn. No sooner had he departed and completed his journey to "a far country" than he squandered his property in loose living. The bulk of the first act is a rapid and escalating depiction of his decline: he spends everything; a famine arises; he works for a Gentile; he feeds unclean animals and would even have eaten their food; "no one gave him anything"—perhaps he tried begging, but unsuccessfully; he is dying of hunger. For both Jesus' and Luke's audience his decline and fall evoke evils worse than physical death. The Jewish diaspora included well-organized systems of almsgiving for Jewish travelers and émigrés in need.[53] The son, however, does not turn to his own but "joined himself" to a Gentile, and his degradation is highlighted by his work as a swineherd, an occupation no Jew would assume. He has lost his familial, ethnic, and religious identity.

The son's change of heart or "coming to himself" begins in a somewhat self-serving manner with a fear of death and hope for a better situation, but finds expression in the confession "Father, I have sinned against heaven and before you."[54] The use of the soliloquy and the switch from narrated action to narrated discourse

---

52. Jeremias, *Parables*, 129.
53. See *Mishnah, Peah* 8:7, Danby, *The Mishnah*, 20; Schürer, *History of the Jewish People*, 2:437; also Posner, "Charity," *EncJud* 4:338–44.
54. Jeremias (*Parables*, 130) argues that behind *eis heauton de elthōn* ("he came to himself") is an Aramaic expression for "repentance." Bailey (*Poet.* 173–75) argues that "repentance" is too strong a description of the son's motivation.

underscore the importance of vv. 17–19 for interpreting the parable. We must not be too quick to join the older brother in identifying this sin as sexual dalliance. In both the narrative of 15:13 and in the older brother's outburst of 15:30 the sin of the younger son is that he "dissipated" or "devoured" the living of the father. The sin of the younger son is one key to the meaning of the parable.

According to the law of the time, a father could dispose of his property during his lifetime, so that the younger son's request is legitimate, even if inappropriate.[55] But possession of his share did not give him rights to total disposal. He was allowed to invest the property and to use it to earn more income—an economic situation reflected in the parable of "the Pounds" (Luke 19:11–27 = Matt. 25:14–30). He was forbidden, however, to jeopardize the capital. In a society with no benefits for the aged, the future of a parent was assured only by retention of property within the family circle (cf. Jesus' criticism of corban [Mark 7:9–13], a gift of money to the temple rather than reserved for care of the parents). By dissipating the property, the younger son severs the bonds with his father, with his people, and hence with God; he is no longer a son of his father and no longer a son of Abraham.

The parable prevents us from trivializing the sin of the younger son. He acts as if his father were dead, and he too in a real sense is dead—"I am perishing" (v. 17, au. trans.). The father will later say, "For this my son was dead, and is alive again" (vv. 24, 32). Both his actions, working in an unclean occupation for a Gentile, and his confession, "I am no longer worthy to be called your son," show that the son is aware of the depth of his sin. Awareness of sin and accepting personal responsibility for it are the beginning of his return.

Act Two: The Return of the
Younger Son (15:20–24)

While the confession of the son serves as the literary link between the two acts of the parable (15:18, 20), the action of the father dominates the second act. The reader is immediately shocked by the

---

55. The legal situation is complex and disputed. I follow the position of Jeremias (*Parables*, 129), Derrett (*Law*, 104–12), and Fitzmyer (*Luke X—XXIV*, 1087). Bailey (*Poet*, 158–68) argues that such a request made by a son during a lifetime is not legitimate and that the son is in a hurry for his father to die.

action of the father—not simply by his welcome of the son or his forgiveness but by his action—running. In oriental culture the idea of the *paterfamilias* (i.e., male head of the house) running for any reason would occasion ludicrous shock.[56] The narrative image prepares the readers for the subsequent religious shock. The father's actions are described with a rapidity similar to the rapid downfall of the son in act one. He sees, has compassion, runs, embraces, and kisses. Like the Samaritan, he crosses the bridge to the world of the son *from* "seeing" through compassion *to* personal contact. He then issues a flurry of orders culminating in the double exclamation that the son who was dead is alive and the one who was lost is found. As in the Lost Sheep and the Lost Coin, act two of this parable ends with a celebration.

The speech of the son in vv. 18, 21 discloses one of the major motifs of the parable. Its repetition at the outset and conclusion of the son's return permits the reader to imagine him rehearsing it as he makes his way back. The wording is virtually the same: in v. 18, the son says, *(a)* "Father, I have sinned against heaven and before you"; *(b)* "I am no longer worthy to be called your son"; *(c)* "Treat me as one of your hired servants." Upon his return (v. 21), however, though he repeats the first two clauses, *he is not allowed to finish his prepared speech; in the embrace of his father (v. 20) he never says,* "Treat me as one of your hired servants."[57] The narrative shifts immediately to a counterspeech of the father, and it does not allow the son to call himself hired servant in the father's presence. The father orders that the best robe, the ring, and the sandals be brought quickly. These are not simply festive adornments but evoke deeper meanings. The robe is a symbol of authority and the ring is a signet ring (Isa. 22:21; Gen. 41:41–42), so that the son can now act with the father's authority; sandals are worn only by free people; hired servants and slaves went barefoot.[58] The son wants to return with the understanding that he live as a slave or hired servant. The father's action shatters this understanding. The request of the son is not really granted; it is

---

56. Jeremias, *Parables*, 130; and Bailey, *Poet*, 181.

57. Some excellent manuscripts such as Vaticanus and Sinaiticus (fourth century) add in v. 21, "treat me as one of your hired servants." But an early manuscript of Luke, Papyrus Bodmer (P[75], third century) omits it and its addition seems due to harmonization.

58. Jeremias, *Parables*, 130; and Derrett, *Law*, 113–15.

transcended. He is not only restored as son but symbolically raised to a position greater than when he left with his share of the property.

Act Three: The Older Brother and the Father (15:25-32)

The traditional title renders this act of the parable almost superfluous. Jeremias ranks it among the few parables with a double application and argues that the grumbling Pharisees and scribes (15:1) are to see themselves reflected in the older brother.[59] Other commentators claim that it is an addition to the original parable.[60] Both the first verse, "There was a man who had two sons," and stylistic uniformity between the parts militate against this view, however, as does the whole literary and theological thrust of the parable.

The third act begins with another return, that of the older son from the fields, presumably in the evening (cf. Matt. 20:8), only to hear the unexpected celebration in full swing. His authority and status within the household are indicated by the orders he gives to the servants. Upon learning that the celebration was called by his father for the return of his brother, he is angry and refuses to go in. The action of the father also provides the shock of act three. He comes out and entreats the son. The cultural gap between the first century and ours softens this shock. According to ancient Jewish law, parents had the right to put rebellious sons to death (Deut. 21:18-21), and maxims about the sorrow caused by foolish sons and the need to discipline rebellious children are frequent in the wisdom literature.[61] The image of the father, leaving a celebration at which he is host to cajole an angry son, upsets the cultural expectations of the audience no less than his earlier running.

As with the younger son, the dialogue points to the interpretation. The older brother does not address his father with respect but immediately blurts out his complaint. Just as the confession of his brother is threefold, so is his complaint: (a) many years I have served you and never disobeyed your command, (b) you never gave me a

---

59. Jeremias, Parables, 131.
60. This position, which goes back to Wellhausen, is strongly argued by J. T. Sanders, "Tradition and Redaction in Luke xv. 11-32."
61. E.g., Prov. 10:1; 17:21, 25; 19:18, 26; 20:20; 22:15; 23:22-25; 28:24.

kid that I might make merry with my friends, and *(c)* when this "son of yours" came who had devoured your living "with harlots," you killed the fatted (i.e., the most valuable) calf. Rather ironically, the older son now sounds and acts very much like his brother. His understanding is also that of a slave; literally, "he has slaved" for his father many years and apparently never even asked for a kid to celebrate. *Just as the younger son felt that the way to restore the severed relationship was to become a servant, the older brother maintained it by acting as a servant. Between the dutiful son and the prodigal is a bond much deeper than is visible on the surface.*[62]

The older brother in his way also kills. He never refers to "my brother" but to "this son of yours." His self-righteousness destroys the family bonds as effectively as the squandering of the inheritance by his brother. Just as in act two the father's action cuts off the servile self-identification of the younger son and emphasizes his dignity within the family, here too the father responds with the simple word "son," states that "all that is mine is yours," and speaks of "your brother." He treats him as equal in authority and dignity and counters angry and divisive language with images of reconciliation and unity. The father summons the elder son also to a feast of life.

As text, then, the parable is not simply the parable of the prodigal son, or of the churlish older brother, nor even of the "prodigal father" who is lavish and wasteful in the love expended to both sons.[63] The father's surprising action toward both sons is the literary center where the meaning must be sought. The father shatters the self-identity of both sons. Both define sonship in terms of servile obligations; each in his own way destroys the family. The parable does not allow this to happen but redefines the conditions under which "family" can happen. A relationship with the father worked out in terms of servility leads to destruction. The relationship as redefined by the father leads to life and joy.

---

62. Two different terms appear for "servant" in the Greek text. The younger son's request is to be treated as a *misthios* (i.e., a hired day laborer). The older brother acted as a *doulos* (i.e., servant or slave). According to Bailey (*Poet,* 176), the *doulos* was often considered a member of the family and of higher status than the *misthios.* See also Oesterley, *The Gospel Parables,* 185–87.

63. This title was first suggested to me by Dr. David McCarthy. It was used also in a sermon by McLeod, "The Parable of the Prodigal Father."

The Parable in the Ministry of Jesus

Jeremias has argued strongly that the Lukan context is the original context of the parable—a vindication through parable of Jesus' fellowship with outcasts, and a challenge to the Jewish leaders not to be like the elder brother. But even Jesus' fellowship with tax collectors and sinners is itself parabolic of his proclamation that the reign of God is near. The reign of God which is enacted in the ministry of Jesus is the offer of God's mercy and love which shatters the categories of servility by which people seek God's favor. It also destroys those destructive categories which people erect between each other and between themselves and God. Both sons are jolted out of their self-understanding and invited to a celebration of life out of death. The understanding of God as "king" and "father," with its accompanying images of power and dominance, is challenged and transformed when one enters the world of this parable. The parable speaks of that change of heart (*metanoia*) which is necessary to respond to the presence of God. More important, it creates an imaginative world which makes *metanoia* possible. It summons to a deep faith that one is loved as son or daughter and created as such, not according to conditions of acceptance which are dictated in advance, but because of the shocking, surprising, and outgoing love of God.

The Lukan Context and Beyond

The parables of Luke 15 have a number of resonances with the larger context. They continue the motif of chapter 14, the "good news for the outcast" and the summons to celebrate meals that shatter conventional norms. As I will indicate later, they also provide a link with the parables of chapter 16 where the use of material goods becomes metaphoric of deeper realities. The immediate context is a triad of parables that conclude with a celebration of the "joy of finding." The celebration in chapter 15, however, is cosmic in scope, comparing an earthly feast with heavenly joy. In pastoral terms today, the churches must find ways to celebrate "returns" and "findings."

In each parable the stress is on the one who finds rather than on what is lost. Obviously, neither the sheep nor the coin is active in

the finding; but even the return of the son is not stressed so much
as that "he was lost, and is found" (15:24, 32). In more explicit
theological terms, Luke stresses the gratuity and unmerited quality
of God's favor. He presents in narrative form the Pauline theology
of the justification of sinners by the unmerited gift of God. Such is
the celebration which the good news brings to all humanity. Luke
stresses this not only in the three parables of chapter 15, but he
prepares for the following parable of the Unjust Steward, who, like
the younger son, lives on the fringes of conventional morality but in
the end is granted acceptance.

On a level that may not be even conscious to Jesus or Luke but
that is part of their religious heritage, the parable is another instance
of the biblical motif of the choice of the "younger child." Throughout
the OT a series of younger sons—Jacob (Gen. 27:1–45), Joseph
(Genesis 37—48), Gideon (Judg. 6:1–23), David (1 Sam. 16:6–13),
and Judas Maccabeus (1 Macc. 3:1–9)—are chosen by God for
important roles in sacred history. J. Duncan Derrett notes that such
people achieve fame only because they are chosen.[64] Like the women
of the OT who are chosen by God at important moments in salvation
history (e.g., Deborah and Judith), they live apart from the expected
lines of power and authority, and in choosing them God reverses
normal human expectations. Such people are symbols of those who
receive the unexpected and unmerited favor of God. Luke's awareness
of this tradition appears in the infancy narratives where God takes
the side of the 'anāwîm, the lowly of the earth—a priest of one of
the minor grades, a childless couple, or shepherds.

This motif has contacts with Pauline theology. In speaking of his
Jewish heritage in Romans 9—11, Paul notes that Jews and Christians
are descendants of the "younger son" (Jacob) who are chosen not
because of their works but because of God's call (Rom. 9:6–13).
Christians, like Jews, are heirs of the "younger brother."

The more striking parallel is the contrast between servility and
being a child of God which characterizes Luke's parable and Paul's
theology. In conclusion to one of his arguments with the Galatians
about the primacy of faith, Paul cites what most scholars think is an
early Christian baptismal formula:

64. Derrett, *Law*, 116–19.

> For in Christ Jesus you are all sons and daughters of God, through faith. For as many of you as were baptized into Christ have put on Christ. There is neither Jew nor Greek, there is neither slave nor free, there is neither male nor female; for you are all one in Christ Jesus. And if you are Christ's, then you are Abraham's offspring, heirs according to the promise. (Gal. 3:26–29, au. trans.)

Through baptism Christians "put on" Christ, like a robe, and receive a new status (cf. Luke 15:22) and new identity, that of the free person united with other Christians whatever their sex, race, or social status. Such people are "heirs according to the promise." They have Jesus as brother and with him can call God "Abba" (Gal. 4:6). Both the older and the younger children can now live in unity and freedom.

In the following verses Paul amplifies this formula by the use of the language of adoption to describe the effects of the Christ event—the salvation and liberation achieved through the life, death, and resurrection of Jesus. Paul writes:

> But when the fullness of time had come, God sent forth his Son, born of woman, born under the law, to ransom those who were under the law, so that we might receive adoption as sons and daughters. And because you are sons and daughters, God has sent the Spirit of his Son into our hearts, crying, "Abba! Father!" So through God you are no longer a slave but a son or daughter, and if so then an heir. (Gal. 4:4–7, au. trans.)

The parallels between Paul's theology and Luke 15:11–32 are striking. In Gal. 4:7, Paul says that it is "through God" that the Christian is freed from servility to become a child of God. Exactly this occurs in the parable. The father's love shatters the conditions of servility by which both sons wish to rule their lives. While Gal. 4:7 describes the conclusion of God's saving action, vv. 4–6 describe its stages. The initiative is from God, whose action liberates and creates a new relationship—adoption. This new relationship empowers the Christian to address God with the familiar "Abba" which characterized Jesus' prayer.

The parable of the "prodigal father" and Paul's theology bear on a crucial social and religious issue today—the challenge of addressing God as "father." Even though the parable of Luke 15:11–32 is not an "allegory" with one to one correspondences between the father and God, the images evoked suggest the relation of God to humanity.

Readers are to think about how God acts in comparison with the father in the parable. Feminist exegesis has raised our consciousness about the problems of patriarchy latent in such an image of God, has underscored the difficulty that many women have in praying to God as "father," and has called attention to maternal images in the biblical tradition often neglected by male scholars.[65] Patriarchy and the ability to pray to God as "Abba" or father are problems also for men in Christianity. No one can live after Sigmund Freud and not realize the problems surrounding the relation of son to father. Feminist exegesis constantly states that its concern is human liberation, not simply "women's liberation."

Even though the characteristic Christian prayer, the "Our Father," is said to sum up biblical piety, the term "father" is not used very frequently of God in the OT.[66] Some examples are Exod. 4:22; Deut. 32:6; Jer. 3:19; Isa. 45:9–11; 64:8; Mal. 2:10. Where God is so called, it is usually not in the context of dominating power but of communicating life in becoming a "father" to the people or by care for the people. The "patriarchal" father arises more out of other OT language applied to God.[67]

Neither the parable of Luke 15:11–32 nor Paul offers a "patriarchal" father, concerned about dominating power, and both likewise summon Christians to a freedom from those cultural influences and personal traumas which surround the image of God as father and make it into a symbol of servility. Both also state that being a free member of the family is a "gift." Paradoxically, attempts to earn acceptance increase servility. Sandra Schneiders captures well the power of the parable:

> Jesus' parable about the father actually constitutes a radical challenge to patriarchy. The divine father who has been understood as the ultimate justification of human patriarchy is revealed as the one who refuses to own us, demand our submission or punish our rebellion. Rather, God

65. See above, n. 42; and Trible, *God and the Rhetoric of Sexuality*, 22–23; 31–72. Trible notes (p. 22) God the pregnant woman (Isa. 42:14), the mother (Isa. 66:13), the midwife (Ps. 22:9), and the mistress (Ps. 123:2). See also pp. 31–72 for more extensive treatment of feminine language for God, esp. "the compassion of God" (where the Hebrew and Greek terms for compassion are also used for "womb"; cf. Luke 15:20).

66. Ringgren, "'abh," *TDOT* 1:16–19.

67. See most recently Schneiders, *Women and the Word*, 37–50. For a NT critique of "patriarchy," see Hamerton-Kelly, *God the Father*.

is the one who respects our freedom, mourns our alienation, waits
patiently for our return and accepts our love as pure gift.[68]

To address God as "father" is the result of a profound experience
of liberation, not the first step. Paul and Luke both suggest that
ultimately this liberation will be experienced only in community, a
community where divisiveness ceases (Gal. 3:28) and where people
can celebrate together the joy of being found. The parable of Luke
15:11–32, however, is open-ended and leaves us with a challenge.
It does not tell us whether the older brother joined the celebration.
It does not tell us whether he chose reconciliation over alienation
or whether he continued to live as a slave, or accepted the risk of
freedom. Its final words are an invitation; will it be accepted?

THE PARABLES OF LUKE 16 AND
RICH AND POOR IN LUKE'S GOSPEL

The Unjust Steward (Luke 16:1–13)

The Parable as Text

Very few chapters in the NT pose as many exegetical challenges
as does Luke 16. Without an explicit change of setting from 15:1–
2, a gathering of Pharisees and scribes, it begins in 16:1 with an
inclusion of disciples as the addressees of the parable of the Unjust
Steward (16:1–8) and the appended sayings (16:9–13). As 16:14
states, however, the Pharisees hear these; moreover, they are the
principal audience in the rest of the chapter, beginning with its bitter
characterization of them as "lovers of money" (16:14–15), continuing
with sayings on the validity of the law and divorce (16:16–18), and
concluding with the parable of the Rich Man and Lazarus (16:19–
31). Though two major Lukan parables anchor the chapter (16:1–
8, 19–31), the middle section contains seemingly unrelated Q material
(16:16–18), and apart from a concern for material possessions, no
thread emerges that gives it thematic unity.[69]

Initial problems are the relation of the appended sayings (16:8b–

---

68. Schneiders, *Women and the Word*, 47.
69. Fitzmyer, *Luke X—XXIV*, 1095.

13) to the parable, the identity of the "master" in 16:8 (*kyrios*), and the extent of the initial parable. Working backward from 16:13, we can find a rough literary unity without consistency of content, so much so that C. H. Dodd has characterized the section as notes for three separate sermons on the parable.[70] The saying of 16:13, "No servant can serve two masters . . . ," from Q (= Matt. 6:24), while tangential to the economic milieu of the parable, is scarcely its interpretation, since the steward of 16:1–8 succeeds at what the saying prohibits—he serves two masters. The previous sayings are united by "catchword" composition (e.g., "mammon," 16:9, 11, 13; "faithful," *pistos*, 16:10, 11, 12). The saying about the children of this world in 8b is a generalized conclusion not usually found in parables but joined also by "catchwords" (obscured by the RSV translation of "shrewdness" for *phronimōs* in 16:8a and "wiser" for *phronimōteroi* in 16:8b; for consistency, the Greek of 16:8b should be translated "shrewder"). Clearly, Luke and the pre-Lukan tradition experienced as much difficulty understanding the parable as did succeeding generations.

The question of the identity of the "master" and the extent of the parable are related. Since Luke frequently uses *ho kyrios* ("the Lord"), both when speaking of the earthly Jesus (e.g., 7:13, 19; 10:1, 39, 41; 11:39; 12:42a; 13:15; 17:6) and in describing the risen Christ (24:34; cf. Acts 1:21; 2:36; 4:33; 5:14; 8:16), scholars have claimed that the "master" who commends the steward in 16:8 is Jesus and represents an editorial comment by the evangelist.[71] While the majority identify the *kyrios* of 16:8 with the rich man of 16:1, the ending is also a problem, with 16:7, 8, 8a and 9 all being proposed. Most recently, J. Dominic Crossan has joined those who opt for 16:7 and has located it among "the parables of action" where the "point" is simply decisive action in the face of a crisis.[72] My working hypothesis is that literary and thematic concerns dictate an ending at 8a, that is, with the commendation by the same master who appears in the initial verse.

A close reading of the text challenges its traditional title of "the

70. Dodd, *Parables*, 17.
71. For discussion of *kyrios* in Luke-Acts, see Fitzmyer, *Luke I—IX*, 201–4. For identification of *kyrios* with Jesus, see Jeremias, *Parables*, 45–46; and Marshall, *Luke*, 619.
72. Crossan, *In Parables*, 108–11; 115–19.

Unjust Steward," since it is not clear that he is unjust nor that it is his story. Like many Lukan parables, it begins with the generalized *anthrōpos tis* (someone, a person) but adds that he was rich (16:1; cf. 16:19). The principal characters are immediately juxtaposed in a situation of reckoning, much like the parable of the Unmerciful Servant in Matt. 18:23–35. Like Matthew's steward (18:23), Luke's is caught in a situation of mismanagement but is simply to be fired rather than imprisoned. He apparently has some leeway before the removal becomes public, which explains the urgency and rapid action of the following verses (esp. v. 6, "sit down quickly"). During the dismissal the steward makes no defense; and his character emerges from the soliloquy of 16:3, couched in mocking self-parody, since the audience would not expect a person of his status either to work or to beg. He then embarks on a plan to extricate himself, hoping that his master's debtors will be so impressed that he will be welcomed into their houses. His plan succeeds apparently beyond his wildest hopes, since the master "commends" (*epaineō*, lit., "praise," with an overtone of approval) what he has done—even though we do not know for sure whether he was restored as manager.

Since patristic times the major problem of interpretation has been how Jesus could commend the apparent dishonesty and chicanery of the steward. The standard casuistic solution has been to focus on the "prudence" (or shrewdness) of the steward and argue that the master praises this while overlooking the dishonesty.[73] Christians are to be equally prudent (16:9) without being equally dishonest. The smiles of the congregation which greet this explanation from the pulpit or podium show that this fine distinction is a bit more than the text or human imagination can bear. A more basic problem is that it fractures the narrative logic of the parable. If the steward is dishonest, what are the grounds of his hope that he will be welcomed into the homes of his accomplices? Would the debtors hire someone to oversee their estates who was recently dismissed for mismanagement due to dishonesty? Would they jeopardize future relationships with the rich man in 16:1 on whom they are in their own way economically dependent? Three principal solutions have emerged in addressing this conundrum.

73. E.g., Creed, *St. Luke*, 201: "The emphasis falls upon the steward's prudence."

*A Solution in Terms of the
Economic Background*

Recent studies by Derrett and Joseph A. Fitzmyer argue that the steward is not really "dishonest."[74] The key, they feel, lies in an understanding of the casuistry surrounding the application of the OT prohibitions against lending money at interest.[75] While this is a complex and controverted discussion, I will attempt to summarize their conclusions. By the law against usury, an owner (the rich man of 16:1) could not lend money at interest. There was, however, a legal fiction which allowed this in practice. If, for example, the contract stated that $100 was to be lent at 6 percent interest, the contract was usurious. If, however, the projected rate of interest was written into the original loan, then there was no usury in the technical sense. If the contract stated "I lend you $106" when you receive only $100, then the contract was not usurious. Since even this practice was frowned upon, people of respect or authority would avoid tainting their hands by direct dealing. The finances and skirting of the law were managed by their stewards, who could be called "stewards of injustice" (16:8)—a literal translation of *oikonomos tēs adikias* (an "objective" genitive, much like "secretary of defense," who need not be a defensive secretary). The steward was not paid a formal salary but derived his income from the interest charged after bringing a profit to the master (cf. Matt. 25:14–30).

According to this understanding of the legal situation, by telling the debtors to reduce the stated amount of the loan (16:6, "a hundred measures . . . write fifty"), the manager simply reduces the loan to its real amount (minus the interest). By so doing, he hopes that the debtors will see him as resourceful and ready to sacrifice his own gain when caught in a difficult situation. Such a person they might welcome into their homes. Fitzmyer finds here the "point" of the parable: when faced with the crisis of the kingdom proclaimed by Jesus, we are summoned to decisive action and to forsake our own advantage.[76]

---

74. Derrett, *Law*, 48–77; and Fitzmyer, "Dishonest Manager."
75. E.g., Exod. 22:24; Lev. 25:35–37; Deut. 23:19–20; cf. Ezek. 18:8, 13, 17; Ps. 15:5.
76. Fitzmyer, "Dishonest Manager," 37 (as in *TS*).

*A Solution in Terms of
Literary Criticism*

The interpretation of this parable by Dan O. Via, more than any other, has captured the imagination of commentators.[77] Via numbers it among the "comic" parables where a character, caught in a difficult or threatening situation, emerges as successful—but with a twist. He describes the steward as "picaresque," a roguish character who lives by wits, often on the fringes of society.[78] Not immoral, but often amoral, such people are humanly attractive and provide a counter to an overly serious view of life. The steward is a model for those who must accept the full human dilemma of surviving amid ambiguous situations and not collapsing when faced with destruction. The steward may also provide comic relief from the "dead seriousness" of Jesus' teaching, and the happy outcome of his story hints that "our well-being does not rest ultimately on our dead seriousness."[79]

Bernard Brandon Scott turns to folklore to explain the parable.[80] The parable satirizes the powerful and makes the crafty steward into a hero of decisive action. For Scott neither character in the parable is a model of virtue. The master has acted unjustly toward the steward and the steward is "getting even." The original hearers would identify with the roguish steward. While the steward is the victim of the rich man's injustice, he is victim of the steward's cleverness. These folkloric motifs are transformed by Jesus into a parable that provides a "counter-world" to the readers' expectations. In the normal world, "power and justice" are coordinates (i.e., those with power are expected to be just), but not so in the parable. The rich man exercises power without justice, and the steward the power of the victim. By so upsetting this normal world the parable functions so that "the reader in the world of the kingdom must establish new coordinates for power, vulnerability and justice."[81]

77. D. O. Via, *Parables,* 155–62; see the review by Perrin, "Biblical Scholarship in a New Vein."
78. D. O. Via draws on the characterization developed by Lewis, *The Picaresque Saint.*
79. D. O. Via, *Parables,* 162.
80. Scott, "A Master's Praise."
81. Ibid., 188.

Solution in Terms of the Lukan Context

This parable (16:1–8) clearly continues to intrigue and mystify, and no agreed-upon solution may be found. Here I offer some suggestions about Luke's understanding of it. Whatever its original form and wording, Luke has rewritten it—the Greek is stylistically consistent with other parts of the Gospel—and its present location is due to Luke. Most striking and somewhat neglected is its similarity to the preceding parable (Luke 15:11–32).[82] The major parallels are the following:

• Both are *anthrōpos tis* parables, that is, introduced by generic statements, "someone, a certain person" (15:11; 16:1).

• In both parables there is a central character who determines the narrative flow and who speaks in the final verse of the parable: the father (15:11, 32); the master (16:1, 8).

• In both parables the character who provides the dramatic interest squanders (*dieskorpisen*) property (15:13; 16:3).

• In both parables this character confronts life-threatening alternatives (15:15–17; 16:3).

• In both parables the resolution begins when the narrative switches to discourse in the form of a soliloquy (15:17–19; 16:3–4).

• The motivation in each case is rather self-serving.

• In both cases the hope for changed fortune is couched in the form of acceptance into a "house."

• In both cases literary devices increase the narrative tension—the return journey of the son and the negotiations of the steward.

• Most important, in both cases the plan is not realized but transcended by the surprising action of the *anthrōpos* mentioned in the first verse. Both characters in difficulty think in terms of reestablishing a proper order of justice or obligation, and both receive surprising acceptance. Both are rescued from danger by what they receive, not by what they accomplish.

• Both parables are open-ended; we do not know whether the

82. Bailey (*Poet*, 109) offers a partial list which is more "theological" than the one proposed here.

older brother joined the party or whether the steward rejoined the master's household, though this is implied.

Such parallels suggest that the parable is not really the parable of the "unjust steward" but of the "foolish master." While he appears in 16:1–2 as potentially harsh in demanding an account and in dismissing the steward, he moves out of the picture and leaves time for the steward to act. The surprise and shock come not in the successful completion of the steward's plan but in the master's praise. Like the father in the previous parable, he is somewhat uninterested in the plan proposed to get out of the difficult situation. Unlike subsequent interpreters, he is blithely unconcerned over the supposed dishonesty.

As in the previous parable (15:11–32), Luke transforms the images under which people relate to figures of power. Both the term "father" in the previous parable and "master" (kyrios, 16:3, 5, 8) are used analogously of God. But, just as normal expectations of how a father would act were challenged in the previous parable, the "master" of Luke 16:1–8 evokes a world where God does not exact punishment but gives time and cancels debts even in the midst of human machinations. Also, since "steward" is used by Luke (12:41–48) and the early church as part of the terminology of Christian ministry and discipleship, often in contexts of warnings about faithful stewardship (cf. 1 Cor. 4:1–2; Titus 1:7; 1 Pet. 4:10), Luke may use this parable to counter fear and anxiety in Christian leaders, in the same fashion that Luke 15:11–32 countered rigidity in Jewish leaders (and perhaps in Christian "Pharisees").

The appended sayings (16:8b–13), whatever their original meanings, are now governed by Luke's understanding of the parable (16:1–8a). Free of a demanding and harsh God, the children of light can be as shrewd as the children of this world; they are not to flee engagement with "unrighteous mammon" but to remain faithful in its midst. Luke ends these sayings with the somewhat ambiguous phrase "You cannot serve God and mammon" (16:13b). Matthew (6:24) may preserve better the original context of this Q saying by appending to it a series of warnings against anxiety (6:25–33). Luke may also play subtly on the etymology of mammon (= that on which one relies or trusts). Although both the son and the steward seem to place their faith in possessions (i.e., either obtaining or securing them), it is the free acceptance of the father/master which provides security. Christian disciples are summoned to be freed from slavery to wealth *and* from servile fear of God.

The Parable of the Rich Man and Lazarus and the Prefaced Sayings (Luke 16:14–31)

The second half of chapter 16 is addressed directly to the Pharisees, who "heard all this" (16:14), that is, the previous parables and sayings. After a number of sayings that seem to have little relation to the context, Luke presents the parable of the Rich Man (often called Dives, from the Latin translation of "rich man") and Lazarus. The proper use of possessions which was present in the two previous parables is now central. I will first discuss this parable and then return to the more difficult issue of the prefaced sayings.

The Parable as Text

This parable has certain unique features: only here does a character have a proper name, Lazarus, and only here is the action mythological, that is, taking place in both the earthly and heavenly spheres. Its atmosphere is strongly folkloric and evocative of Egyptian tales about the reversal of fates after death. One contender for such background is the rabbinic parable of the rich tax collector, Bar Ma'jan and the poor scholar.[83] When Bar Ma'jan dies, he receives a splendid funeral, generally a sign of divine approval, while the poor scholar dies unnoticed. The question posed by the rabbis is how a just God could allow such injustice. The reply, which may have also influenced the Q parable of the Great Supper, is that once the tax collector held a great banquet and, when the invited guests declined, he invited the poor and was rewarded for this one good deed by the funeral, while the poor scholar is taken to paradise.

Derrett offers another contender for the folkloric background.[84] In Greek the name *Lazaros* contains the same root consonants as the Semitic *Eliezer*, who is a servant of Abraham in Gen. 15:2. According to Derrett, in the midrashic tales Eliezer was thought to walk in

83. Jeremias, *Parables*, 182–83.
84. Derrett, *Law*, 78–99.

disguise on this earth and report back to Abraham on how his children observed the Torah, especially regarding the treatment of the poor and on hospitality to strangers. This is reflected in the picture of Lazarus as a poor beggar (16:20), in his return to Abraham's bosom (16:22), and especially in the request of the rich man (16:27) to send *him* (Lazarus) to his brothers' house.

Both the unique elements of this parable and the folkloric contacts suggest that this parable does not go back to the historical Jesus but originated among those groups which brought to Luke the traditions about the dangers of wealth and a God who puts down the mighty and exalts the lowly (1:52).[85] Luke adopts and sharpens these traditions.

The narrative falls into three major parts: rich and poor in this life (16:19–21); the death of each protagonist and the reversal of fates in the afterlife (16:22–26); and a parenetic dialogue between Abraham and the rich man over the fate of those still alive (16:27–31). The parable achieves its initial effect by a vivid contrast between the main characters. The man is rich (*plousios*); Lazarus is a destitute beggar (*ptōchos*). The rich man is clothed in purple and fine linen (i.e., he lives like a king; cf. Prov. 31:22; 1 Macc. 8:14); Lazarus is covered with sores. The man feasts sumptuously every day (*euphrainomenos*, lit., "splendidly making merry every day"); Lazarus desires (the Greek, *epithumōn chortasthēnai*, suggests a constant and unfulfilled longing) to be fed with scraps normally given to animals and has these as his only companions. His plight is described in virtually the same terms as the younger son's (cf. 15:16, *epethumei chortasthēnai*). Despite the vivid contrast, the audience would not necessarily see the rich man as evil and Lazarus as virtuous. Abundant possessions are a gift from God (Gen. 24:35; Job 42:10–17; Eccles. 3:10–13; 1 Tim. 4:4–5), and the condition of Lazarus, like the pitiable state of Job, could be interpreted as a sign of divine disfavor.

The surprising reversal of fates is quick and immediate. The poor man dies and, without a funeral, is carried to Abraham's bosom; the rich man dies and has a decent burial (*etaphē*, v. 22)—which is important to the final section of the parable, since his remaining brothers presume he has received divine favor. The shock comes

85. R. Brown (*Birth of the Messiah,* 350–55) argues that behind these narratives stand the traditions of the ʿanāwîm, the poor of the Jerusalem church.

when we see him in Hades (16:23). The physical description underscores the reversal of fates: in contrast to sumptuous feasting, he is in great thirst; in contrast to his splendid garb, he is surrounded by flames. As Lazarus "desired" to eat the scraps from his table, he now begs Abraham to have Lazarus offer him a drop of water. The answer of Abraham in v. 25 simply puts in discourse what the narrative has portrayed: the fates are reversed; signs of power and favor in this life are no guarantee of joy in the afterlife. The time for decision and resolute action is past; now is the time only for realizing the consequences of one's action (cf. Matt. 25:31–46). As a parable of the reversal of fates, it could end in v. 26, but the final verses, which show strong Lukan redaction (esp. vv. 30–31), are important for a deeper understanding of the text.

The story has different emphases. If it ended at v. 26, then it could be simply a continuation of the OT polemic against the misuse of material possessions. The rich man is condemned not because he is rich but because he never even saw Lazarus at his gate; the first time he sees him is from Hades, emphasized by the somewhat solemn phrase "He lifted up his eyes, and saw" (v. 23). Here the text is bitterly ironic. In life there was a chasm between himself and Lazarus because of his wealth and power; in death this chasm still exists (16:26). As we will see below, one of the prime dangers of wealth is that it causes "blindness."

These dangers provide the backdrop for the dialogue between the rich man and Lazarus. Too late, the rich man realizes that in neglecting Lazarus he was neglecting the Torah. He asks that Lazarus again be sent to warn the brothers. The reply of Abraham is also ironic. The brothers have Moses and the prophets, with their prescriptions on care for the poor, the orphan, the widow, and the stranger. They would be as blind to Lazarus as was their brother now in torment. The second request of the rich man (16:27) implies that he too understands this and he says that they will repent "if someone goes to them from the dead" (16:30).

The response of Abraham (v. 31) that the brothers will not be convinced "even if some one should rise from the dead" provides a solemn conclusion to the narrative and shows considerable sign of Lukan redaction. Whereas the rich man wants someone to "go to them" (*poreuthē*, v. 30) from the dead, the answer of Abraham uses the technical Christian language of resurrection (*anastē*). The reference to "Moses and the prophets" occurs here and in Luke's narrative of the appearance of the risen Jesus where he teaches his followers how his suffering and death were predicted in "Moses and the prophets" (Luke 24:27, 44). Luke directs the final verse to those in his community who by neglecting the poor do not heed the teaching or follow the example of Jesus who rose from the dead.

Luke also gives a christological nuance to the final verse of the parable. Jesus is the rejected outcast and the poor one, who has risen from the dead. In an early kerygmatic sermon of Acts all the people are summoned through proof from Moses and the prophets (Acts 3:11–26) to repent and believe in the risen Jesus.[86] If they do not, then it may be too late for them, as it was for the child of Abraham in the parable.

The Sayings of Luke 16:14–18

No satisfactory explanation exists for the relation of these sayings to their context. To propose a convincing one could take us too far afield, but I will offer some suggestions as an invitation to further reflection. The introduction (16:14) is quite harsh. The Pharisees are called "lovers of money" (*philargyroi*), and they "sneer at Jesus." Both are surprising. Historically, the Pharisees, unlike Sadducees and many of the scribes, were not from the upper class and represented a popular movement within Palestine. Though Luke hands on the disputes between Jesus and the Pharisees (e.g., Luke 5:17–39 = Mark 2:1–22), he has nothing comparable to the harsh polemic of Matthew 23. He also portrays Jesus frequently at meals with the Pharisees (7:36; 11:37; 14:1) and depicts them in a favorable light (13:31; cf. Acts 5:34; 23:6).[87]

A solution to the harsh statement of 16:14 may be found in the understanding of possessions in Luke. As Luke Johnson has cogently argued, wealth and riches in Luke are both literal and metaphoric.[88] Luke is concerned about the actual poor and the danger of wealth: at the same time, wealth is a symbol of power and dominance; and

---

86. On proof from prophecy in Luke, see Fitzmyer, *Luke I—IX*, 179–80.
87. See Ziesler, "Luke and the Pharisees."
88. Johnson, *The Literary Function of Possessions*; idem, *Sharing Possessions*.

poverty is a symbol of vulnerability. In chapters 15—16 Luke portrays the Pharisees as people of power and influence who grumble because Jesus accepts the outcast. Their "money" is power expressed in self-confidence which brings human esteem (16:15, "You are those who justify yourselves before men"). They are miserly in their possession of virtue. Conversely, neither the younger son nor the steward is careful or grasping; their attitude toward possessions is metaphoric of a certain freedom and prodigality. Jesus continues the polemic against the assurance of the Pharisees in the following verse (16:16) by affirming that the law and the prophets, which maintain their enduring validity (16:17), are to be interpreted under the ethic of the kingdom as proclaimed by his parables and enacted in his fellowship with the outcasts. Response to this proclamation requires a "violent" break with past values and norms.[89]

The most puzzling material in this whole section is the seemingly unrelated saying on divorce (16:18).[90] One clue to its presence arises from the literary structure. Luke creates here a chiastic structure to stress that Jesus is both the fulfillment of the law and its authentic interpreter. It assumes the following form:

A   Saying on relation of law and prophets to proclamation of good news of kingdom (16:16)

  B   Saying on abiding validity of law (16:17)

  B'   Saying on divorce as instance of abiding validity of law (16:18)

A'   Parable of Rich Man and Lazarus as embodying the law and the prophets (16:29), now interpreted by the proclamation of Jesus (16:19–31)

Thus both the abiding validity of the law and the prophets and the gospel of the kingdom (16:16) are illustrated and defended. The chiasm, which is at the center of the chapter, both defends, in Pharisaic terms of appeal to the law and the prophets, Jesus' action which has been under attack since 15:2 and also calls attention to

89. On this understanding of "violently," see Fitzmyer, *Luke X—XXIV*, 1115–16; and Marshall, *Luke*, 630–31.
90. Fitzmyer, *Luke X—XXIV*, 1119–24 (with bibliography).

the "gospel of the kingdom" (16:16) which is manifest in Jesus' concern for the marginal and defense of the poor.

Another consideration is that in the cultural milieu of the Gospels, divorce is more an economic issue than a breakup of an interpersonal relationship, so a saying on divorce is not out of context in a section that deals with the proper use of possessions. Divorce legislation, as known from texts of that time, is very much concerned with the disposition of property, and often the woman suffered deprivation.[91] The woman was in danger of becoming as poor and vulnerable as Lazarus. The thread then that unites all the material from 15:1 to 16:31 is Jesus' defense of those on the margin of society who can be victimized by the rich and powerful. This defense is "the good news of the kingdom" which has been preached since John (Luke 16:16).

The Wider Context: Rich and Poor in Luke

No NT writings deal more extensively than Luke-Acts with the dangers of wealth, the proper use of possessions, and concern for the poor. As the Christian churches today become more aware of the gap between rich and poor, as well as of the challenge to discipleship amid economic prosperity, and as they are summoned to an "option for the poor," the message of Luke becomes ever more urgent.[92] Within the past decade there have been an increasing number of excellent discussions of the pertinent texts.[93] Even a

91. On Jewish laws, see Brooten, "Konnten Frauen im alten Judentum die Scheidung betreiben?"; and Fitzmyer, "Divorce among First-Century Palestinian Jews." In a "deed of divorce" from Alexandria dated 13 B.C. between a Jewish woman, Apollónia, and a Gentile, Hermogenes, half the contract deals with disposition of the dowry; see Tcherikover and Fuks, *Corpus Papyrorum Judaicarum* 2.10–12, no. 144.

92. The term "option for the poor" is associated with Latin American liberation theology and was used by the Latin American bishops in their meetings at Puebla. In an excellent survey of the origin and use of the term, Dorr (*Option for the Poor,* 1) notes that it may be as controversial for our age as was "justification by faith" for a previous one. On its biblical basis, see Dupont and George, *Gospel Poverty,* which contains essays on OT and NT understandings of the poor. See also Gelin, *The Poor of Yahweh;* and Lohfink, *Option for the Poor.*

93. The other important places are 2 Corinthians 8—9 (the collection) and James. Some helpful studies of Luke are Johnson, *The Literary Function of Possessions;* idem, *Sharing Possessions;* Mealand, *Poverty and Expectation in the Gospels;* Pilgrim, *Good News to the Poor;* Seccombe, *Possessions and the Poor in Luke-Acts;* and Stegemann, *The Gospel and the Poor.*

cursory survey of Lukan special material or of Luke's editing of the tradition shows the extent of the concern.

- The infancy narratives show a special concern for the ʿanāwîm, people without money and power. In her Magnificat, Mary praises a God who puts down the mighty from their thrones, fills the hungry with good things, and sends the rich away empty (Luke 1:52–53). The sacrifice offered at the presentation is that determined by law for poor people (Luke 2:24).
- Luke adds to the Q tradition about John's preaching an exhortation that the one who has two coats or food should share with those who have none (3:10).
- Luke begins the public ministry of Jesus not with the proclamation of the imminence of the kingdom (cf. Mark 1:15; Matt. 4:17) but with Jesus citing Isa. 61:1–2, "the good news to the poor" (Luke 4:17–19; cf. 7:22).
- Only in Luke does Levi leave everything when he follows Jesus (5:28; cf. Mark 2:14; Matt. 9:9).
- In Luke it is simply "the poor" who are blessed, and Luke adds woes against the rich and powerful (6:20, 24–26).
- Only Luke contains the parable of the Rich Fool (12:13–21) as well as the parable of the Rich Man and Lazarus (16:19–31).
- Upon his conversion, Zacchaeus is willing to give half his goods to the poor (19:8).
- Luke presents Jesus in the form of an OT prophet who takes the side of the widow (7:11–17; 18:1–8), the stranger in the land (10:29–37; 17:16), and those on the margin of society (14:12–13, 21).
- The early Christian community is one which shares its goods in common and where there is no needy person (Acts 2:41–47; 4:32–37).
- In both the Gospel and Acts almsgiving is stressed (Luke 11:41; 12:33; 19:8; Acts 10:2, 4, 31; 24:17).

The recent awareness of the importance of these texts and of their roots in the OT has not solved all the connected issues. Basic is the question "Who are the poor?" Are they the economic poor, or is poverty a metaphor for powerlessness and vulnerability? Why are the poor called "blessed"? Is it because they are not blinded by wealth and hence are open to God, or because they are to be the beneficiaries of the kingdom as proclaimed by Jesus, which will reverse the structures of poverty and oppression?[94] Is the community addressed by Luke composed mainly of the poor who are to be heartened by the message of Jesus, or of relatively well off people who are to be confronted by it?[95] Does Luke urge common possession, dispossession, or almsgiving as the most fundamental Christian posture toward wealth?

The discussion of such questions is beyond the scope of this study, but we want to highlight some guidelines from Luke's Gospel in parable. In treating the Rich Man and Lazarus we noted that the evil of the rich man is that he is blinded by his wealth; he does not see Lazarus. The parable of the Rich Fool (Luke 12:13–21), also special Lukan material, offers an added perspective. The parable appears in the context of a long sermon (12:1—13:9) by Jesus "to his disciples" (12:1, 22, 41) and to the multitude (12:1, 13, 54; 13:6). Much of the Q material found in Matthew's Sermon on the Mount and omitted from Luke's Sermon on the Plain is given here. The parable of the Rich Fool (12:13–21), which is sandwiched between groups of sayings to the disciples on trust and fearless confession (12:2–12, 22–31), is introduced by a question from the multitude. If the disciples are symbolic of those who have responded and followed Jesus and of the multitudes of those who are still being summoned to respond, then this parable has relevance for both groups. It will address both the conditions and consequences of discipleship.

The Parable of the Rich Fool
(Luke 12:13–21)

Though this parable is introduced by a request from one of the multitude for Jesus to settle the question of a disputed inheritance (12:13), like the Good Samaritan it does not really respond to this request but speaks of the deeper issue involved. Kenneth E. Bailey notes that the request is peremptory, since the questioner asks Jesus

---

94. A major influence on all subsequent writings has been the massive study of Dupont, *Les béatitudes*. Dupont rejected "otherworldly" interpretation of the beatitudes and argued that the poor were to be the beneficiaries of the reign of God as proclaimed and enacted by Jesus (see esp. 2:80–85).

95. See Karris, "Poor and Rich."

to decide in his favor.[96] Jesus responds somewhat harshly, "Who made me judge or divider over you?" and then underscores the real issue: "Beware of covetousness, for a human life does not consist in the abundance of possessions" (12:14–15, au. trans.).

The phrasing of verse 15 is significant. "Covetousness" (*pleonexia*, lit., "the desire for more"), also translated as avarice or greed, is one of the vices most scorned by Hellenistic moralists. They call it "the metropolis of all evil deeds" (Diodorus Siculus) or "the greatest source of evil" (Dio Chrysostom).[97] It is found in the early Christian "vice lists" (Rom. 1:29; *1 Clement* 35:5). In Col. 3:5 it is equated with "idolatry," which Rom. 1:24–25 describes as serving "the creature rather than the Creator." It is a vice that turns its victim away from both God and neighbor. While the first half of the introductory verse is a warning, the second is a maxim: human life does not consist in an "abundance" (*en tō perisseuein*). The Greek literally means "in what is more than enough," with pejorative overtones, since moderation and having nothing in excess (*mēden agan*) was prized in the Hellenistic world. It is not the mere possession of material goods which will spell the downfall of the rich man but his constant desire for more which leads to surplus possession, which today we might call "conspicuous consumption."

As often in Luke, the following parable illustrates the saying. The protagonist is another *anthrōpos tis* (12:16), who like the owner of 16:1 and the person in 16:19, is rich (*plousios*). His land has brought forth "plentifully," and now the narrative switches to the soliloquy (12:17–19)—which makes up the bulk of the parable. Instead of thanking God for the bountiful harvest, he decides to build ever larger barns in which to store all acquired grain and goods. The soliloquy is enhanced by a staged dialogue with "his soul." The text here is very subtle. While this is a dramatic parable (i.e., with a human character rather than about nature), there is no interaction with any other human being. The rich man can dialogue only with his own soul (his *psychē* or self, 12:19). Bailey comments, "This speech is sad: having 'made it' the rich man does not share his joy with his friends, but only with his own 'soul,' which will soon be

96. Bailey, *Through Peasant Eyes*, 59.
97. See the examples in BAGD, 667.

snatched away" (12:20).[98] His wealth has isolated him from all human contact. He continues: "Soul, . . . take your ease; eat, drink, be merry"—in both language and image paralleling the action of the rich man in 16:19.

Despite his assurance of goods for many years and his careful plans for security, his soliloquy is rudely interrupted: "God said to him, 'Fool! This night your soul is required of you; and the things you have prepared, whose will they be?' " This explosive introduction shocks the original hearers more than us. In no other parable does "God" enter so explicitly into the narrative and speak in a manner forbidden to human beings (cf. Matt. 5:21–22). The word "fool" also recalls the wide OT polemic against "folly" (e.g., Pss. 14:1; 53:1, "The fool says in his heart, 'There is no God' "; cf. also Ps. 49:10; Sir. 11:19–20). The Greek (a-phrōn, lit., "without sense") is from the same root as the words associated with faithful and prudent (phronimos) stewardship (Luke 12:42; 16:8; cf. Matt. 7:24; 24:45; 25:2, 4, 8, 9). The contrast between his complacency in his riches and the danger they pose is enhanced by the phrase "This night your soul is required of you" (lit., "They are demanding [apaitousin] your soul from you"). The word "demand" (apaitousin) is commonly used for collecting a loan.[99] The rich man did not realize that the fruits of his harvest were "on loan" from God and not to be used for his own gratification.

The final question by God, "The things you have prepared, whose will they be?" (12:20) provides an inclusio with the dispute over an inheritance which evoked the parable (12:13). The covetousness of the rich person in the parable has so isolated him that he has not even provided for his heirs. Given the importance of family and heirs in first-century culture, his condition is pitiable. He is isolated amid his wealth, dies alone, and leaves only what will be a bitter dispute over the inheritance (cf. 12:13). The parable then has a "second application": such will happen to those who lay up treasure for themselves and are not rich toward God (12:21). The following verses, which urge trust in God and almsgiving, spell out what it means to be "rich toward God" (12:22–34).

98. Bailey, *Through Peasant Eyes*, 66.
99. Ibid., 67.

Rich and Poor in Luke

While the more elaborate Rich Man and Lazarus parable under-scores one danger of riches, that they cause blindness to the presence of the suffering and needy neighbor, the Rich Fool, in its short compass, offers a paradigm of the dangers of "the desire for more" and "superfluous possession." First of all, riches isolate one from community. The imagery of the parable is powerful: a rich man surrounded by material possessions, living and dying alone. Second, they blind one to God's presence—God has to interrupt his material musings. In the Bible the good things of the earth are to be enjoyed; God's love is manifest in material blessings and God brings oppressed people to a land flowing with milk and honey. Their possessors, however, are to pray in thanksgiving for God's gifts, but wealth has been given also to benefit the poor and the needy, never for the sole good of its possessors.[100]

These two parables then provide a handy summary of Luke's concern for the dangers of wealth. Jesus comes to the lowly of the earth and announces the good news to the poor. The conditions under which they live will be reversed by the proclamation of the good news, and the life of the community is to reflect this. Banquets are to be celebrated with the poor and needy; the suffering person at one's doorstep cannot be ignored. In Luke's somewhat idyllic picture of the Jerusalem community in Acts 2:44, he speaks of the community having "all things in common," using the classic Hellen-istic term for friendship.[101] The sharing of material goods is symbolic of a deeper level of community; gross inequalities of goods destroy community.

At the same time Luke does not wage as strong a polemic against wealth as is found, for example, in some of the apocalyptic litera-ture.[102] In Acts especially, people further the growth of the early community by offering hospitality and providing out of their means (Acts 16:14; 18:27), and Luke frequently urges almsgiving. Luke then leaves Christianity with a manifold legacy regarding discipleship in the world of material possessions: riches can cause blindness to

100. See the excellent short treatment by Mott, "Wealth."
101. Pilgrim, *Good News to the Poor*, 191 n. 11; Karris, "Poor and Rich," 116.
102. Nickelsburg, "Riches, the Rich, and God's Judgment."

God and to the presence of the neighbor; they can isolate people from community; the Christian community must embody the good news to the poor; material possessions, which are a gift from God, are to be used in service of the poor.

TRIAL BY PRAYER: THE PARABLES OF
THE WIDOW AND THE JUDGE
AND
THE PHARISEE AND THE TAX COLLECTOR

In 18:1–14 Luke concludes that section of the travel narrative which incorporates material from his own source, L, or from Q; in 18:15 he returns to the Markan content and order. This conclusion is in the solemn form of twin parables, in the familiar woman/man pattern. Both parables are concerned with prayer: the first due to Luke's addition of 18:1, ". . . to the effect that they ought always to pray and not lose heart"; and the second because of the setting, "Two men went up into the temple to pray" (18:10). Both parables also deal with "trials," the first explicitly and the second implicitly since one person is pronounced "justified" (18:14).[103] These parables offer paradigms of prayer which is to mark the life of the community during its pilgrimage. Earlier I have alluded to prayer as one of the major themes of Luke-Acts; now it can be treated in more detail.

The Widow and the Judge (18:1–8)

The Parable as Text

Behind this "deceptively simple story" are a complex of literary and interpretive problems.[104] Initially one must determine the extent of the original parable. The introduction (18:1) reflects Luke's understanding of "parable" as paradigm of action and, like the Rich Fool (12:15), begins with an application. The formal narrative comprises vv. 2–5; vv. 6–8 offer different applications of the parable.[105] The relation of these to the parable itself is similar to the

103. In my description of these parables, I intend "trial" in a double sense as found in Luke: (1) the juridical situation envisioned in the two parables; (2) the sense of "testing" (*peirasmos*) which is to characterize the community prior to the parousia. For Luke's community as an *ecclesia pressa*, a church undergoing "testing," see Conzelmann (*St. Luke*, 12–17) and S. Brown (*Apostasy and Perseverance*).
104. Bailey, *Through Peasant Eyes*, 127.
105. Fitzmyer, *Luke X—XXIV*, 1176.

problem of the relation of the appended sayings to the Unjust Steward. Perhaps those who added the verses were "scandalized" by the implicit comparison of God with such a judge, as they were earlier by the action of the steward. Verse 6 simply calls attention to the action of the judge. Verses 7–8a compare the vindication of the widow to the eschatological vindication of the elect. Verse 8b asks whether the Son of man will find faith on the earth at the parousia.

I follow Fitzmyer in regarding the parable proper as vv. 2–6, even if Luke or an earlier editor has substituted "Lord" in v. 6 for "he" or "Jesus."[106] Though he argues that the inclusion of v. 6 makes the parable into one of "the dishonest judge" rather than of "the importunate widow," I contend that it is as much the "widow's story" as that of the judge. Verses 7–8a with their "imminent eschatology" are in tension with Luke's realization of the delay of the parousia and stem most likely from the same source used by Luke in 17:20–34. The final verse, which provides an inclusio to v. 1, is from the hand of Luke and represents his reinterpretation of eschatology. This short parable provides an excellent example of a text that reflects the three levels of the synoptic tradition: (a) Jesus; (b) the early church; (c) the evangelist, and the progressive reinterpretation of tradition.

In the Greek word order (in contrast to the RSV) the parable proper begins with the introduction of the judge (lit., a "certain [tis] judge there was in a certain city [tini]"). In contrast to the usual lack of moral evaluations in the parables, the judge is described as one "who neither feared God nor regarded man." Such a person is the direct opposite of the instructions given by Jehoshaphat to judges in 2 Chron. 19:5–6.[107]

> He appointed judges in the land . . . and said to the judges, "Consider what you do, for you judge not for man but for the Lord; he is with you in giving judgment. Now then, let the fear of the Lord be upon you; take heed what you do, for there is no perversion of justice with the Lord our God, or partiality, or taking bribes."

Both in the OT (Amos 2:6–7; 5:10–13) and in NT times, the venal or corrupt judge appears frequently.[108] As the rich man was blinded

106. Ibid.
107. I owe the reference to Bailey, *Through Peasant Eyes*, 131.
108. Bailey (ibid.) cites Edersheim (*The Life and Times of Jesus the Messiah*, 2:287) that the judges in Jerusalem were often called "robber judges."

by his wealth, this judge is blinded by his power; he has no fear of God and is not even moved by the cries of the poor which are heard by God (e.g., Pss. 69:33; 72:12; Prov. 22:22–23).

The next verse begins in direct parallel to the previous one: the Greek reads literally, "But a widow there was in that city" (18:3a). A stark and direct confrontation is set up. In the ancient Near East and throughout the OT and the NT the widow not only is a symbol of powerlessness but was de facto a victim of injustice and exploitation.[109] In imagining the world of this parable, we should also avoid thinking of the widow as aged and infirm. In a culture with short life spans where women married in their early teens, the "widow," as the subsequent narrative presumes, would most likely be young and vigorous. The second half of the verse (3b) then describes her action. She "kept coming" and saying, "Vindicate [ekdikēson, i.e., give me justice] me against my adversary." The shock of the parable comes here, not in the exploitation of widows, which was common, but in her public and persistent cry for justice. In the cultural context a woman would rarely, if at all, claim her rights by appearing constantly, and presumably alone, in public, raising a public outcry. She also refuses to resort to bribery—a common recourse in a situation such as hers. The woman speaks of an "adversary," who could be an in-law, her own son or a stepson by her husband's previous marriage. The Greek apo tou anti dikou suggests a male adversary. The issue is most likely a dispute over an inheritance or a dowry—that portion remaining after her husband's death.[110] The situation of the woman could be one of life and death; she is faced with poverty and starvation if her rights are not respected.

At this point the reader expects no easy solution to the woman's plight. A judge who does not fear God would not be expected to be moved by the OT exhortations on consideration of the widow. The woman's continual coming implies continual refusal, which is explicit in the next verse (4a): "for a while" (or better, "for a long time")

109. On God's concern for the widow and other powerless people (e.g., orphan and stranger in the land), see Exod. 22:21–23; Deut. 10:14–19, "He [the Lord] executes justice for the fatherless and the widow" (v. 18); Deut. 14:28–29; Jer. 49:11; Pss. 68:5; 146:9; on exploitation of the widow, Isa. 1:16–17; Ps. 94:1–7; Job 22:9–11; cf. Luke 20:46–47 = Mark 12:40 for polemic against scribes who devour the houses of widows.

110. Jeremias, Parables, 153; and Bailey, Through Peasant Eyes, 133–35.

he refused.[111] The change comes, as it frequently does in the parables, when the narrative moves to dialogue, in this case a soliloquy ("he said to himself"). Since this is our first inside look at the judge, we might wonder whether the characterization of v. 2 is fair. The answer comes quickly in the first words from his mouth; he unabashedly says that he does not fear God, nor regard other people (v. 4), but "because this widow is 'working me over' I will recognize her rights, so she doesn't give me a black eye by her unwillingness to give up" (v. 5, au. trans.).

The translation of 18:5 is difficult and disputed. I have tried to capture the rather earthy metaphors of the original. "Working me over" translates the Greek *to parechein moi kopon* (lit., "because she gives me labor or toil"). The RSV "bothers me" is too weak, and while Fitzmyer's "because this widow is a nuisance"[112] is stronger, it tends to minimize the seriousness of the struggle. My rendering is also influenced by the second consideration of the judge in v. 5b: *mē . . . hypōpiazē me* (RSV: "lest she will wear me out"). The verb *hypōpiazō*, translated as "wear me out," is a metaphor from boxing and literally means "strike a blow below the eye" or "blacken my eye," another shocking expression, since people in few cultures image women as boxers. Though it is used in the contemporary Greek for "blacken my reputation," there is no hint in the text that the judge is ever worried about his poor reputation. He seems rather to enjoy it. Finally, I have translated *eis telos erchomenē* (lit., "by her coming forever"; RSV: "by her continual coming") "by her unwillingness to give up."[113]

The original Greek better captures both the humor and the shock of the situation. A complacent and fearless judge is pummeled like a faltering boxer by a woman fighting for her rights. The action of the woman is as shocking as the running father and the compassionate Samaritan and is an instance of the power of the parable to orient by disorienting (Ricoeur).[114]

The parable concludes with a summons to attend to the dialogue of the unjust judge (v. 6). For those who hold that the parable in substance comes from Jesus, it is primarily an instance of the rabbinic

111. On translation of *epi chronon* as "for a long time" rather than "for a while," see Fitzmyer, *Luke X—XXIV*, 1179.
112. Ibid., 1175.
113. Bailey (*Through Peasant Eyes*, 136) notes that the woman will never give up. Manson (*Sayings*, 306) calls it "a war of attrition" (cited in Bailey, *Through Peasant Eyes*, 136).
114. See above, chap. 1, pp. 15–16.

mode of argument "from the lesser to the greater" (*qal waḥomer*). If such a judge will vindicate perseverance, how much more will God. Jeremias then locates it among those parables in which Jesus assures his disciples of vindication in the face of suffering and persecution.[115] Pheme Perkins treats it with those parables which "assure the righteous that God does hear, that suffering does not pass for nothing."[116] I suggest that the parable be seen under the aegis of the proclamation of the kingdom with its reversal of human expectations.

In both his parable and parabolic actions—fellowship with tax collectors and sinners and with other marginal groups—Jesus challenges the way people are to think of the reign or activity of God. This parable is rife with reversal and paradox. The widow, who from the OT evokes the image of the powerless and vulnerable victim of more powerful people, while here a subject of injustice, is hardly powerless and vulnerable. She shatters convention by going alone and directly confronting the judge; she is publicly persistent in demanding her rights, and the imagery from one of the more violent athletic contests (boxing) shatters the stereotype of the vulnerable widow. The hearers are confronted with a new vision of reality, inaugurated by God's reign, where victims will claim their rights and seek justice—often in an unsettling manner.

The Appended Sayings (18:7-8)

The first application (v. 7) then asks rhetorically, "Will not God vindicate [*ekdikēsin*] his elect, who cry to him day and night? Will he delay long [*makrothymei*] over them?" The response follows: "I tell you, he will vindicate them speedily [*en tachei*]." Generally interpreters apply the parable to the delay of the parousia and allegorically identify the judge with God and the widow with the community (the elect), anxious for vindication in the face of evil. Despite the delay (cf. vv. 4, 7), vindication is assured.[117] The final

---

115. Jeremias, *Parables*, 153–57.
116. Perkins, *Hearing*, 194–95.
117. Like the parable itself, these verses mask a host of problems. The major problem for interpreters is the punctuation and meaning of the phrase "Will he delay long over them?" The verb *makrothymei* can mean (1) wait patiently or (2) delay. Jeremias (*Parables*, 154–55) punctuates it differently and offers: "And will not God hasten to the help of his elect, even if he puts their patience to the test?" In an extensive treatment of the phrase, Bailey (*Through Peasant Eyes*, 137–40) argues that

verse takes us back to the introduction ("not lose heart") by asking whether the Son of man will find faith (*pistis*) at his coming. Luke evidently adapts the parable to the situation of his community, aware now of the delay of the parousia and undergoing *peirasmos* (trial or testing; cf. Luke 11:4). Only through prayer can fidelity (faith) be assured. By inserting the parable of the Widow and the Judge (18:2–7) between the exhortation to prayer (18:1) and an admonition to fidelity (18:8), Luke understands continual prayer not simply as passive waiting but as the active quest for justice..

The Friend at Midnight
(Luke 11:5–8)

The parable of the Unjust Judge has often been compared to the parable of the Friend at Midnight, since the latter is in a context of instruction on prayer and since the main characters in each do not give up in the face of opposition.[118] The Friend at Midnight appears in a collection of sayings (Luke 11:5–13) attached to Luke's version of the Lord's Prayer (11:1–4) and illustrates the attitude that should characterize Christian prayer.

The Parable as Text

On initial reading, the parable seems to be relatively simple. An unexpected visitor arrives in the middle of the night, and, according to the demands of hospitality, his friend must offer a meal. Caught unawares, he then goes to "his friend" who is fast asleep with his family in the one-room house and asks for three loaves of bread. The latter, obviously perturbed (11:7, "Do not bother me," the same Greek phrase found in Luke 18:5), initially refuses, since he does not want to rouse his sleeping family. The narrative does not recount the granting of the request but quickly shifts to an application that the sleeping man will answer the request not out of friendship but because of "his importunity."

---

makrothymei evokes the God of the covenant who is patient and slow to anger. It counters a desire of the elect for precipitous punishment of persecutors (cf. Luke 13:1–5) and says that God's slowness to anger is a period of grace which should evoke faith and patience (citing F. Horst, *TDNT* 4:381). See also Fitzmyer, *Luke X—XXIV*, 1180; and Marshall, *Luke*, 674–75.

118. Jeremias (*Parables*, 157) calls it a "doublet" of 18:1–8. See also Fitzmyer, *Luke X—XXIV*, 910.

Though the parable seems deceptively simple, there are major exegetical problems, the solutions to which determine the central thrust of the parable. Is it the parable of the "persistent friend," or is rather the main character the sleeping man who finally answers the request? The final verse (11:8), which the RSV translates "because of his importunity" (*anaideia*), could also be translated "because of his shameless persistence" (i.e., of the person knocking) or "because of his 'loss of face' " (i.e., the man in bed does not himself want to be shamed because he turned down the request of a friend).

The principal proponent that the main thrust is on the "friend who is roused from sleep" is Jeremias. His main evidence is the somewhat rhetorical question that introduces and dominates the parable (vv. 5–7). He translates it as follows:[119]

> Can you imagine that, if one of you had a friend who came to you at midnight and said to you, "My friend, lend me three loaves, because a friend has come to me on a journey and I have nothing to set before him," you would call out, "Don't disturb me . . ."? Can you imagine such a thing?

The expected answer to such a question would be, "Unthinkable, I can't imagine such a situation." The parable, then, like that of the unjust judge, proposes an argument "from the lesser to the greater," that is, if such a cranky human will answer a request, then how much more so will God.[120]

The Parable in Context

While this interpretation may have merit if the parable is read independently of its context, Luke shifts the emphasis to the "persistence" of the man seeking bread. The parable as a whole is interposed between a prayer of petition and a saying on the need for petition. The specific request for three loaves (11:5, *treis artous*) recalls the petition for "bread" (*arton*) from the Lord's Prayer (11:3). The following verses (vv. 9–13), taken from Q and added here by Luke, stress the need for "asking" and "knocking," a recollection of the petitioner's action in the parable. Finally, even the promise that the Father will give the Holy Spirit to those who ask, which concludes

119. Jeremias, *Parables*, 158.
120. This interpretation is also strongly defended by Bailey, *Poet*, 119–33.

the whole instruction of prayer of 11:1–13, is connected with the "persistence" of the man in the parable. This "persistence" (*anaideia*) has overtones of "shameless boldness." The Holy Spirit in both the Gospel (Luke 12:12) and Acts (4:8, 29–31) enables people to speak out boldly with confidence in the face of opposition (see also 2:29; 28:31; cf. John 14:26).

These two parables, one of which (11:5–8) Luke locates among the initial scenes of the travel narrative and the other (18:2–7) near its conclusion, depict in imaginative form distinctive attitudes that should characterize Christian prayer. It is to be bold and courageous whether arising out of the need to help a friend or to seek justice in the face of evil. Prayer is to be persistent in the face of opposition, without losing heart, and with the confidence that the Father will grant the Holy Spirit.

The Pharisee and the Tax Collector
(Luke 18:9–14)

The second scene in the "trial by prayer" of Luke 18 is the story of two men (*anthrōpoi duo*, a variation on Luke's usual generalized "someone, a certain person") who offer two different prayers with surprising results. As in the previous parable, its introductory verse (18:9) is also an application, and it concludes with a variation of the application "Those who exalt themselves will be humbled, but those who humble themselves will be exalted" (18:14b, au. trans.), a generalized aphorism found throughout the synoptic tradition (Luke 14:11; Matt. 23:12; cf. 18:4). The parable proper consists of the narrative of 18:10–14, with the short application of 14a, "This man went down to his house justified rather than the other."

The Parable as Text

Contemporary Christians read this parable with a distinct bias against the Pharisee, based more often on Matthew 23 than on Luke. The parable begins abruptly in a manner designed to shock the hearers. It is not surprising that two people go to the temple to pray, nor that one is a Pharisee; shocking is the presence of the tax collector. This was one of the occupations forbidden to Jews. Tax collectors were ritually impure through contact with Gentiles at forbidden times, generally thought to be dishonest, and hardly popular in a country suffering economic exploitation through widespread taxation.[121]

The Pharisee "stands"—the normal position for private prayer in Judaism and in early Christianity. The next phrase (18:11b, "and prayed thus with himself") is obscure, since commentators and the manuscript tradition differ whether *pros heauton* modifies "pray" and should be translated "prayed thus with himself" (RSV) or "about himself" (Fitzmyer), or whether it modifies "stood" and then would mean "he stood by himself" (Bailey) or "he took up a prominent position" and uttered this prayer (Jeremias).[122] In favor of "with himself" would be the connection with the soliloquy of the judge in the previous parable (18:4) and elsewhere (7:39; 12:17; 16:3; cf. 15:17). Bailey notes, however, that soliloquies always use *en heautō* ("within himself") and never *pros heauton*.[123] The significance of the debate transcends translation. When the phrase is translated as "with himself," the Pharisee utters a private prayer not heard by others, but when it is rendered as "stood by himself" (Jeremias and Bailey), a situation of public worship is envisioned where the Pharisee conspicuously steps apart from the other worshipers and utters a prayer heard by all. He thus accentuates his piety and humiliates the tax collector.

The prayer of the Pharisee has become for Christians a caricature of boasting or exalting oneself before God. The original hearers would not have been as appalled by its content. It is twofold: (*a*) a prayer of thanksgiving (*eucharistō*) to God for preservation from sin, and (*b*) an account of his fidelity in observing the fast and in giving tithes. Even the converted Pharisee Paul can "boast" of his piety and observance of the law and contrast them with others (Phil. 3:4–6; Gal. 1:14; 2:15, "not Gentile sinners"). Jeremias calls attention to a prayer from the Talmud:

> I thank thee, O Lord my God, that thou hast given me my lot with those who sit in the seat of learning, and not those who sit at the street-corners; for I am early to work, and they are early to work; I am early to work on the words of the Torah, and they are early to work on things of no moment. I weary myself and they weary themselves. I weary myself and profit thereby, while they weary themselves to no profit. I run and they run; I run towards the life of the Age to Come,

121. See above, n. 41.
122. Fitzmyer, *Luke X–XXIV*, 1186; Bailey, *Through Peasant Eyes*, 147–49; and Jeremias, *Parables*, 140.
123. *Through Peasant Eyes*, 148–49.

and they run towards the pit of destruction. (*Babylonian Talmud, b. Ber.* 28b)[124]

In one of the psalms from Qumran, we read:

> I praise thee, O Lord, that thou hast not allowed my lot to fall among the worthless community, nor assigned me a part in the circle of the secret ones. (1QH 7:34)[125]

To thank God for election and to speak of one's devotion do not of themselves make a prayer hypocritical or self-congratulatory.

As the parable unfolds, the Pharisee's prayer is rejected. This has been anticipated in the formulation of the prayer. Most striking is the concentration of verbs in the first person nominative: "I thank," "I am not like others," "I fast," "I tithe" from what "I possess." When it is the tax collector's turn to speak, he avoids the nominative but simply says, "Be merciful to me a sinner!" The Pharisee's language is of egocentric achievement; the tax collector hopes that he will be given God's mercy. Also the Pharisee explicitly contrasts his virtue with the tax collector, which the flow of the sentence accentuates. He states his fidelity to the Decalogue in a negative sense; he is not a "robber" (*harpax*; more accurate than the RSV: "extortioner"), an unjust person or an adulterer (cf. Exod. 20:14–15; Deut 5:17–19), "or even," he then adds, "like this tax-collector." The deprecatory pronoun (*houtos*, "this") could be paraphrased as "like this immoral and unclean tax collector." The images accentuate the contrast. The Pharisee steps apart from the assembled worshipers and virtually proclaims his virtue, while humiliating the tax collector. His virtue is as destructive of real community as was the wealth of the rich man. Perhaps this is why Luke earlier (16:14) called Pharisees "lovers of money."

The scene then shifts immediately to "this tax collector." In contrast to the Pharisee, whose posture is described only by one word ("he stood up") and whose prayer occupies considerable space, his physical position is accentuated and his prayer is very short. He is "standing far off," most likely ostracized by other worshipers because of his suspected ritual impurity. He is conscious of his sinfulness and will

---

124. As quoted in Jeremias, *Parables*, 142.
125. The translation is by Jeremias (ibid., n. 55). Vermes (*Dead Sea Scrolls*, 175) translates: "[I thank] Thee, O God, for Thou hast not cast my lot in the congregation of Vanity, nor hast Thou placed my portion in the council of the cunning."

not lift up his eyes to heaven (cf. *1 Enoch* 13:5, "They did not raise their eyes to heaven out of shame for the sins for which they had been condemned").[126] Finally "he beats his breast," which is attested to as a sign of compunction or contrition (Luke 23:48). His bodily gestures are themselves a prayer, so the words are simple: "God, be merciful to me a sinner!" He does not unroll a catalogue of sins, like the Pharisee's catalogue of virtues, nor does he compare himself with others. His hope is in God alone. Like the other powerless outsiders in Luke and the OT—the poor, the widow, the stranger in the land— he casts his lot with God.

The shock as well as the meaning of the parable comes with the somewhat solemn "I tell you"; "this one [*houtos*, repeating ironically the deprecatory pronoun of v. 11] went down to his house justified rather than the other" (au. trans.). This is the only use in the Gospels of "justified" (*dedikaiōmenos*) applied to an individual. Though some authors hear a "Pauline ring" here, the motif that one is accepted by God, not by one's own activity, that is, justified, pervades such Psalms as 51 and 24:3–5 in the OT (cf. *2 Esd.* 12:7).[127] The terminology of "justice" and "justification" is rooted in the language of the law court and supports our claim that we have in these two parables a "trial by prayer." The verdict rendered by the narrative is that the prayer of the tax collector is acceptable. The penalty is that those who exalt themselves will be humbled, while those who humble themselves will be exalted.

Though the parable now functions as part of a double instruction on prayer, when uttered by Jesus it coheres with his kingdom proclamation and praxis. The kingdom reverses normal standards of divine approval and how this approval is experienced. The Pharisee is a moral person who in fasting and tithing even goes beyond legal requirements. Yet, as with the older brother, his God exacts dutiful service, which isolates him from others. The tax collector simply asks forgiveness. The justice of God accepts the unjust and the ungodly and judges the virtuous. The paradox of the kingdom is supported by the paradox of the two protagonists. The widow who is expected to be weak and powerless is aggressive and courageous; she is described with metaphors from the boxing ring. The tax collector,

126. I owe this reference to Fitzmyer, *Luke X—XXIV*, 1188.
127. Ibid., 1185.

who represents a class who were aggressive and often even brutal, seems submissive and deferential. His gesture of striking the breast, which is not attested to in the OT, is, according to Bailey, more characteristic of women than men in a Near Eastern culture.[128] Just as in his practice Jesus shocked his culture by having women followers, so in his parables he shatters stereotypical sex roles and challenges all people to a deeper understanding of God's empowering and merciful love.

The Lukan Context

The immediate context is a dual illustration, made through a parable, on prayer, following the eschatological parenesis of 17:20–37. Though the return of Jesus will be sudden and threatening, the community is not to lose heart but to pray continually with the courage of the woman and the trust of the tax collector. In his two-volume work Luke shows a strong interest in prayer, as an overview of material peculiar to Luke indicates.[129]

All important moments in salvation history
are in the context of prayer

Gospel: People are praying when an angel appears to Zechariah (1:10). Jesus prays at his baptism (3:21–22). Jesus prays for those who crucify him (23:34). Jesus' final words are a prayer of trust in God (23:46 = Ps. 31:5). The Gospel ends with disciples returning to the temple to pray (24:51–52; cf. 1:10).

Acts: The post-resurrection community is gathered in prayer (1:14). Prayer precedes the choice of Matthias (1:24–25). The community is at prayer before the gift of the Spirit (2:1–4, cf. 4:31). "The seven" are chosen so that the twelve can devote themselves to prayer (6:1–7). In Luke's "missionary geography" of Acts 1:8, the gospel spreads from Jerusalem through Judea and Samaria to the ends of the earth. Each stage is marked by prayer: prayer before the conversion of Samaria (8:15, 22, 24); prayer before the conversion of Cornelius which is "the Pentecost of the Gentiles" (10:2–4, 9, 30–31; 11:5); prayer before the mission of Paul and Barnabas (13:1–3); and prayer before the appointment of presbyters (14:23). Paul thanks God in prayer when he arrives at Rome (28:15).

128. Bailey, *Through Peasant Eyes*, 153.
129. There is no attempt to be comprehensive here. The best survey is Trites, "The Prayer Motif in Luke-Acts," 168–86. See also Fitzmyer, *Luke I—IX*, 244–46.

*Prayer characterizes Jesus and other significant figures
in the Gospel and Acts*

Gospel: Elizabeth blesses Mary, and Mary offers a hymn of praise (1:46–
55). Zechariah utters a canticle of blessing (1:67–79). The angels praise God
(2:13). Simeon utters a prayer (2:28–32), and Anna is at prayer (2:37).
Mary/Zechariah and Anna/Simeon are also female/male parallels, here at
prayer. Jesus prays at his baptism (3:21–22) and after miracles retreats to
the wilderness for prayer (5:16). Disciples of John fast, as in Matthew and
Mark, but in Luke they also pray (5:33). Jesus prays all night before the
choice of the disciples (6:12)—a Lukan addition to Mark 3:13. Only in Luke
does Jesus pray before Peter's confession (9:18). Jesus prays before the
transfiguration, which occurs when he is at prayer (9:28–29; cf. baptism,
3:20–21). In twin parables, prayer is central (18:1–14; cf. 11:5–8). Luke's
eschatological discourse adds a saying on prayer (21:36). Jesus prays for
Simon that his faith does not fail (22:31–34), and it does not even though
he denies Jesus. Luke's additions to the agony at Gethsemane stress the
prayer of Jesus (22:44–45). Jesus prays that his Father forgive those who
crucify him (23:34), and the disciples on the way to Emmaus recognize him
when he blesses and breaks the bread (24:30–31).

Acts: The idealized picture of the early Christian community is one of
friendship and devotion to prayer (2:42). Disciples go to the temple at the
hour of prayer (3:1). Stephen, the first "witness," prays for his enemies in
words similar to those of Jesus before his death (7:59–60). Paul is at prayer
after his conversion (9:11). While Peter is in prison, the community is at
prayer (12:5). Prior to the conversion of Lydia, Paul meets the women at
the place of prayer (16:13). Paul prays during his final meeting with the
Ephesian elders (20:36). Paul prays before leaving Tyre (21:5). Paul takes
bread, blesses it, and breaks it (27:35). Paul prays before laying hands on
the father of Publius, who is then healed (28:8).

Luke offers examples of different kinds of prayer

There is thanksgiving (e.g., 1:46–55; 2:29–32; 10:21–22); praise (e.g.,
1:67–79; 2:13–14, 20); petition and intercession (esp. 11:1–4) for a variety
of needs—for daily sustenance and help in the time of trial (11:3, 4), for
boldness (*parrēsia*) in speaking the word of God (Acts 4:29–30), and for
Peter's release from prison (Acts 12:5–12). Especially strong in Luke is prayer
for enemies (6:27 = Matt. 5:44, but Luke adds 6:35 where Luke says that
love of enemies will make one a child of the Most High [cf. Luke 23:34;
Acts 7:60]).

Prayer has a manifold importance for Luke. It opens human beings
to communion with God, and God becomes present at moments of

prayer. Through prayer, Christians, to use Pauline language, take on the mind of Christ (Phil. 2:5). As Jesus prepares for important moments in following God's will, so too must the pilgrim community as it makes its way to the end of the earth. The early church is characterized by *koinōnia* (communal life) expressed in the breaking of the bread, in prayer, and in concern for the poor in the community (Acts 2:42–47; cf. 4:32–37).

The beginning and the end of the special material of Luke's travel narrative are marked by groups of parables (the Good Samaritan/ Martha and Mary; the Friend at Midnight; the Unjust Judge/the Pharisee and the Tax Collector) in which prayer is central and which therefore anchor Jesus' teaching on "the way" of Christian discipleship as he himself makes his "way" to Jerusalem. These parables, which shock the sensibilities of the hearers, open them to a new understanding of the way of discipleship. It comprises compassionate entry into the world of the suffering neighbor, along with the rhythm of listening to the word and quiet presence before God, just as a similar rhythm characterized Jesus and the early church. Prayer, however, does not lead to passive acquiescence to evil. Under persecution the early community pray for "boldness"; their prayer is answered and they confront brutal power. The exhortation "always to pray and not lose heart" (18:1) is illustrated by the story of a widow who aggressively seeks justice.

Luke's theology is especially pertinent for an issue that concerns many Christians today: the relation between specifically religious activity—meditation on Scripture, prayer, and worship—and individual or social action on behalf of the suffering neighbor. At times these are polarized between "liberals" who identify religion with "the doing of works of justice and charity" and "conservatives" who stress that religion is to lead us beyond this earth to the transcendent God. The Gospel of Luke counters such facile polarization by juxtaposing the Samaritan who fulfills the law by showing mercy in concrete deed with Mary who listens to the word, and by placing together a widow who raises her voice in protest against injustice with a tax collector who quietly asks for God's mercy. For Luke, listening to the word of God, prayer for forgiveness, and concern for alleviating suffering and injustice are wedded inseparably, and no human being should put them asunder.

5

THE
GOSPEL
IN
PARABLE

In examining major parables of the Synoptic Gospels as texts in context, I have attempted to show how the parables simultaneously influence and reflect the major theological motifs of the individual Gospels. Now I would like to draw some of the diverse threads together and offer brief suggestions on contemporary proclamation of the gospel in parable.

THE GOSPEL OF MARK:
CHRISTOLOGY AND DISCIPLESHIP
IN PARABLE

One of the more intriguing questions in Gospel research is the origin of the narrative form "gospel." While there is a growing admission that Mark creates the form, there is little consensus on what models he followed (e.g., OT historical narrative; aretalogies, i.e., stories of the mighty deeds of heroic figures; Hellenistic biography).[1] In a short and challenging study Paul Ricoeur has argued for a continuity of form and internal dynamism between the parables of Jesus, the proclamation (*kerygma*) of his death and resurrection, and the narrative form of gospel.[2] Ricoeur agrees with Ernst Käsemann and Norman Perrin that the parables put us in touch not only

1. See esp. Kee, *Community of the New Age*, 14–49; Kelber, *Oral and Written Gospel*, 117–29; and Talbert, *What Is a Gospel?*, 1–23.
2. Ricoeur, "From Proclamation to Narrative," esp. 510–12.

with the teaching of Jesus about the kingdom but with the self-understanding of Jesus as he proclaims the kingdom. They offer a paradoxical vision where expectations are overturned and simple beginnings have great endings. When the early community proclaims the paradox of the cross and when Mark puts this proclamation into narrative form, the gospel itself becomes parabolic. The narrative parables told *by* Jesus provide the model for the narrative dynamics of the story *about* Jesus. Mark not only contains the parables of Jesus; it is a "written parable."[3] Three central features of the parables characterize also Mark's narrative of Jesus' ministry: *(a)* realism, *(b)* paradox and wonder, and *(c)* a challenge to freedom.[4]

Realism

The realism of Mark emerges in a number of ways. Though the shortest of the Synoptics, in narratives common to the three, especially in the miracle stories, Mark is generally longer, with a wealth of realistic detail such as the violent condition of the Gerasene demoniac (Mark 5:4–6), details of the illness of the woman who touched Jesus' garment (5:25–26), and the spontaneous reaction of the man healed of blindness (10:50–51). Mark depicts Jesus with strong emotions: pity (1:41), violent displeasure (1:43), anger (3:5), indignation (10:14), groanings and deep sighs (1:43; 8:12), surprise at unbelief (6:6), and love (10:21)—all of which Matthew and Luke omit in retelling the same stories. There are also places where Jesus shows ignorance—for example, about who touched him (5:30–32) or of what the disciples were discussing (9:33), also altered by Matthew and Luke. Matthew and Luke also omit the statement by Jesus' relatives that he is "out of his mind" (Mark 3:21, au. trans.).

In contrast to Matthew and Luke, a sober realism permeates the passion narrative. Where Matthew and Luke simply say that Jesus prayed in Gethsemane (Matt. 26:39; Luke 22:41), Mark writes that Jesus prayed "that, if it were possible, the hour might pass from him" (Mark 14:35). While Luke omits some of the more brutal

---

3. For this description of Mark, see Kelber, *Oral and Written Gospel*, 117.
4. I have developed Mark's parabolic quality in more detail in "Jesus as the Parable of God." See also the interesting study by Williams, *Gospel against Parable*. Williams integrates recent study of Mark and contemporary literary theory in an extensive study of mystery and parable in Mark. I did not encounter his work in time to incorporate his insights into the present work.

aspects of the passion such as the scourging (Mark 15:15) and the mocking by the soldiers (Mark 15:16–20), Matthew, though retaining these, stresses the "lordly" aspects of Jesus in the passion. Jesus can command more than twelve legions of angels (Matt. 26:53), and his innocence is revealed in a dream—which tells the readers that God is near to Jesus, even during his suffering (Matt. 27:19; cf. 2:19). In Mark the passion of Jesus is the radical emptiness of one who dies as a slave.

The realism that characterizes the parables of Jesus influences Mark's picture of Jesus, the parable giver. As Vincent Taylor has remarked, "The sheer humanity of the Markan portraiture catches the eye of the most careless reader."[5] In Mark the way to God is not through any docetic circumvention of the human Jesus. In the case of Jesus himself, no less than in the parables he utters, the scandal of the human is the starting point for the unfolding mystery of God.

Paradox and Wonder

Long recognized as the most realistic of the Gospels, Mark is also a "mysterious Gospel." Throughout the Gospel the actions of Jesus evoke reactions of wonder, surprise, and awe. Jesus' first mighty work engages the audience who "were all amazed, so that they questioned among themselves, saying, 'What is this?' " (1:27).[6] The teaching of Jesus likewise causes astonishment (6:2; 10:26; 11:18) and amazement (10:24; 12:17). The Gospel echoes with questions about the nature and identity of Jesus (1:27; 2:7; 4:41, "Who then is this?"; 5:7; 6:2; 8:27, 29; 11:28). Mark's theology of fear and wonder emerges especially in the resurrection account (16:5, 8) and in the jarring ending of the Gospel, "They were afraid" (16:8). This motif, which throughout the Gospel establishes rapport with the readers and dictates how they should respond to Jesus, now becomes a symbolic reaction to the Gospel as a whole. Mark's readers are left not even with the assurance of a resurrection vision but simply with numinous fear in the face of a divine promise. These reactions of wonder and surprise accompany the revelation of God in Jesus, and

---

5. Taylor, *St. Mark,* 121.
6. This is a standard reaction to miracle stories; cf. Mark 2:12; 4:41; 5:15, 20, 33, 42; 6:50, 51; 7:37.

they signify the power of this revelation to unsettle and challenge human existence. At the same time, this wonder is fascinating and attracting; it invites people to confront mystery. Such motifs call for a parabolic reading of Mark; for an approach to Mark's Jesus with a sense of wonder, awe, and holy fear; for an openness to the extraordinary in the midst of the ordinary; for a suspension of belief that faith may occur.

Mark communicates vividness and strangeness by the use of irony and paradox, understood as language or situations that express a meaning opposite to that intended, or seeming contradictions that conceal a deeper truth. Mark's picture of Jesus is both ironic and paradoxical. The day of the Lord's rest becomes, through Jesus, the day of the Lord's labor (2:27—3:5). Clean is declared unclean (7:1–23); children who do not even yet bear the yoke of the kingdom (the law) are to enter God's kingdom (10:13–16). The one who wishes to rule must become the lackey; the last will be first (10:42–45). The chosen disciples are blind (8:18); and the blind become disciples (10:52). Jesus is mocked as a false prophet at the very moment when his prophecy of Peter's denial is being fulfilled (14:65, 72). Pilate and the bystanders mockingly call him king (15:2, 32), while the centurion expresses the true meaning of his kingship (15:39). The women and Joseph take great pains to bury him whom no tomb will hold (15:42–43; 16:6). Women, who in the culture of the time could not be legal witnesses, are the first witnesses to the message of the resurrection (16:1–8). Mark's Gospel challenges the readers to have their preconceptions shattered and to engage Jesus himself as "the mystery of the kingdom of God" (4:11). Like the parables themselves, the Gospel as a whole presents a world where the familiar is put askew and where our normal way of viewing life is challenged so that we can be open to the newness of God's gift.

A Challenge to Freedom

Mark's Gospel has a distinct open-ended quality, most clearly evident from its two rewritings by Matthew and Luke. Just as the parable functions as an event of revelation when the hearers freely enter its world, and appropriate its challenge, the Gospel of Mark as both realistic and paradoxical is also inviting and open-ended. The

often discussed Messianic Secret, that series of texts in which Jesus
counsels silence or forbids people to reveal who he is, creates suspense
about his identity, which is resolved only by the centurion's confession.[7] The understanding of titles for Jesus that are used early in the
Gospel, such as Son of God (1:1, 11) and Son of man (2:10, 28), is
refined and revised as the Gospel unfolds.[8] The figure who is addressed
directly by God (1:11; 9:7) and whose mighty works disclose God's
power (e.g., 1:24; 5:7) dies powerless and seems to be abandoned
by God (15:26–39).

The disciples move from spontaneous response (1:18, "immediately
they . . . followed") through fearful uncertainty (4:41; 6:50) and
misunderstanding (8:18, 32; 9:32) to flight and denial (14:50, 66–
72). Readers must then ask themselves what it means to follow Jesus
and whether they will be caught up in the same fate as the disciples.
Mark recounts predictions in the Gospel that are fulfilled (8:31;
9:31; 10:32), but the narrative is silent on other important predictions—for example, that Jesus will baptize in the Spirit (1:8), that
the community will undergo persecution and betrayal (13:9–13),
and that Jesus will meet his disciples in Galilee (14:28; cf. 16:7).
Readers are challenged to see how they are fulfilled in their lives.
Like the parables, then, the Gospel invites its readers into its world;
its summons to conversion and its offer of grace are also a challenge
to freedom.

With justification, then, Mark can be called a "parabolic narrative"
and the Jesus of Mark "a parable of God." The parable form uttered
by Jesus became the form par excellence for discourse about Jesus.
Parabolic narrative is a caution against absolutizing the Gospel itself.
Like the parables, the Gospel points beyond itself to the ultimate
mystery of the divine-human encounter; not even the picture of
Jesus in Mark exhausts this encounter; like the parables, the Gospel
must be adapted to new situations. Precisely this happens when both
the parables of Jesus and the parabolic Gospel are rewritten and
transformed by Matthew and Luke. Though their rewritings take
different directions, Matthew and Luke compose by "inclusive rein-

7. The literature on the Messianic Secret is immense; see above, chap. 2, n. 28.
8. See Perrin, A Modern Pilgrimage, chap. 4, "The Creative Use of the Son of Man
Traditions by Mark," and chap. 8, "The Christology of Mark: A Study in Methodology."

terpretation," taking over virtually all of Mark. They also supplement Mark's parables with extensive parables from their own traditions. Nonetheless, these Gospels too remain parabolic, but like their parables, offer a distinct appropriation of parabolic language.

ESCHATOLOGY, ETHICS, AND THE
GOOD NEWS OF THE KINGDOM:
MATTHEW'S GOSPEL IN PARABLE

Though Mark has been at the center of study of the Synoptic Gospels in recent decades, for the bulk of church history Matthew has been the Gospel for church life and teaching. Christians have been nurtured on Matthew's version of the Lord's Prayer and the Beatitudes; the Sermon on the Mount has been called the Magna Charta of Christian life.[9] Even the much maligned "fire and brimstone" preaching draws its imagery almost exclusively from Matthew. Matthew's well-organized collection of the sayings and deeds of Jesus fitted the Gospel for catechetical use. Its concern for observance of the law, its stress on proper teaching, its attention to community order, and even its warnings against the misuse of authority make Matthew a natural focus for NT ecclesiology. It is the only Gospel that calls the community an *ekklēsia* (16:18; 18:17).

Matthew is a more complex literary phenomenon than Mark and reflects a social setting equally more complex. The traditions that Matthew appropriates often stand in tension within the Gospel itself. It contains some of the most anti-Jewish statements in the NT (e.g., 23:2–36; 27:25) while being the most Jewish in tone and content—evident in Matthew's extensive quotation of the OT and his affirmation of the validity of the law (5:17–20). He incorporates the traditions of that radical wing of Christianity, the wandering charismatics who preserved and observed Jesus' sayings on homelessness, radical poverty, and the imminent end.[10] At the same time, Matthew is concerned with Christians of less radical disposition, those "of little faith," and is aware that a community must have structures of reconciliation. Divisions in the community may arise, not simply

---

9. See the discussion in R. Brown, *The Churches the Apostles Left Behind*, esp. 124–25.
10. Theissen, *Sociology of Early Palestinian Christianity*, esp. 7–16.

from different theological understandings of Jesus but from differences in cultural and social status.[11] Whereas Mark presents a radically egalitarian view of authority in the community, Matthew, while not abandoning an egalitarian ideal (23:8–11), is aware of different levels of authority and different responsibilities (16:18–20; 18:15–20).[12] Matthew, like Mark, is concerned about external persecution, but the situation seems more complex with opposition from both Gentiles and Jewish groups with whom he is engaged in a struggle over a common heritage.

Matthew's collection of parables, as I noted earlier, is more extensive than Mark's, since he supplements Mark with Q parables and those from his special source, M, or of his own composition. Matthew's parables are also more ornate, heavily allegorical, and concerned with the disclosure of good and evil at the final judgment. The literary style and the theological thrust of the parables are reflected in the Gospel itself. Matthew's "book of origins" (1:1) speaks in elaborate detail of the birth of Jesus, and Jesus' death is accompanied by apocalyptic signs (27:51–54, the earthquake and the opening of the tombs). Matthew's parables, as we saw in detail, are dramatic parables in which human beings determine their fate in response to surprising opportunities (e.g., the remission of a debt; unexpected hiring and payment; a gift of talents).

Eschatology and Ethics

Matthew's parables are heavily ethical, concerned with human decisions and their consequences, but an ethics that is eschatologically determined. Only at the end time will the good and the evil be separated and will the nature of true goodness be disclosed. Christians are to look to this end, to live in the light of its disclosure of true reality, but to act responsibly in the world prior to the end. Matthew presents an ethics qualified by eschatology which is in service of leadership and ministry in the community.

The structure of Matthew supports this union of ethics and eschatology. Jesus speaks in five major discourses which culminate

11. On understanding the development and structure of Matthew's community I follow Kingsbury, *Matthew*, 78–106; and R. Brown and Meier, *Antioch and Rome*, 45–72.

12. On Mark's egalitarian understanding of community, see Donahue, *Theology and Setting of Discipleship*, 42–46; and Schüssler Fiorenza, *In Memory of Her*, 316–23.

in a long eschatological discourse. The vast majority of Matthew's parables fall in these discourses, with the exception of the Laborers in the Vineyard (20:1–16), the Two Sons (21:28–32), the Wicked Tenants (21:33–45), and the Marriage Feast (22:1–14). These five discourses serve in a special way to instruct the disciples, who are the sole audience of chapters 10, 18, and 24—25. In chapters 5—7, the Sermon on the Mount, though the crowds are present (5:1; cf. 7:28), Jesus addresses the discourse primarily to the disciples. The first major section (vv. 1–35) of chapter 13 is to the crowd, but the disciples are the sole audience in the second half (vv. 36–52).

The picture of discipleship in Matthew is more nuanced than in Mark. Whereas Mark stresses "following," Matthew (building on the literal meaning of *mathētai*, "learners") stresses Jesus as teacher and the disciples as learners, "little ones" to whom Jesus reveals the mysteries of God (11:25–30). The Twelve are not portrayed in as negative a light as in Mark; Peter, though he will deny the Lord, is also the one whom Jesus assists when he is weak (14:28–32; 17:24–27), and he promises Peter a special role among the Twelve (16:13–19). Unlike Mark, which contains only a promise of the resurrection, Matthew recounts an appearance to the disciples (28:16–20). Though in Mark the contrast between belief and unbelief and between following or denying Jesus is stark, with little middle ground, Matthew knows those "of little faith" and is concerned with the weak in the community. The disciples and especially the Twelve in Matthew seem to be more typological, standing for leaders in the Matthean community (see 23:1–12).[13]

The dramatic parables offer a consistent defense of the lowly and vulnerable in the community; the oppressed debtor is vindicated; the eleventh hour workers receive equal pay; uninvited guests feast at the marriage banquet; the wandering sheep (= weak Christian) becomes an object of special concern; and ultimately Jesus is hidden in the "least of his brothers and sisters." The parables also take up the world of those in authority. A king remits an unpayable debt and punishes a person who does not do to others as was done to him; a vineyard owner gives equal reward for unequal work; returning masters punish abusive stewards, and departing masters

13. A strong advocate of this view is Zumstein, *La condition du croyant dans l'Evangile selon Matthieu.*

freely distribute large sums of money. The parables likewise contain vivid warnings about the misuse of authority or gifts. Unfaithful tenants are destroyed; those who receive the vineyard must produce fruit; and unprepared guests and presumptuous maidens find the door of the wedding feast closed to them. Irresponsible stewards and timid guardians of a trust are cast into outer darkness. Neglect of the least brings eternal exclusion.

As we move from image to ethic we see a Jesus who commissions his disciples to make disciples by "teaching them to observe all that I have commanded you" (28:20). Matthew's Gospel in parable remains a caution against interpreting this legacy in a too legalistic or imperious fashion. To observe what Jesus has commanded is to enter the world of Matthew's parables and to risk identification with both the good and the bad (Matt. 5:45). As imaginative constructs rather than literal examples the parables paradoxically allow their readers an "ethical holiday" where they can identify with characters and attitudes that would be destructive in real life. Ordinary Christians can confront their own unwillingness to forgive and murmur with those who have worked throughout the day. When church leaders live through the pitfalls and experience the dire warnings of misuse of authority in the parables, they can be moved by the warnings about the pomp and pretensions of authority in Matt. 23:1–7. The shattering "but you" of 23:8–12 summons them to a style of life marked by service rather than by the trappings of power. Those Christian leaders who neglect the weak and the marginal, when entering the parables, find themselves confronted by a God who seeks out and protects such people. Those who claim special authority in the name of Jesus and boast of mighty works may be shocked to find that the true disciple is hungry, homeless, and imprisoned.

Though drawing on a ready store of apocalyptic images, Matthew's parables are not subservient to apocalyptic speculation about the end time. Matthew uses the pictures of judgment to give a view of history in reverse—from history's end to the present, with the emphasis on how people are to live in the present. Nor does Matthew use apocalyptic allegory, as found frequently in other apocalyptic writings, simply to offer the elect images of their own vindication and the punishment of their persecutors.[14] Matthew turns apocalyptic escha-

---

14. One of the acknowledged characteristics of apocalyptic literature is that it is

tology on its head by telling the elect that when the ultimate separation of good and bad takes place, they may be the outsiders. Election is a gift; it is also a challenge.

The Good News of the Kingdom

Matthew's ethics is not, however, simply a collection of parabolic exhortations or warnings. In Jesus, the parable giver, God has drawn near to humanity; he is "God with us" (1:23; 18:20; 28:20). Matthew stresses also the nearness of the heavenly Father who knows the needs of the community (6:25–33) and gives "good things to those who ask" (7:10). In Matthew's ethical vision those who respond to the gospel are called members of God's family. The peacemakers will be sons and daughters of God (5:9), as will be those who pray for their persecutors (5:44–45).

Just as the members of the community are to speak to each other in the language of familial unity (23:8–9), Matthew stresses the close bond between Jesus and the disciples. In a significant addition to a traditional saying that "a disciple is not above his teacher, nor a servant above his master" (10:24; cf. Luke 6:40; John 13:16; 15:20), Matthew adds: "It is enough for the disciple to be like his teacher, and the servant like his master" (10:25). The context is encouragement in the face of persecution, with the assurance that the fate of Jesus and that of the disciple are closely aligned. In a narrative rich with typological overtones of the church battered by persecution, Jesus hears the prayer of the disciples who are about to be submerged by the waves (8:23–27).[15] He later promises his heavily burdened disciples "rest for your souls" (11:28–30). Parables such as the Unmerciful Servant and the Laborers in the Vineyard image a God who summons people to live out of experienced graciousness. Matthew's ethics proceeds out of a gracious response to the mercy and love of God made present in the life and teaching of Jesus. This life and teaching is to be proclaimed by Christian missionaries to all nations through a gospel rich in parables.

"persecution literature." Often those persecuted are heartened by the vivid descriptions of the punishment of persecutors (e.g., Rev. 18:1–20). See A. Y. Collins, "Persecution and Vengeance in the Book of Revelation," 729–49. The same attitude permeates *1 Enoch* 92–105. See Nickelsburg, "The Apocalyptic Message of 1 Enoch 92–105"; idem, "Riches, the Rich, and God's Judgment."

15. Bornkamm, "The Stilling of the Storm in Matthew," in *Tradition and Interpretation in Matthew*, 52–57.

PARABLES AND PARADIGMS FOR A
COMMUNITY IN MISSION:
LUKE'S GOSPEL IN PARABLE

The world of Luke's parables is very different from that of Mark and Matthew (see above, pp. 29–30, 63). Luke's parables are more realistic and more dramatic. The vivid images of the final judgment found in Matthew are absent. A more varied cast of characters move on Luke's stage. Soliloquies invite readers to enter the world of these characters. We have also seen that Luke contains a great number of "example stories" or "paradigmatic narratives" which provide models for "the way" of Christian discipleship. The parables of Luke are in harmony with major theological directions of the Gospel as a whole.[16] Without attempting to be exhaustive, I call attention to three aspects: (a) Luke's shift in eschatology, (b) the summons to conversion in Luke's thought, and (c) the importance of "witness" (martyria) to Luke's understanding of the Christian life.

The Shift in Eschatology

The eschatology of Luke has been called "the most difficult and most controverted aspect of Lucan theology today."[17] Many scholars have followed Hans Conzelmann's position that Luke "has definitely abandoned belief in the early expectation of the end time."[18] The evidence for this is impressive. Luke omits Mark 1:15, "The kingdom of God is at hand," and substitutes a generalized statement about the teaching of Jesus and his being praised in all the synagogues (4:14–15). Luke alters what may be one of the most difficult eschatological sayings of the synoptic tradition (Mark 9:1): "There are some standing here who will not taste death before they see that the kingdom of God has come with power" (cf. Matt. 16:28, "before they see the Son of man coming in his kingdom"). In his rewriting, Luke omits any reference to "coming," substituting "who will not taste death before they see the kingdom of God" (9:27), thus making it into a generalized statement about the death of a Christian. In his introduction to the parable of the Pounds (= talents in Matthew),

16. See below, n. 36, on surveys of Luke.
17. Fitzmyer, Luke I—IX, 231. My discussion follows Fitzmyer closely.
18. Conzelmann, St. Luke, 135.

Luke explicitly rejects those who would join Jesus' imminent death in Jerusalem to the coming of the kingdom, by directing the parable to those who "supposed that the kingdom of God was to appear immediately" (19:11) and by inserting a short statement that the nobleman went to a far country, which evokes the continued absence of Jesus. Luke lacks Matthew's more threatening images of the future judgment—outer darkness, weeping and gnashing of teeth. Judgment occurs at death (12:20; 16:22–23), and Jesus promises the criminal, "Today you will be with me in Paradise" (23:43). By his addition of a second volume (the Acts of the Apostles) to the Gospel, Luke portrays a church that is adapting to life in the world, under the guidance of the Spirit, as it makes its way to the end of the earth (Acts 1:8).

While Conzelmann has undoubtedly described an important aspect of Luke's theology, his position is a bit one-sided. As Joseph A. Fitzmyer carefully details, Luke retains a good deal of material, especially from Q, which implies an eschatological crisis inaugurated by the coming of Jesus.[19] John the Baptist threatens imminent judgment (3:7–12), and in the mission charge the disciples (only in Luke 10:9, 11) are to announce, "The kingdom of God has come near to you." Only in Luke does the parable of the Fig Tree conclude with the warning "Realize that the kingdom of God is near" (21:31; cf. Mark 13:29). The instructions of Jesus on reading the signs of the times (Luke 12:49–56) have an eschatological urgency equal to any sayings of the Gospels, as does the portrait of the day of the Son of man in Luke 17:22–37.

Following Fitzmyer, I argue that the mixed eschatological posture of Luke is not due simply to a crisis over the delay of the parousia, nor does it reflect the emergence of an "early Catholicism" which substituted timeless truth for eschatological urgency. Rather, Luke wanted to shift the locus of the saving event from the eschaton, the end time, to the *sēmeron*, the "every day" of Christian life. For Luke, eschatological existence means *daily realization* of the crisis brought to human history by the life and teaching of Jesus rather than preoccupation with the end of history.

Unlike Matthew, Luke does not begin with a long genealogy but

19. Fitzmyer, *Luke I—IX*, 233–35; see also Kümmel, "Current Theological Accusations."

after a short preface (1:1–4) plunges us immediately into God's intervention into ordinary human existence. The infancy narratives (1:5—2:52) offer vignettes of different ways in which people's lives are touched by the Christ event (Elizabeth, Zechariah, Mary, Joseph, the shepherds, Simeon, Anna), and the angels announce that "today is born a savior" (2:11, au. trans.). After the prologue to the public ministry of Jesus (3:1—4:21), Jesus begins his inaugural sermon with a proclamation from Isa. 61:1–2; 58:6 that he has come to proclaim good news to the poor and release to the captives and that "today" this scripture has been fulfilled in your hearing (Luke 4:16–22). The initial chapters of Luke stress the presence of salvation in Jesus. At the risk of oversimplification, I suggest that while Mark places the saving event primarily in the cross and resurrection of Jesus, and Matthew in the cross, resurrection, and return of Jesus, Luke stresses the incarnation. For him, salvation begins with the coming of Christ and his life provides an example of the way to God.

Frequent use of the word "today" or "daily" throughout the Gospel is a literary device to convey this perspective. Those who witness Jesus' mighty works proclaim that they "have seen strange things today" (5:26). In a narrative that is a paradigm of Christian conversion, Jesus announces that he will come to Zacchaeus's house "today," and after Zacchaeus announces his plans for almsgiving and restitution of injustice, Jesus says, "Today salvation has come to this house" (Luke 19:5, 9). Jesus responds to the "fox," Herod, that he casts out demons and cures "today and tomorrow" (13:32). Luke reinforces the immediacy with which salvation touches daily life by altering sayings from the tradition. Those who would follow Jesus must take up their crosses "daily" (9:23; cf. Mark 8:34), and in Luke's version of the Lord's Prayer the petitioner is to ask, "Give us each day our daily bread" (11:3).

The parables of Luke reflect this perspective. With an earthy realism they depict the everyday lives of ordinary people which become the place where life is lost or gained. Luke's parables give examples of the challenges and demands of Christian existence and invite their hearers to see their lives reflected there. Luke writes the most elegant Greek of the evangelists and is most influenced by Hellenistic literary conventions. His presentation of the gospel in parable reflects such a milieu. In Hellenistic education and rhetoric, teaching by example occupies a central place.[20] Luke's narrative parables, along with the stories of the first Christian missionaries and their communities in Acts, may be the earliest example of a Christian *paideia*, instruction through example of the fundamental values which inform Christian life.

The Summons to Conversion

Mark (1:15) and Matthew (4:17) begin Jesus' public ministry with a call for "change of heart" (*metanoia*, or repentance). Although Luke omits this call, not only does he use the technical language of conversion more extensively (*metanoia* and *epistrophē*, lit., "turning toward" in the religious sense of turning to God or to the Lord) but also conversion is a central motif in his theology.[21] The mandate given to the disciples by the risen Jesus in Luke 24:44–49, like Matthew's Great Commission (Matt. 28:16–20), picks up key themes of the Gospel and reveals Luke's understanding of the post-resurrection mission of the church. The disciples are to be witnesses of the cross and resurrection of Jesus, and repentance (*metanoia)* and the forgiveness of sins are to be preached in Christ's name to all the nations.

This commission takes the readers back to the angel's proclamation of the mission of John "to turn many of the children of Israel to the Lord their God" (1:16, au. trans.) and "to turn . . . the disobedient

20. See esp. Marrou, *A History of Education in Antiquity*, 160–70, 235, 277–81. Kennedy (*New Testament Interpretation through Rhetorical Criticism*, 16) notes the similarity of Jesus' parables to examples used in Hellenistic rhetoric.

21. In **Mark** the noun is found only once (1:4, John's baptism of "repentance") and the verb twice (1:15; 6:12). In **Matthew** the noun appears twice (3:8, 11, describing the preaching of John) and the verb appears five times (3:2; 4:17; 11:20–21; 12:41); only in 4:17 does Jesus summon anyone to repent; 3:2 contains John's proclamation; 11:20 is a comment by the narrator; 11:21 refers to Tyre and Sidon which would have repented had they seen the mighty works done in Chorazin and Bethsaida; 12:41 refers to the repentance of Nineveh at the preaching of Jonah. In the **Lukan** writings the noun appears five times in the Gospel (3:3, 8; 5:32; 15:7; 24:47) and six times in Acts (5:31; 11:18; 13:24; 19:4; 20:21; 26:20). The verb appears nine times in the Gospel (10:13; 11:32; 13:3, 5; 15:7, 10; 16:30; 17:3, 4) and five times in Acts (2:38; 3:19; 8:22; 17:30; 26:20). *Epistrephō/epistrophē* in a religious sense appears in Luke 1:16–17; 17:4; 22:32; Acts 3:19; 9:35; 11:21; 14:15; 15:19; 26:18–20; 28:27 (citing Isa. 6:9–10). See Fitzmyer, *Luke I—IX*, 237–38. For a fine study of conversion in the NT with emphasis on Acts, see Gaventa, *From Darkness to Light*.

to the wisdom of the just" (1:17). Later Zechariah will prophesy that the visitation of the "Lord God of Israel" will bring about knowledge of salvation and the forgiveness of sin through the tender mercy of our God (1:77–78), and the public ministry of Jesus is prefaced by John's call for conversion (3:1–16). The post-resurrectional Lukan commission also looks forward to Acts. After the promise is fulfilled and they are filled with the power from on high (24:49; cf. Acts 2:1–4), the original disciples, and Paul after his own conversion, conclude their missionary sermons with a call for conversion (Acts 2:38–41; 3:19–20; 14:15; 17:30; 26:20). In confrontation with opponents they repeat this commission (5:31; 8:22), and the conversion of numbers of people is a sign of the Spirit-directed spread of the church (Acts 2:41–42; 11:21–26; 15:19). For Luke, conversion is one of the signs of the church.

Luke's theology of conversion is epitomized in the defense speech of Paul before Agrippa (Acts 26:2–24). Paul describes the effect of his own conversion as a mission from "the Lord" to open the eyes of the Gentiles, "that they may turn from darkness to light and from the power of Satan to God, that they may receive forgiveness of sins and a place among those who are sanctified by faith in me" (Acts 26:18). Conversion, for Luke, involves a prior act where God offers forgiveness in Jesus. The response in faith involves a new way of living and a new view of the world. As Beverly Gaventa notes, conversion in the NT "requires a life of obedience."[22]

It is here that I suggest a connection with Luke's Gospel in parable. Through the parables the Lukan converts are invited to enter a world ruled now by grace in which the consequences of a graced life unfold. Through the "tragic" parables the Christian community can also experience the consequences of a halfhearted conversion. The realism of Luke's parables shows that the consequences of conversion touch all areas of human life—family life, the use and danger of wealth, legal disputes and banquets, journeys and the management of estates. In the Lukan parables "every man and every woman" realize that salvation is at stake precisely in the everyday unfolding of human life. Salvation is a gift for the now; it can be won and lost in every now.

22. Ibid., 150.

A Theology of Witness

The motif of witness or testimony (*martys/martyria*) is generally associated with the Johannine writings, where it plays a major role. Among the Synoptics, Luke makes important use of the motif in two important places. In the resurrection appearance noted above, Jesus tells the disciples that they are to be "witnesses of these things" (Luke 24:48), that is, of the death and resurrection of Jesus and the consequent offer of forgiveness. It is then repeated prior to the ascension in Acts 1:8 where the disciples are told that the Holy Spirit will "come upon you; and you shall be my witnesses in Jerusalem and in all Judea and Samaria and to the end of the earth." It remains an important refrain throughout Acts (esp. Acts 1:22; 2:32; 3:15; 5:32; 10:39–41; 13:31; 22:15; 26:16, 22). "Witness" defines the posture of the Christian in the world for Luke and evokes the legal arena where the authenticity of the words and deeds of the defendant is at stake. Luke's picture of the early church is, as Conzelmann has emphasized, that of an *ecclesia pressa*, a community under trial (*peirasmos*).[23] The ethics of the Gospel prepares the disciple for a life of faithful witness.

The theological importance of witness is in accord with Luke's stress on the social impact of the teaching of Jesus. In the Gospel, Jesus proclaims good news to the poor and warns against the danger of wealth; he confronts those deep hatreds which divide people (e.g., Jew from Samaritan) and takes the part of the marginal in society. The early Christians in Acts gather in community as friends who share their goods in common so that there is not a needy person among them (Acts 2:42–47; 4:32–37).[24] The earliest Christian mission in Acts beyond the confines of Jerusalem is to the Samaritans (Acts 8:1–25), a witness to the transforming power of Jesus' teaching on the Samaritan as neighbor (Luke 10:29–37) and as a model of grateful praise (Luke 17:11–19). As in the ministry of Jesus, people from all segments of society benefit from the proclamation of the good news: for example, Jewish leaders (Acts 2:38); a crippled man

---

23. Conzelmann, *St. Luke*, 209.
24. When Luke describes the community as having "all things in common" (Acts 2:44), he uses the classic Greek description of friendship. A community not divided by social inequality can be such a community. See Johnson, *Sharing Possessions*, 119–39.

(3:1–10); a multitude of men and women, the sick and those afflicted with unclean spirits (5:12–16); an Ethiopian "stranger in the land" (8:26–40); a persecutor (9:1–30); a Gentile (10:1–45).

Witness involves not only faith and conversion but action. In treating the Good Samaritan and Martha and Mary, I noted that Luke stresses the importance of both "listening" to the word of God and being a "doer of the word."[25] Throughout the Gospel, Luke involves the reader quickly in the quest for right action by having important characters ask, "What shall I do?" Those who listen to John's preaching ask, "What shall we do?" (3:10). The rich man musing about his wealth asks, "What shall I do?" (12:17), as do the unjust steward (16:3) and the ruler summoned to abandon his wealth and follow Jesus (18:18). The question of "doing" permeates the parable of the Good Samaritan, which begins with the lawyer's question, "What shall I do to inherit eternal life?" (10:25). Jesus responds that "doing" the command to love God and neighbor will bring life and then tells the lawyer to "do" the same act of mercy to a neighbor as the Samaritan did (10:37).

I would not want to claim here that Luke offers a "justification by works," but that, in addition to offering an earthy realism, Luke's parables present a form of "Christian pragmatism." In the parables real people make real decisions, and it is their actions which determine their fate. The Samaritan "does mercy"; the errant son comes to himself and returns to the father; the unjust steward takes decisive action; the callous judge finally gives in to the widow. The parables offer an imaginative world where reflection is translated into action, for better (15:17–18) or for worse (12:15–21).

Luke does not sanction an understanding of the Christian life that would devolve into quietism, fideism, or any false mysticism. His understanding of Christian witness is counter to any attempt to separate the world of religion from the world of everyday life or to erect a spiritual, religious realm opposed to the secular. Disciples who are introduced into the pedagogy of the parables are forced to ask, "What shall we do?" The answer they give in their ordinary and daily lives determines whether they will be faithful witnesses of the gospel in parable.

25. See above, chap. 4, pp. 136–40.

While recent Gospel scholarship has rightly stressed the literary and theological diversity within the Synoptic Gospels, there is a fundamental unity of perspective. Each Gospel is a narrative presentation of the Christ event, that is, the significance that the person, teaching, ministry, death, and resurrection of Jesus of Nazareth had and still has for human history. In the Gospel contexts the ethics of the parables is in response to the mercy and love of God manifest in the Christ event.

Luke shapes the contours of the Christ event in his own distinctive manner. The canticles of Mary (1:46–55) and Zechariah (1:67–79), couched in the rhythmic cadences of the psalms, resonate with the gracious mercy and compassion of God. Compassion motivates God's entry into human history (1:78) and moves Jesus to the side of those suffering (7:13). While Matthew has, "Be perfect, as your heavenly Father is perfect" (Matt. 5:48), Luke writes simply, "Be merciful, even as your Father is merciful" (Luke 6:36). Mercy and compassion when received and when extended to others bring people into the family of God. Jesus himself, who offers parables that are paradigms of life before God, dies as a model of such a life. He consoles the widows of Jerusalem (23:28–31), prays that God forgive those who crucify him (23:34), and commits his last breath to his Father (23:46). In his ministry, as presented by Luke, Jesus is himself "the compassion of God," showing compassion to those in need and telling parables where through compassion people become bearers of God's mercy and love.[26]

PROCLAIMING THE GOSPEL
IN PARABLE

Ernst Fuchs, Rudolf Bultmann's pupil and the successor to his chair at Marburg University, has urged that all exegesis should be concerned with how texts, which originally functioned in proclamation, can again become "the texts of a sermon."[27] Fuchs's concern is especially true of the parables but should not be limited to preaching the parables. It applies equally to the use of parables in service of

26. For a theological development of this motif, see Hellwig, *Jesus: The Compassion of God.*

27. Fuchs, *Studies of the Historical Jesus,* 8. For an excellent discussion of Fuchs and the "New Hermeneutic," see Perrin, *Jesus and the Language,* 120–27.

the communication of the gospel in a wide variety of contexts: preaching, teaching, personal and group reflection on the Bible, pastoral counseling, and spiritual direction. These latter contexts may be surprising to some, but in religious traditions where parables play a large part, such as rabbinic Judaism, Sufism, and Buddhism, they are an integral part of the director-student relationship in communicating a tradition, in the quest for self-understanding and in directing a person to the mystery of God.[28]

In speaking of proclaiming the gospel in parable, we confront immediately the problem of the relation of exegesis and the religious use of biblical texts. Without attempting to address the complex hermeneutical issues involved, I propose that exegesis, especially of the parables, can offer the parameters of correct interpretation and can disclose patently false interpretation. But since the parables are imaginative texts with open-ended applications, exegesis cannot exhaust those possibilities of fruitful interpretation and appropriation which extend the original meaning of the text. Because the parables come from a time and culture foreign to us, historical criticism of the language and social context of the parables is an unending task. Virtually every direction in NT exegesis has had implications for understanding the parables. The more recent methods that employ social analysis and cultural anthropology, when applied to the parables, will continue to bring life to the parables and their world.[29]

Since the parables are literary and poetic texts, all the methods of both ancient and modern literary criticism which help to grasp the power of imaginative language should be appropriated. In proclaiming the parables, it is crucial that the hearers engage their images.[30] Today this is not an easy task, for we live often in a desert of the imagination, with a special resistance to the application of the imagination to biblical texts. Fundamentalism, which conceives of

28. Collections in English can be found in A. Feldman, *The Parables and Similes of the Rabbis;* Newman, *The Hasidic Anthology;* Burlingame, *Buddhist Parables;* and Shah, *Tales of the Dervishes.*

29. For the social context of Jesus' teaching, see esp. Freyne, *Galilee;* Vermes, *Jesus the Jew;* idem, *Jesus and the World of Judaism.* For cultural anthropology, see Malina, *The New Testament World;* idem, *Christian Origins and Cultural Anthropology.* The integration of new methods of social and cultural analysis is becoming increasingly important for study of the parables.

30. Close reading of the imagery of specific books has been neglected by biblical scholars. See Goulder (*Midrash and Lection in Matthew,* 95–115) for an interesting treatment of Matthean imagery; for a general approach, see Caird, *The Language and Imagery of the Bible.*

the Bible as a storehouse of historical facts and clear religious truth, is the most obvious example of life in this desert. More positively, people must be assisted and allowed to be captured by the images of the parables. The images of the parables present a paradox. On the one hand' they are strange and foreign, especially to modern urban dwellers; on the other hand they are too familiar and sedimented by centuries of interpretation. In my attempts to have students engage the parables, I have often begun with parables from other religious traditions or asked them to rewrite a familiar parable using different images. Liberation of the imagination can be an important first step to hearing the liberating voice of the parables.

The parables must be proclaimed as texts in context, which is a major challenge to those who preach on the parables. Actually this is a problem when any individual "text" is chosen for a sermon. Virtually no part of the Bible was ever intended to be read or heard in isolation. Every pericope or section was part of a larger whole. Preaching, as it occurs today in most Christian denominations, encourages misuse of the Bible. One text is made to bear the whole weight of how the preacher wants his or her understanding of Christianity to touch the lives of the congregation on a given Sunday. Every text is forced to become "a gospel within a gospel."

I urge that those who preach on the parables practice an "expanding contextual analysis."[31] A fundamental choice is between the context of the parable within the larger context of Jesus' ministry and teaching or within the Gospel in which it is found. The first is fraught with the difficulties of how the life and teaching of Jesus is understood. The work of Jeremias remains an invaluable resource for uncovering the earliest stages of the tradition and for their cultural context, despite the criticism that his reconstruction of Jesus' teaching reflects "a rather conservative Lutheran piety."[32] The recent explosion of Jesus studies, especially those by Edward Schillebeeckx, John Riches, and Edward P. Sanders, offer contemporary preachers rich resources for combining the presentation of the parables with a better understanding of the social context and impact of Jesus' ministry.[33] The studies of Jesus emerging from Third World liberation

---

31. See above, chap. 1, pp. 25–27.
32. Perrin, *Jesus and the Language,* 106.
33. Schillebeeckx, *Jesus;* Riches, *Jesus and the Transformation of Judaism;* and E. P. Sanders, *Jesus and Judaism.*

theology challenge a Jesus made in the image and likeness of the First World.[34] Whatever shape the quest for Jesus may take, scholar and preacher alike must remember Albert Schweitzer's warning about his predecessors that each epoch "found its reflection in Jesus; each individual created Him in accordance with his own character."[35]

A more certain context, and one that I have tried to develop, is the context in the Gospels. This context is important not only for preaching the parables but for all preaching from the Gospels. Preaching of the parables should involve proclaiming the parables in the Gospels and the gospel in the parables. For those denominations which use a lectionary cycle, attention should be given to the relation of a text for a given Sunday to its context in the Gospel and in the lectionary cycle, which often leaves out important sections. Those who choose a text for a sermon (who are always in special danger of making their own canon within a canon) should examine what comes before and what comes after a given text and how the text fits into the theology of the book from which it is taken. Over the past twenty years redaction criticism has proved to be an invaluable resource in uncovering the distinctive literary characteristics and theological motifs of the individual Gospels.[36] There is no better preparation for proclaiming the gospel in parable than serious and intense study of the Gospels.

Finally, proclamation of the parables should itself be parabolic. Following C. H. Dodd, I have stressed the four qualities of Jesus' parables, the qualities of being (a) realistic, (b) metaphorical, (c)

34. On Jesus and liberation theology, see the fine survey by Bussmann, *Who Do You Say?* See also the multivolume Christology by Segundo, *Jesus of Nazareth Yesterday and Today,* esp. vol. 2, *The Historical Jesus of the Synoptics.*
35. Schweitzer, *The Quest of the Historical Jesus,* 4.
36. Helpful surveys of the results of such scholarship are: **Mark:** D. Harrington, "A Map of Books on Mark (1975–1984)"; Kee, "Mark's Gospel in Recent Research"; Kealy, *Mark's Gospel: A History of Its Interpretation;* Kingsbury, "The Gospel of Mark in Current Research." **Matthew:** Stanton, "Matthew's Gospel: A New Storm Center," in *The Interpretation of Matthew,* 1–18. See also his more detailed and scholarly survey "The Origin and Purpose of Matthew's Gospel: Matthean Scholarship from 1945–1980." **Luke:** Fitzmyer, *Luke I—IX,* 3–34, 143–270; Kodell, "The Theology of Luke in Recent Study"; Talbert, "Shifting Sands: The Recent Study of the Gospel of Luke." Most standard introductions to the NT integrate the results of redaction criticism, esp. Perrin and Duling, *The New Testament: An Introduction;* and Johnson, *The Writings of the New Testament.* For insight into the theology of the evangelists, see Kingsbury, *Jesus Christ in Matthew, Mark, and Luke.*

paradoxical or surprising, and *(d)* open-ended. These could serve as guidelines for effective preaching. Jesus addressed his hearers in their everyday lives with an unabashed realism. The parables are now proclaimed in the "Sunday morning world" of a church service, a world that becomes an escape from everyday life. Professional ministers are in danger of living in this world seven days a week. Realistic proclamation of the parables demands an awareness not only of their context in the Gospels but of the context of the hearers.

Preaching should also embody some of the paradoxical, upsetting, and shocking quality of the teaching of Jesus. Religion in our society often has been a bastion of the expected, often serving to enforce the values of the dominant majority. People do not want to be either surprised or upset on Sunday. The routine of Sunday worship encourages a certain gracious uniformity. Jesus, the friend of tax collectors and sinners, told parables that took the side of the outcast, provoked the proud, and unsettled the complacent. Can his parables continue to do this today?

Metaphorical and open-ended parabolic preaching are related. Much Christian preaching has become so moralistic that there is little doubt at the end of a sermon what should be done, even if it will not be done. Metaphorical preaching points beyond the sermon to engagement with the mystery of God, and God's relation to the world. It does not hesitate to point to those deeper problems and fears which lie below the surface even in our overly prosperous contemporary culture. Issues such as the possibility and viability of faith itself; the ominous presence of death behind the statistic of nations armed with over 20,000 nuclear warheads; fears of external and internal violence; the challenges to family life in contemporary society—all these and more are often hidden behind the stolid faces of a Sunday congregation. The challenge is to let parables point beyond themselves to the mystery of God and to the good news proclaimed and embodied by the parable giver.

Finally, and perhaps the greatest challenge to the preacher, is to preach in an open-ended fashion. Jesus chose a form of discourse that appealed to the freedom of his hearers. Both he and his preaching were rejected by the majority of his contemporaries and continue to be, even by many who today invoke his name. We are accustomed to thinking that every good sermon must have a conclusion or an application. Rather paradoxically, I have written perhaps too many pages suggesting how certain parables could be interpreted. The last thing I expect is that my interpretations become normative. They present starting points and suggestions. How and if they can be presented is itself an open question. Perhaps the best "application" in proclaiming the parables is to help people to be so captured by a biblical text that they will wonder what it really means and will wrestle with it. Like Jacob (Gen. 32:22–32), in the struggle they may even be touched by God's power and presence.

ABBREVIATIONS

AB   Anchor Bible
AnBib   Analecta Biblica
ANRW   *Aufstieg und Niedergang der römischen Welt.* Hildegard Temporini and Wolfgang Hase, eds. Multivolume. Berlin and New York: Walter de Gruyter, 1972–.
BAGD   Walter Bauer, William F. Arndt, and F. Wilbur Gingrich. *A Greek-English Lexicon of the New Testament and Other Early Christian Literature.* 2d ed. rev. F. Danker.
BETL   Bibliotheca Ephemeridum Theologicarum Lovaniensium
Bib   *Biblica*
BJRL   *Bulletin of the John Rylands University Library of Manchester*
BTB   *Biblical Theology Bulletin*
CBQ   *Catholic Biblical Quarterly*
CBQMS   Catholic Biblical Quarterly—Monograph Series
EKKNT   Evangelisch-katholischer Kommentar zum Neuen Testament
EncJud   *Encyclopaedia Judaica* (1971)
EvQ   *Evangelical Quarterly*
EvT   *Evangelische Theologie*
ExpTim   *Expository Times*
FRLANT   Forschungen zur Religion und Literatur des Alten und Neuen Testaments

HTKNT	Herders theologischer Kommentar zum Neuen Testament
IDBSup	*Interpreter's Dictionary of the Bible, Supplementary Volume*
Int	*Interpretation*
IRT	Issues in Religion and Theology
JBL	*Journal of Biblical Literature*
JR	*Journal of Religion*
JSNT	*Journal for the Study of the New Testament*
JSNTSup	Journal for the Study of the New Testament—Supplement Series
JSOT	*Journal for the Study of the Old Testament*
JTS	*Journal of Theological Studies*
LCL	Loeb Classical Library (Cambridge: Harvard University Press)
LXX	Septuagint or Greek Translation of the Old Testament
NovT	*Novum Testamentum*
NovTSup	Novum Testamentum, Supplements
NT	New Testament
NTAbh	Neutestamentliche Abhandlungen
NTM	New Testament Message
NTS	*New Testament Studies*
OBO	Orbis Biblicus et Orientalis
OBT	Overtures to Biblical Theology
OT	Old Testament
RelSRev	*Religious Studies Review*
RSV	Revised Standard Version of the Bible, 1973 ed.
SBL	Society of Biblical Literature
SBLDS	SBL Dissertation Series
SBLMS	SBL Monograph Series
SBLSP	SBL Seminar Papers
SBS	Stuttgarter Bibelstudien
SBT	Studies in Biblical Theology
SJT	*Scottish Journal of Theology*
SNTSMS	Society for New Testament Studies Monograph Series
SNTU	Studien zum Neuen Testament und seiner Umwelt
SS	Semeia Supplements
ST	*Studia Theologica*
SUNT	Studien zur Umwelt des Neuen Testaments
TD	*Theology Digest*

TDNT	*Theological Dictionary of the New Testament.* G. Kittel and G. Friedrich, eds.
TDOT	*Theological Dictionary of the Old Testament.* G. J. Botterweck and H. Ringgren, eds.
TS	*Theological Studies*
ZNW	*Zeitschrift für die neutestamentliche Wissenschaft*
1QH	*Hôdāyôt (Thanksgiving Hymns)* from Qumran
1QM	*Milḥmāh (War Scroll)* from Qumran
1QS	*Serek hayyaḥad (Manual of Discipline)* from Qumran
1QSa	*Rule of the Congregation,* appendix A to 1QS

BIBLIOGRAPHY

BOOKS ON PARABLES

Bailey, Kenneth E. *Poet and Peasant: A Literary-Cultural Approach to the Parables in Luke* and *Through Peasant Eyes: More Lucan Parables, Their Culture and Style.* 2 vols. in 1. Grand Rapids: Wm. B. Eerdmans Pub. Co., 1984.

Boucher, Madeleine I. *The Mysterious Parable: A Literary Study.* CBQMS 6. Washington, D.C.: Catholic Biblical Association of America, 1977.

————. *The Parables.* NTM 7. Wilmington, Del.: Michael Glazier, 1981.

Breech, James E. *The Silence of Jesus: The Authentic Voice of the Historical Man.* Philadelphia: Fortress Press, 1983.

Carlston, Charles E. *The Parables of the Triple Tradition.* Philadelphia: Fortress Press, 1975.

Crossan, J. Dominic. *Cliffs of Fall: Paradox and Polyvalence in the Parables of Jesus.* New York: Seabury Press, 1980.

————. *The Dark Interval: Towards a Theology of Story.* Niles, Ill.: Argus Communications, 1975.

————. *Finding Is the First Act: Trove Folktales and Jesus' Treasure Parable.* SS 9. Missoula, Mont.: Scholars Press; Philadelphia: Fortress Press, 1979.

————. *In Parables: The Challenge of the Historical Jesus.* New York: Harper & Row, 1973.

Dodd, C. H. *The Parables of the Kingdom.* New York: Charles Scribner's Sons, 1961.

Drury, John. *The Parables in the Gospels: History and Allegory.* New York: Crossroad Pub. Co., 1985.

Funk, Robert W. *Language, Hermeneutic and the Word of God.* New York: Harper & Row, 1966.

————. *Parables and Presence.* Philadelphia: Fortress Press, 1982.

Granskou, David M. *Preaching on the Parables.* Philadelphia: Fortress Press, 1972.

Harrington, Wilfrid J. *Key to the Parables*. New York: Paulist Press, 1964.

————. *Parables Told by Jesus*. New York: Alba House, 1974.

Hunter, A.M. *Interpreting the Parables*. London: SCM Press; Philadelphia: Westminster Press, 1960.

Jeremias, Joachim. *The Parables of Jesus*. 2d rev. ed. New York: Charles Scribner's Sons, 1972.

Jones, Geraint Vaughan. *The Art and Truth of the Parables*. London: S.P.C.K., 1964.

Jülicher, Adolf. *Die Gleichnisreden Jesu*. 2 parts in 1. Darmstadt: Wissenschaftliche Buchgesellschaft, 1976 [1888, 1899].

Kingsbury, Jack Dean. *The Parables of Jesus in Matthew 13*. Richmond: John Knox Press, 1969. Reprinted. St. Louis: Clayton Pub. House; London: S.P.C.K., 1977.

Kissinger, Warren S. *The Parables of Jesus: A History of Interpretation and Bibliography*. Metuchen, N.J.: Scarecrow Press and American Theological Library Association, 1979.

Klauck, Hans-Josef. *Allegorie und Allegorese in synoptischen Gleichnistexten*. NTAbh 13. Münster: Verlag Aschendorff, 1978.

Lambrecht, Jan. *Once More Astonished: The Parables of Jesus*. New York: Crossroad Pub. Co., 1981.

Linnemann, Eta. *Jesus of the Parables*. New York: Harper & Row, 1966.

Oesterley, W. O. E. *The Gospel Parables in the Light of Their Jewish Background*. London: S.P.C.K., 1938.

Perkins, Pheme. *Hearing the Parables of Jesus*. New York: Paulist Press, 1981.

Perrin, Norman. *Jesus and the Language of the Kingdom: Symbol and Metaphor in New Testament Interpretation*. Philadelphia: Fortress Press, 1976.

Scott, Bernard Brandon. *Jesus, Symbol-Maker for the Kingdom*. Philadelphia: Fortress Press, 1981.

Tolbert, Mary Ann. *Perspectives on the Parables: An Approach to Multiple Interpretations*. Philadelphia: Fortress Press, 1979.

Via, Dan O. *The Parables: Their Literary and Existential Dimension*. Philadelphia: Fortress Press, 1967.

Weder, Hans. *Die Gleichnisse Jesu als Metaphern*. FRLANT 120. Göttingen: Vandenhoeck & Ruprecht, 1978.

Wilder, A. *Jesus' Parables and the War of Myths: Essays on Imagination in the Scriptures*. Philadelphia: Fortress Press, 1982.

————. *The Language of the Gospel: Early Christian Rhetoric*. New York: Harper & Row, 1964. Reissued as *Early Christian Rhetoric*. Cambridge: Harvard University Press, 1971.

OTHER WORKS CITED

Achtemeier, Paul J. "The Origin and Function of the Pre-Marcan Miracle Catenae." *JBL* 91 (1972): 198–221.

————. "Toward the Isolation of Pre-Markan Miracle Catenae." *JBL* 89 (1970): 265–91.

Ballard, P. H. "Reasons for Refusing the Great Supper." *JTS* 23 (1972): 341–50.

Batey, Richard A. *New Testament Nuptial Imagery*. Leiden: E. J. Brill, 1971.

Best, Ernest. *Following Jesus: Discipleship in the Gospel of Mark*. JSNTSup 4. Sheffield: JSOT Press, 1981.

Bird, Phyllis A. "Images of Women in the Old Testament." In *Religion and Sexism*, edited by Rosemary R. Ruether, 41–88.

Bonhoeffer, Dietrich. *The Cost of Discipleship*. New York: Macmillan Co., 1966 [1937].

Bornkamm, Günther, Gerhard Barth, and Heinz Joachim Held. *Tradition and Interpretation in Matthew*. Philadelphia: Westminster Press, 1963.

Bowker, J. W. "Mystery and Parable: Mark iv. 1–20." *JTS* 25 (1974): 300–17.

Brandenburger, Egon. *Das Recht des Weltenrichters. Untersuchung zu Matthäus 25, 31–46*. SBS 99. Stuttgart: Katholisches Bibelwerk, 1980.

Brooten, Bernadette. "Konnten Frauen im alten Judentum die Scheidung betreiben? Überlegungen zu Mk 10, 11–12 und 1 Kor 7, 10–11." *EvT* 42 (1982): 65–80.

Brown, Frank Burch, and Elizabeth Struthers Malbon, "Parabling as a *Via Negativa*: A Critical Review of the Work of John Dominic Crossan." *JR* 64 (1984): 530–38.

Brown, Raymond E. *The Birth of the Messiah: A Commentary on the Infancy Narratives in Matthew and Luke*. New York: Doubleday & Co., 1977.

———. *The Churches the Apostles Left Behind*. New York: Paulist Press, 1984.

———. *The Gospel according to John I—XII*. AB 29. Garden City, N.Y.: Doubleday & Co., 1966.

———. *The Semitic Background of the Term "Mystery" in the New Testament*. Facet Books. Philadelphia: Fortress Press, 1968.

Brown, Raymond E., and John P. Meier. *Antioch and Rome: New Testament Cradles of Catholic Christianity*. New York: Paulist Press, 1983.

Brown, Schuyler. *Apostasy and Perseverance in the Theology of Luke*. AnBib 36. Rome: Biblical Institute Press, 1969.

———. "The Matthean Apocalypse." *JSNT* 4 (1979): 2–27.

———. " 'The Secret of the Kingdom of God' (Mark 4:11)." *JBL* 92 (1973): 60–74.

Bultmann, Rudolf. *The History of the Synoptic Tradition*. New York: Harper & Row, 1963.

———. *This World and the Beyond: Marburg Sermons*. London: Lutterworth Press, 1960.

Burlingame, E. W. *Buddhist Parables*. New Haven: Yale University Press, 1922.

Burnett, Fred W. *The Testament of Jesus-Sophia: A Redaction-Critical Study of the Eschatological Discourse in Matthew*. Washington, D.C.: University Press of America, 1981.

Bussmann, Claus. *Who Do You Say? Jesus Christ in Latin American Theology*. Maryknoll, N.Y.: Orbis Books, 1985.

Caird, George B. *The Language and Imagery of the Bible.* Philadelphia: Westminster Press, 1980.

Carlston, Charles E. "Parable and Allegory Revisited: An Interpretive Review." *CBQ* 43 (1981): 228–42.

Cave, C. H. "Lazarus and the Lukan Deuteronomy." *NTS* 15 (1968–69): 319–25.

Chilton, Bruce. *God in Strength: Jesus' Announcement of the Kingdom.* SNTU 1. Linz: SNTU, 1979.

Ciardi, John. *How Does a Poem Mean?* Boston: Houghton Mifflin Co., 1960. 2d rev. ed. with Miller Williams, 1975.

Collins, Adela Yarbro. *The Apocalypse.* NTM 22. Wilmington, Del.: Michael Glazier, 1979.

———. "Persecution and Vengeance in the Book of Revelation." In *Apocalypticism in the Mediterranean World and the Near East*, edited by Hellholm, 729–49.

Collins, John J. *The Apocalyptic Imagination: An Introduction to the Jewish Matrix of Christianity.* New York: Crossroad Pub. Co., 1984.

Compton, J. E. "The Prodigal's Brother." *ExpTim* 42 (1930–31): 287.

Conzelmann, Hans. *The Theology of St. Luke,* New York: Harper & Row, 1960.

Cope, Lamar O. *Matthew: A Scribe Trained for the Kingdom of Heaven.* CBQMS 5. Washington, D.C.: Catholic Biblical Association, 1976.

———. "Matthew XXV: 31–46, 'The Sheep and the Goats' Reinterpreted." *NovT* 11 (1969): 32–44.

Cousar, Charles B. "Eschatology and Mark's *Theologia Crucis:* A Critical Analysis of Mark 13." *Int* 24 (1970): 321–35.

Creed, J. M. *The Gospel according to St. Luke.* New York: St. Martin's Press; London: Macmillan & Co., 1965.

Crossan, J. Dominic. *Four Other Gospels: Shadows on the Contours of Canon.* Minneapolis: Winston-Seabury, 1985.

———. *A Fragile Craft: The Work of Amos Niven Wilder.* Chico, Calif.: Scholars Press, 1981.

———. *In Fragments: The Aphorisms of Jesus.* San Francisco: Harper & Row, 1983.

———. "Mark and the Relatives of Jesus." *NovT* 15 (1973): 81–113.

———. "Parable and Example in the Teaching of Jesus." *NTS* 18 (1971–72): 285–307.

———. "Parable as Religious and Poetic Experience." *JR* 53 (1973): 330–58.

———. "The Parable of the Wicked Husbandmen." *JBL* 90 (1971): 451–65.

———. *Raid on the Articulate: Comic Eschatology in Jesus and Borges.* New York: Harper & Row, 1976.

———. *Sayings Parallels: A Workbook for the Jesus Tradition.* Philadelphia: Fortress Press, 1986.

———. "The Seed Parables of Jesus." *JBL* 92 (1973): 244–66.

Dahl, Nils A. "The Parables of Growth." *ST* 5 (1951): 132–66.

Danby, Herbert. *The Mishnah*. Oxford: Clarendon Press, 1954.

D'Angelo, Mary Rose. "Images of Jesus and the Christian Call in the Gospels of Luke and John." *Spirituality Today* 37 (1985): 196–212.

Davies, Stevan. *The Gospel of Thomas and Christian Wisdom*. New York: Seabury Press, 1983.

Davies, W. D. *The Setting of the Sermon on the Mount*. Cambridge: Cambridge University Press, 1964.

Derrett, J. Duncan M. *Law in the New Testament*. London: Darton, Longman & Todd, 1970.

———. *Studies in the New Testament*. Volume 1, *Glimpses of the Legal and Social Presuppositions of the Authors*. Leiden: E. J. Brill, 1977.

———. *Studies in the New Testament*. Volume 3, *Midrash, Haggadah, and the Character of the Community*. Leiden: E. J. Brill, 1982.

Dewey, Joanna. *Markan Public Debate*. SBLDS 48. Chico, Calif.: Scholars Press, 1980.

Dibelius, Martin. *Botschaft und Geschichte*. Vol. 1. Tübingen: J. C. B. Mohr (Paul Siebeck), 1953.

Didier, M., ed. *L'Evangile selon Matthieu: Rédaction et théologie*. BETL 19. Gembloux: J. Duculot, 1972.

Dillon, R. J. "Towards a Tradition-History of the Parables of the True Israel (Matthew 21,33—22,14)." *Bib* 47 (1966): 1–42.

Donahue, John R. *Are You the Christ? The Trial Narrative in the Gospel of Mark*. SBLDS 10. Missoula, Mont.: Scholars Press, 1973.

———. "Biblical Perspectives on Justice." In *The Faith That Does Justice*, edited by Haughey, 68–112.

———. "Jesus as the Parable of God in the Gospel of Mark." *Int* 32 (1978): 369–86. Also in *Interpreting the Gospels*, edited by Mays, 148–67.

———. "A Neglected Factor in the Theology of Mark." *JBL* 101 (1982): 563–94.

———. "The 'Parable' of the Sheep and the Goats: A Challenge to Christian Ethics." *TS* 47 (1986): 3–31.

———. "Tax Collectors and Sinners: An Attempt at Identification." *CBQ* 33 (1971): 39–61.

———. *The Theology and Setting of Discipleship in the Gospel of Mark*. Milwaukee, Wis.: Marquette University Press, 1983.

Donfried, Karl P. "The Allegory of the Ten Virgins (Matt 25:1–13) as a Summary of Matthean Theology." *JBL* 93 (1974): 415–28.

Dorr, Donal. *Option for the Poor: A Hundred Years of Vatican Social Teaching*. Maryknoll, N.Y.: Orbis Books, 1983.

Douglas, Mary. *Natural Symbols*. New York: Random House, Vintage Books, 1973.

———. *Purity and Danger: An Analysis of Concepts of Pollution and Taboo*. London: Routledge & Kegan Paul, 1966.

Duling, Dennis C. "The Therapeutic Son of David: An Element in Matthew's Christological Apologetic." *NTS* 24 (1977–78): 392–410.

Dupont, Jacques. *Les béatitudes.* 3 vols. Louvain: Nauwelaerts, 1958–73.
————. "Le point de vue de Matthieu dans le chapitre des paraboles." In *L'Evangile selon Matthieu,* edited by Didier, 221–59.
Dupont, Jacques, and A. George, eds., *Gospel Poverty: Essays in Biblical Poverty.* Chicago: Franciscan Herald Press, 1977.
Dupont-Sommer, A. *The Essene Writings from Qumran.* Cleveland: World Pub. Co., 1961.
Eagleton, Terry. *Literary Theory: An Introduction.* Minneapolis: University of Minnesota Press, 1983.
Edersheim, A. *The Life and Times of Jesus the Messiah.* 2 vols. New York: Longmans, Green & Co., 1896.
Edwards, Richard A. *A Theology of Q: Eschatology, Prophecy, and Wisdom.* Philadelphia: Fortress Press, 1976.
Evans, C. F. "The Central Section of St. Luke's Gospel." In *Studies in the Gospels: Essays in Memory of R. H. Lightfoot,* edited by D. E. Ninehan, 37–53. Oxford: Basil Blackwell, 1955.
Farmer, William R. "Modern Developments of Griesbach's Hypothesis." *NTS* 23 (1976–77): 275–95.
————. *The Synoptic Problem: A Critical Analysis.* New York: Macmillan Co., 1964. Slightly revised edition, Dillsboro, N.C.: Western North Carolina Press, 1976.
Feldman, Asher. *The Parables and Similes of the Rabbis: Agricultural and Pastoral.* Cambridge: Cambridge University Press, 1924.
Feldman, E. *Biblical and Post-Biblical Defilement and Mourning: Law as Theology.* New York: Yeshiva University Press and Ktav Pub. House, 1977.
Feldman, Louis H. *Josephus: Jewish Antiquities.* LCL 9. Cambridge: Harvard University Press, 1965.
Fitzmyer, Joseph A. "Anti-Semitism and the Cry of 'All the People' (Mt 27:25)." *TS* 26 (1965): 667–71.
————. "Divorce among First-Century Palestinian Jews." In *H. L. Ginzburg Volume,* 103*–110*. Eretz Israel 14. Jerusalem: Israel Exploration Society, 1978.
————. *Essays on the Semitic Background of the New Testament.* Missoula, Mont.: Scholars Press, 1974.
————. *The Gospel according to Luke I—IX* and *The Gospel according to Luke X—XXIV.* AB 28 and 28A. Garden City, N.Y.: Doubleday & Co., 1981, 1985.
————. "The Priority of Mark and the 'Q' Source in Luke." In *To Advance the Gospel,* 3–40.
————. "The Story of the Dishonest Manager (Lk 16:1–13)." *TS* 25 (1964): 23–42. Reprinted in *Essays on the Semitic Background of the New Testament,* 161–84.
————. *To Advance the Gospel: New Testament Studies.* New York: Crossroad Pub. Co., 1981.
Flender, Helmut. *St. Luke, Theologian of Redemptive History.* Philadelphia: Fortress Press, 1967.

Fletcher, A. *Allegory: The Theory of a Symbolic Mode.* Ithaca, N.Y.: Cornell University Press, 1964.

Ford, J. Massyngbaerde. *My Enemy Is My Guest: Jesus and Violence in Luke.* Maryknoll, N.Y.: Orbis Books, 1984.

———. "The Parable of the Foolish Scholars (Matt. xxv, 1–13)." *NovT* 9 (1967): 107–23.

Fowler, Robert. "Who Is 'the Reader' of Mark's Gospel?" SBLSP 1983. Chico, Calif.: Scholars Press, 1983, 31–53.

Freyne, Sean. *Galilee from Alexander the Great to Hadrian, 323 B.C.E. to 135 C.E.* Wilmington, Del.: Michael Glazier; Notre Dame, Ind.: University of Notre Dame Press, 1980.

Fuchs, Ernst. *Studies of the Historical Jesus.* SBT 42. London: SCM Press, 1964.

Funk, Robert W. "Beyond Criticism in Quest of Literacy: The Parable of the Leaven." *Int* 25 (1971): 149–70.

———. "The Looking-Glass Tree Is for the Birds: Ezekiel 17:22–24; Mark 4:30–32." *Int* 27 (1973): 3–9.

———, ed. *New Gospel Parallels.* Volume 1, *The Synoptic Gospels.* Foundations and Facets. Sonoma, Calif.: Polebridge Press, 1985.

Furnish, Victor. *II Corinthians.* AB 32A. Garden City, N.Y.: Doubleday & Co., 1984.

Garland, David. *The Intention of Matthew 23.* NovTSup 52. Leiden: E. J. Brill, 1979.

Gaventa, Beverly Roberts. *From Darkness to Light: Aspects of Conversion in the New Testament.* OBT 20. Philadelphia: Fortress Press, 1986.

Gelin, A. *The Poor of Yahweh.* Collegeville, Minn.: Liturgical Press, 1964.

Gnilka, Joachim. *Das Evangelium nach Markus (Mk 1—8, 26),* EKKNT 2. Zurich: Benziger Verlag; Neukirchen-Vluyn: Neukirchener Verlag, 1978.

Goulder, Michael. "Characteristics of the Parables in the Several Gospels." *JTS* 19 (1968): 51–69.

———. *Midrash and Lection in Matthew.* London: S.P.C.K., 1974.

Grayston, K. "The Study of Mark XIII." *BJRL* 56 (1973–74): 371–87.

Grube, G. M. A., ed. *Aristotle: On Poetry and Style.* Indianapolis: Bobbs-Merrill Co., 1958.

Gundry, Robert H. *Matthew: A Commentary on His Literary and Theological Art.* Grand Rapids: Wm. B. Eerdmans Pub. Co., 1982.

Hamerton-Kelly, Robert. *God the Father: Theology and Patriarchy in the Teaching of Jesus.* OBT 4. Philadelphia: Fortress Press, 1979.

Hare, Douglas. *The Theme of Jewish Persecution of Christians in the Gospel according to St. Matthew.* SNTSMS 6. Cambridge: Cambridge University Press, 1967.

Hare, Douglas, and D. Harrington. "Make Disciples of All the Gentiles (Mt. 28:19)." *CBQ* 37 (1975): 359–69.

Harrington, Daniel. "A Map of Books on Mark (1975–1984)." *BTB* 15 (1985): 12–16.

Haughey, John C., ed. *The Faith That Does Justice: Examining the Christian Sources for Social Change*. New York: Paulist Press, 1977.

Hellholm, David, ed. *Apocalypticism in the Mediterranean World and the Near East*. Tübingen: J. C. B. Mohr (Paul Siebeck), 1983.

Hellwig, Monika. *Jesus: The Compassion of God*. Wilmington, Del.: Michael Glazier, 1983.

Herbert, A. S. "The 'Parable' (*MĀŠĀL*) in the Old Testament." *SJT* 7 (1954): 180–96.

Heschel, Abraham. *God in Search of Man: A Philosophy of Judaism*. New York: Farrar, Straus and Cudahy, 1955; New York: Jewish Publication Society of America, 1958.

———. *The Prophets*. New York: Harper & Row, 1962.

Hooker, M. D. "Trial and Tribulation in Mark XIII." *BJRL* 65, no. 1 (1982): 78–99.

Howe, Irving, and Ilana Widner Howe, eds. *Short Shorts: An Anthology of the Shortest Stories*. Boston: David R. Godine Pub., 1982.

Johnson, Luke T. *The Literary Function of Possessions in Luke-Acts*. SBLDS 39. Missoula, Mont.: Scholars Press, 1977.

———. *Sharing Possessions: Mandate and Symbol of Faith*. OBT 9. Philadelphia: Fortress Press, 1981.

———. *The Writings of the New Testament: An Interpretation*. Philadelphia: Fortress Press, 1986.

Johnston, R. M. "The Study of Rabbinic Parables: Some Preliminary Observations." SBLSP 10, 337–57. Missoula, Mont.: Scholars Press, 1976.

Karris, Robert. "Poor and Rich: The Lukan *Sitz im Leben*." In *Perspectives on Luke-Acts*, edited by Talbert, 112–25.

Kealy, Sean P. *Mark's Gospel: A History of Its Interpretation*. New York: Paulist Press, 1982.

Kee, Howard Clark. *Community of the New Age: Studies in Mark's Gospel*. Philadelphia: Westminster Press, 1977.

———. "Mark's Gospel in Recent Research." *Int* 32 (1978): 353–68. Also in *Interpreting the Gospels*, edited by Mays, 130–47.

Keegan, Terence J. *Interpreting the Bible: A Popular Introduction to Biblical Hermeneutics*. New York: Paulist Press, 1985.

Kelber, Werner. *The Kingdom in Mark: A New Place and a New Time*. Philadelphia: Fortress Press, 1974.

———. *The Oral and the Written Gospel*. Philadelphia: Fortress Press, 1983.

Kennedy, George A. *New Testament Interpretation through Rhetorical Criticism*. Chapel Hill: University of North Carolina Press, 1984.

Kermode, Frank. *The Classic: Literary Images of Permanence and Change*. New York: Viking Press, 1975. Reprint. Cambridge: Harvard University Press, 1983.

———. *The Genesis of Secrecy: On the Interpretation of Narrative*. Cambridge: Harvard University Press, 1979.

Kilgallen, John J. "The Messianic Secret and Mark's Purpose." *BTB* 7 (1977): 60–65.

Kingsbury, Jack Dean. *The Christology of Mark's Gospel.* Philadelphia: Fortress Press, 1983.

———. "The Gospel of Mark in Current Research." *RelSRev* 5 (1979): 101–7.

———. *Jesus Christ in Matthew, Mark, and Luke.* Proclamation Commentaries. Philadelphia: Fortress Press, 1981.

———. *Matthew.* Proclamation Commentaries. Philadelphia: Fortress Press, 1977.

———. *Matthew as Story.* Philadelphia: Fortress Press, 1986.

———. *Matthew: Structure, Christology, Kingdom.* Philadelphia: Fortress Press, 1975.

Kloppenborg, John S. *The Formation of Q.* Studies in Antiquity and Christianity. Philadelphia: Fortress Press, 1987.

———. "Tradition and Redaction in the Synoptic Sayings Source." *CBQ* 46 (1984): 34–62.

Koch, Klaus. *The Rediscovery of Apocalyptic.* SBT 22. London: SCM Press, 1972.

Kodell, J. "The Theology of Luke in Recent Study." *BTB* 1 (1971): 115–44.

Koenig, John. *New Testament Hospitality: Partnership with Strangers as Promise and Mission.* OBT 17. Philadelphia: Fortress Press, 1985.

Kümmel, Werner G. "Current Theological Accusations against Luke." *Andover Newton Quarterly* 16 (1975): 131–45.

———. *Introduction to the New Testament.* Nashville: Abingdon Press, 1975.

Lambrecht, Jan. *The Sermon on the Mount.* Good News Studies 14. Wilmington, Del.: Michael Glazier, 1985.

Légasse, S. " 'L'antijudaïsme' dans l'Evangile selon Matthieu." In *L'Evangile selon Matthieu,* edited by Didier, 417–28.

Lewis, R. W. B. *The Picaresque Saint.* Philadelphia: J. B. Lippincott Co., 1961.

Lohfink, Norbert. *Option for the Poor: The Basic Principle of Liberation Theology in Light of the Bible.* Edited by Duane Christensen. Bailey Lectures. Berkeley, Calif.: BIBAL Press, 1986.

Luz, U. "The Disciples in the Gospel according to Matthew." In *The Interpretation of Matthew,* edited by Stanton, 98–128.

McArthur, Harvey K. "The Parable of the Mustard Seed." *CBQ* 33 (1971): 198–210.

McFague, Sallie. *Metaphorical Theology: Models of God in Religious Language.* Philadelphia: Fortress Press, 1982.

———. *Speaking in Parables: A Study in Metaphor and Theology.* Philadelphia: Fortress Press, 1975.

McLeod, N. B. "The Parable of the Prodigal Father: A Sermon for Christian Family Sunday." *Princeton Seminary Bulletin* 64 (1971): 43–47.

Malbon, Elizabeth Struthers. *Narrative Space and Mythic Meaning in Mark.* San Francisco: Harper & Row, 1986.

Malina, Bruce J. *Christian Origins and Cultural Anthropology.* Atlanta: John Knox Press, 1986.

———. *The New Testament World: Insights from Cultural Anthropology.* Atlanta: John Knox Press, 1981.

Manson, T. W. *The Sayings of Jesus.* London: SCM Press, 1971 [1937].

Marcus, Joel. "Mark 4:10–12 and Marcan Epistemology." *JBL* 103 (1984): 557–74.

———. *The Mystery of the Kingdom of God.* SBLDS 90. Atlanta, Ga.: Scholars Press, 1986.

Marrou, Henri. *A History of Education in Antiquity.* New York: Sheed & Ward, 1956.

Marshall, I. Howard. *The Gospel of Luke: A Commentary on the Greek Text.* Grand Rapids: Wm. B. Eerdmans Pub. Co., 1978.

Marxsen, Willi. *Mark the Evangelist.* Nashville: Abingdon Press, 1969.

Mays, James Luther, ed. *Interpreting the Gospels.* Philadelphia: Fortress Press, 1981.

Mealand, David L. *Poverty and Expectation in the Gospels.* London: S.P.C.K., 1980.

Meier, John P. *Matthew.* NTM 3. Wilmington, Del.: Michael Glazier, 1980.

———. "Nations or Gentiles in Matthew 28:19?" *CBQ* 39 (1977): 94–102.

Montefiore, Hugh, and H. E. W. Turner. *Thomas and the Evangelists.* SBT 35. London: SCM Press, 1962.

Mott, Stephen. "Wealth." *Harper's Bible Dictionary.* San Francisco: Harper & Row, 1985, 1122–23.

Moule, C. F. D. *An Idiom Book of New Testament Greek.* Cambridge: Cambridge University Press, 1968.

Navone, John. *Themes of St. Luke.* Rome: Gregorian University Press, 1970.

Neirynck, F. "Recent Developments in the Study of Q." In *Logia: Les paroles de Jésus—The Sayings of Jesus. Mémorial Joseph Coppens,* edited by J. Delobel, 29–75. BETL 59. Louvain: University Press, 1982.

Neirynck, F., and F. Van Segbroeck. "Q Bibliography." Ibid., 561–86.

Neusner, Jacob. "The Formation of Rabbinic Judaism: Yabneh (Jamnia) from A.D. 70–100." *ANRW* II.19.2 (1979): 3–42.

———. *The Pharisees: Rabbinic Perspectives.* Hoboken, N.J.: Ktav Pub. House, 1985.

Newman, L. I. *The Hasidic Anthology.* New York: Bloch Pub. Co., 1944.

Neyrey, J. "The Idea of Purity in Mark's Gospel." *Semeia* 35 (1986): 91–128.

Nickelsburg, George W. E. "The Apocalyptic Message of 1 Enoch 92–105." *CBQ* 39 (1977): 309–28.

———. "Riches, the Rich, and God's Judgment in 1 Enoch 92–105 and the Gospel according to Luke." *NTS* 25 (1978–79): 324–44.

Norwood, F. A. " 'Compel Them to Come In': The History of Luke 14:23." *Religion in Life* 23 (1953–54): 516–27.

Ogawa, Akira. "Paraboles de l'Israël véritable? Reconsidération critique de Mt. XXI 28—XXII 14." *NovT* 21 (1979): 121–49.

Patte, Daniel. *The Gospel according to Matthew: A Structural Commentary on Matthew's Faith.* Philadelphia: Fortress Press, 1987.

Pedersen, Johannes. *Israel: Its Life and Culture I–II.* London: Oxford University Press, 1926.

Perkins, Pheme. *Resurrection: New Testament Witness and Contemporary Reflection.* Garden City, N.Y.: Doubleday & Co., 1984.

Perrin, Norman. "Biblical Scholarship in a New Vein." *Int* 21 (1967): 465–69.

———. *The Kingdom of God in the Teaching of Jesus.* Philadelphia: Westminster Press; London: SCM Press, 1963.

———. *A Modern Pilgrimage in New Testament Christology.* Philadelphia: Fortress Press, 1974.

———. *Rediscovering the Teaching of Jesus.* New York: Harper & Row, 1967.

———. *What Is Redaction Criticism?* Philadelphia: Fortress Press, 1969.

Perrin, Norman, and Dennis C. Duling. *The New Testament: An Introduction.* 2d rev. ed. New York: Harcourt Brace Jovanovich, 1982.

Pesch, Rudolf. *Das Markusevangelium.* 2 vols. HTKNT 2. Freiburg/Basel/Vienna: Verlag Herder, 1976, 1977.

———. *Naherwartungen: Tradition und Redaktion in Mk 13.* Düsseldorf: Patmos Verlag, 1968.

Pilgrim, Walter E. *Good News to the Poor: Wealth and Poverty in Luke-Acts.* Minneapolis: Augsburg Pub. House, 1981.

Polk, T. "Paradigms, Parables, and Mĕšālîm: On Reading the Māšāl in Scripture." *CBQ* 45 (1983): 564–83.

Posner, R. "Marriage Ceremony." *EncJud* 11:1032–42.

Przybylski, Benno. *Righteousness in Matthew and His World of Thought.* SNTSMS 41. Cambridge: Cambridge University Press, 1980.

Ramaroson, L. "Le coeur du troisième évangile: Lc 15." *Bib* 60 (1979): 348–60.

Reagan, Charles E., and David Stewart, eds. *The Philosophy of Paul Ricoeur: An Anthology of His Work.* Boston: Beacon Press, 1978.

Rhoads, David, and Donald Michie. *Mark as Story: An Introduction to the Narrative of a Gospel.* Philadelphia: Fortress Press, 1982.

Riches, John. *Jesus and the Transformation of Judaism.* New York: Seabury Press; London: Longman & Todd, 1980.

Ricoeur, Paul. "Biblical Hermeneutics." *Semeia* 4 (1975): 29–148.

———. "From Proclamation to Narrative." *JR* 64 (1984): 501–12.

———. "Listening to the Parables of Jesus." In *The Philosophy of Paul Ricoeur,* edited by Reagan and Stewart, 239–45.

Ringe, Sharon. *Jesus, Liberation, and the Biblical Jubilee.* OBT 19. Philadelphia: Fortress Press, 1985.

Ringgren, H. "*abh.*" *TDOT* 1:16–19.

———. *Israelite Religion.* Philadelphia: Fortress Press, 1966.

Rivkin, Ellis. "Pharisees." *IDBSup*, 657–63.

Robbins, Vernon K. *Jesus the Teacher: A Socio-Rhetorical Interpretation of Mark.* Philadelphia: Fortress Press, 1984.

Robertson, David. "Literature, The Bible as." *IDBSup*, 547–51.

Robinson, James M., ed. *The Nag Hammadi Library in English.* San Francisco: Harper & Row, 1977.

Ruether, Rosemary R., ed. *Religion and Sexism: Images of Women in the Jewish and Christian Traditions.* New York: Simon & Schuster, 1974.

Sanders, Edward P. *Jesus and Judaism.* Philadelphia: Fortress Press, 1985.

Sanders, Jack T. "Tradition and Redaction in Luke xv. 11–32." *NTS* 15 (1968–69): 433–48.

Schillebeeckx, Edward. *Jesus: An Experiment in Christology.* New York: Seabury Press, 1979.

Schneiders, Sandra. *Women and the Word.* New York: Paulist Press, 1986.

Scholes, Robert. *Elements of Fiction.* New York: Oxford University Press, 1968.

Scholes, Robert, and Robert Kellogg. *The Nature of Narrative.* New York: Oxford University Press, 1966.

Schottroff, Luise. "Human Solidarity and the Goodness of God: The Parable of the Vineyard Workers." In *God of the Lowly*, edited by Schottroff and Stegemann, 129–47.

Schottroff, Willy, and Wolfgang Stegemann, eds. *God of the Lowly: Socio-Historical Interpretations of the Bible.* Maryknoll, N.Y.: Orbis Books, 1984.

Schürer, Emil. *The History of the Jewish People in the Age of Jesus Christ.* 3 vols. Rev. ed. by G. Vermes, F. Millar, and M. Black. Edinburgh: T. & T. Clark, 1973, 1979.

Schüssler Fiorenza, Elisabeth. "A Feminist Critical Interpretation for Liberation: Martha and Mary, Luke 10:38–42." *Religion and Intellectual Life* 3 (1986): 21–36.

———. *In Memory of Her: A Feminist Theological Reconstruction of Christian Origins.* New York: Crossroad Pub. Co., 1983.

Schweitzer, Albert. *The Quest of the Historical Jesus.* New York: Macmillan Co., 1961 [1906].

Schweizer, Eduard. *The Good News according to Luke.* Atlanta: John Knox Press, 1984.

———. *The Good News according to Matthew.* Atlanta: John Knox Press, 1975.

———. "Observance of the Law and Charismatic Activity in Matthew." *NTS* 16 (1969–70): 213–30.

———. "The Portrayal of the Life of Faith in the Gospel of Mark." *Int* 32 (1978): 387–99. Also in *Interpreting the Gospels*, edited by Mays, 168–82.

Scott, Bernard B. "A Master's Praise: Luke 16, 1–8ª." *Bib* 64 (1983): 173–88.

Seccombe, David P. *Possessions and the Poor in Luke-Acts.* SNTU 6. Linz: SNTU, 1982.

Segundo, Juan Luis. *The Historical Jesus of the Synoptics.* Volume 2 of *Jesus of Nazareth Yesterday and Today.* Maryknoll, N.Y.: Orbis Books, 1985.

Sellin, G. "Lukas als Gleichniserzähler: Die Erzählung vom barmherzigen Samariter (Lk 10:25–37)." *ZNW* 65 (1974): 166–89; 66 (1975): 19–60.

Shah, Idries. *Tales of the Dervishes*. New York: E. P. Dutton & Co., 1970.

Sider, J. W. "The Meaning of *Parabolē* in the Usage of the Synoptic Evangelists." *Bib* 62 (1981): 453–70.

Sider, Ronald J. "A Plea for Conservative Radicals and Radical Conservatives." *Christian Century* 103, 28 (Oct. 1, 1986), 834–38.

Soden, H. von. "adelphos." *TDNT* 1:144–46.

Sommer, F. *The World's Greatest Short Story: A Study of Present-Day Significance of the Family Pattern of Life*. Oswega, Kans.: Carpenter Press, 1948.

Sparks, H. F. D., ed. *The Apocryphal Old Testament*. Oxford: Clarendon Press, 1984.

Stanton, Graham, ed. *The Interpretation of Matthew*. IRT 3. Philadelphia: Fortress Press, 1983.

———. "The Origin and Purpose of Matthew's Gospel: Matthean Scholarship from 1945–1980." *ANRW* II.25.3 (1984): 1890–1952.

Stegemann, Wolfgang. *The Gospel and the Poor*. Philadelphia: Fortress Press, 1984.

Stewart, R. A. "The Parable Form in the Old Testament and the Rabbinic Literature." *EvQ* 36 (1964): 133–47.

Streeter, B. H. *The Four Gospels: A Study of Origins*. London: Macmillan & Co., 1924.

Talbert, Charles H. *Literary Patterns, Theological Themes, and the Genre of Luke-Acts*. SBLMS 20. Missoula, Mont.: Scholars Press, 1974.

———. "Shifting Sands: The Recent Study of the Gospel of Luke." *Int* 30 (1976): 381–95. Also in *Interpreting the Gospels*, edited by Mays, 197–213.

———. *What Is a Gospel? The Genre of the Canonical Gospels*. Philadelphia: Fortress Press, 1977.

———, ed. *Perspectives on Luke-Acts*. Danville, Va.: Association of Baptist Professors of Religion, 1978.

Tannehill, Robert C. "The Disciples in Mark: The Function of a Narrative Role." *JR* 57 (1977): 386–405.

———. "The Gospel of Mark as Narrative Christology." *Semeia* 16 (1980): 57–95.

———. *The Sword of His Mouth*. SS 1. Missoula, Mont.: Scholars Press; Philadelphia: Fortress Press, 1975.

Taylor, Vincent. *The Gospel according to St. Mark*. London: Macmillan & Co., 1952.

Tcherikover, Victor A., and Alexander Fuks, eds. *Corpus Papyrorum Judaicarum*. 3 vols. Cambridge: Harvard University Press, 1957–64.

Theissen, Gerd. *Sociology of Early Palestinian Christianity*, trans. J. Bowden. Philadelphia: Fortress Press, 1978.

Thompson, William G. "An Historical Perspective in the Gospel of Matthew." *JBL* 93 (1974): 243–62.

———. *Matthew's Advice to a Divided Community.* AnBib 44. Rome: Biblical Institute Press, 1970.

Thompson, William G., and Eugene LaVerdiere. "New Testament Communities in Transition: A Study of Matthew and Luke." *TS* 37 (1976): 567–97.

Tracy, David. *The Analogical Imagination.* New York: Crossroad Pub. Co., 1981.

———. "Theological Classics in Contemporary Theology." *TD* 25 (1977): 347–55.

Trible, Phyllis. *God and the Rhetoric of Sexuality.* OBT 2. Philadelphia: Fortress Press, 1978.

Trites, A. "The Prayer Motif in Luke-Acts." In *Perspectives on Luke-Acts,* edited by Talbert, 168–86.

Trocmé, Etienne. "Why Parables? A Study of Mark IV." *BJRL* 59 (1976–77): 458–71.

Tuckett, Christopher, ed. *The Messianic Secret.* IRT 1. Philadelphia: Fortress Press, 1983.

Vermes, Geza. *The Dead Sea Scrolls in English.* 2d ed. Baltimore: Penguin Books, 1975.

———. *Jesus and the World of Judaism.* Philadelphia: Fortress Press, 1984.

———. *Jesus the Jew: A Historian's Reading of the Gospels.* Philadelphia: Fortress Press; London: William Collins Sons & Co., 1973.

Via, E. Jane. "Women, the Discipleship of Service, and the Early Christian Ritual Meal in the Gospel of Luke," *St. Luke's Journal of Theology* 29 (1985–86): 37–60.

Weeden, Theodore J. *Mark—Traditions in Conflict.* Philadelphia: Fortress Press, 1971.

Wilder, Amos N., "New Testament Studies, 1920–1950: Reminiscences of a Changing Discipline," *JR* 64 (1984): 432–51.

Williams, James G. *Gospel against Parable: Mark's Language of Mystery.* Bible and Literature Series 12. Decatur, Ga.: Almond Press; Sheffield: JSOT Press, 1985.

Wimsatt, William. *The Verbal Icon: Studies in the Meaning of Poetry.* Lexington, Ky.: University of Kentucky Press, 1954.

Wrede, William. *The Messianic Secret.* London: James Clark & Co., 1971 [1901].

Ziesler, J. "Luke and the Pharisees." *NTS* 25 (1978–79): 146–57.

Zumstein, J. *La condition du croyant dans l'Evangile selon Matthieu.* OBO 16. Fribourg: Editions Universitaires; Göttingen: Vandenhoeck & Ruprecht, 1977.

INDEX OF PARABLES*

The Allegory of the Seeds (Mark 4:13–20; Matt. 13:18–23; Luke 8:11–15), 7, 28, 29, 30, 31, 33, 39, 46–47, 48, 50, 61, 65, 135

The Doorkeeper *or* the Waiting Servants (Mark 13:33–37), 28, 53, 58–60, 61, 99

The Faithful and Wise Servant (Matt. 24:45–51; Luke 12:42–46), 98–101, 106

The Fig Tree (Mark 13:28–29; Matt. 24:32–33; Luke 21:29–31), 28, 58, 61, 205

The Friend at Midnight (Luke 11:5–8), 103, 185–87, 192, 193

The Good Samaritan (Luke 10:29–37), 4, 8, 126, 127, 128, 129–34, 136, 137, 138, 146, 152, 175, 176, 193, 209, 210

The Great Supper *or* the Marriage Feast (Matt. 22:1–14; Luke 14:16–24), 5, 86, 92–96 (Matt.), 102, 140–46 (Luke), 169, 201

The Hidden Treasure (Matt. 13:44), 8, 65, 68–69

The Laborers in the Vineyard (Matt. 20:1–16), 4, 13, 18, 70, 72, 79–85, 89, 108, 201, 203

The Leaven (Matt. 13:33; Luke 13:20–21), 5, 65, 67

The Lost Coin (Luke 15:8–10), 140, 146, 147, 148, 149–51, 155, 158, 159

The Lost Sheep (Matt. 18:12–14; Luke 15:4–7), 11, 17, 18, 72–73 (Matt.), 78, 99, 146, 147–49 (Luke), 150–51, 155, 158, 159

The Mustard Seed (Mark 4:30–32; Matt. 13:31–32; Luke 13:18–19), 28, 29, 33, 34, 36–37, 65, 67

The Net (Matt. 13:47–50), 65, 69, 94

The Pearl (Matt. 13:45–46), 13, 17, 65, 68–69

The Pharisee and the Tax Collector (Luke 18:9–14), 19, 126, 180, 187–91, 193

The Prodigal Son (Luke 15:11–32), 4, 5, 24, 126, 140, 146, 151–58, 159, 160, 161, 162, 167, 168

* Index is to each parable as a whole; for individual verses consult the citation index. Biblical references are given only for identification and imply nothing about the original extent of the parable. Page numbers in bold designate the principal treatment of a given parable.

The Rich Fool (Luke 12:13–21),
128, 175, **176–78**, 179, 180
The Rich Man and Lazarus (Luke
16:19–31), 25, 112, 128, 140,
162, **169–72**, 173, 175, 176, 179
The Seed Growing Secretly (Mark
4:26–29), 28, 29, 32, **34–36**, 61,
63, 65, 67
The Sheep and the Goats (Matt.
25:31–46), 95, 98, 104, **109–25**,
171
The Sower (Mark 4:3–9; Matt.
13:3–9; Luke 8:5–8), 4, 28, 29,
30, 31, **33–34**, 35, 40, 46, 48,
64, 66, 68, 137
The Talents *or* the Pounds (Matt.
25:14–30; Luke 19:11–27), 48,
53, 58, 99, **105–9**, 154, 165, 204
The Ten Maidens (Matt. 25:1–13),
63, **101–5**

The Two Debtors (Luke 7:41–43),
19, 126
The Two Sons (Matt. 21:28–32),
86, **87–89**, 201
The Unjust Steward (Luke 16:1–8),
4, 13, 23, 107, 126, 159, **162–
69**, 181
The Unmerciful Servant (Matt.
18:23–35), 8, 23, 24, 70, 71, **72–
79**, 84, 108, 129, 133, 164, 203
The Wheat and the Tares (Matt.
13:24–30, 36–43), 65, **67–68**,
69, 89, 104, 109
The Wicked Tenants (Mark 12:1–
11; Matt. 21:33–45; Luke 20:9–
18), 4, 5, 24, 28, **52–57** (Mark),
86, 87, **89–92** (Matt.), 201
The Widow and the Judge (Luke
18:1–8), 126, 175, **180–84**, 185,
193

INDEX OF CITATIONS

OLD TESTAMENT

Genesis
15:2—169
24:35—170
27:1–45—159
32:22–32—216
37—48—159
41:41–42—155

Exodus
3:7–8—132
4:21—41
4:22—161
8:15—41
8:32—41
9:34—41
20:14–15—189
22:21–27—118n
22:21–23—182n
22:24—165n
34:6—55

Leviticus
19:18—129
21:1–2—131
23:13—132
25:35–37—165n

Numbers
14:18—55
15:37–41—50

Deuteronomy
4:5–6—137
5:15—1
5:17–19—189
6:4–9—50
10:14–19—182n
10:18—182n
11:13–21—50
14:28–29—182n
15:1–11—118n
20:5–7—141
21:18–21—156
23:19–20—165n
24:5—141
28:13–14—137
32:6—161
32:18—149n

Judges
6:1–23—159
9:7–15—5, 37
14:10–18—5

1 Samuel
2:6—1
10:12—5
16:6–13—159

2 Samuel
12:1–4—5, 18
12:3—18
12:5–10—18
12:5—87

1 Kings
18:13—52
18:22–27—52

2 Chronicles
12:6—71
19:5–6—181
24:21—52
36:15–16—52

Nehemiah
9:8—71
9:16—55
9:26—52

Job
22:9–11—182n
22:21 (LXX)—90n
38:4—1
38:8—1
42:10–17—170

Psalms
1:3—37
5:11—151n
7:9—71
11:7—118n
14:1—178
15:5—165n
16:11—151n
20:5—151n
21:1—151n
22:9—161n
24:3–5—190
31:5—191
33:1—151n
33:5—118n
37:28—118n
43:4—151n
49:10—178
51—190
51:8—151n
53:1—178
65:7—49
68:5—182n
69:33—182
72:12—182
78:2—65
80:8–18—52
82:1–5—118n
82:3–4—71
86:15—55
92:13–15—37
94:1–7—182n
96:11—151n
99:4—118n
103:6—71
103:8—55
103:17—71
104:7—49
104:12—37
104:31—151n
107:23–31—49
116:5—71
118:22–23—53
123:2—135n, 161n
145:8—55

146:9—182n

Proverbs
1:1—5
1:6—5
6:6–11—109
6:11—109
10:1–5, 156n
11:30–31—90
17:21—156n
17:25—156n
19:18—156n
19:26—156n
20:20—156n
22:15—156n
22:22–23—182
23:1–12—140
23:22–25—156n
26:7–9—5
28:24—156n
31:22—170

Ecclesiastes
3:1–9—35
3:10–13—170

Isaiah
1:2–20—45
1:16–17—182n
5:1–7—5, 71, 90n
5:1–2—52
5:1—53, 55
5:2—52
5:24–25—94
6:9–13—45
6:9–10—30, 39, 44,
  65, 207n
6:10—40–41, 44
9:6–7—118n
11:3–5—118n
22:21—155
25:6–8—95, 142
28:17–18—71
30:18—118n
42:1–4—71, 116

42:6—121
42:14—149n, 161n
45:9–11—161
45:10—135n
49:13–15—149n
49:14–15—1
49:23—135n
51:2—135n
52:13—53:12—116
55:1–2—142n
58:5–9—132
58:6—206
61:1–2—175, 206
61:1—142
61:8—118n
62:1–5—94
64:8—161
65:13–14—142n
66:7–9—149n
66:13—149n, 161n

Jeremiah
1:9–10—45
1:10—40
2:21—52
3:11–14—55
3:19—161
7:25–26—89
9:24—71
17:7–8—37
22:15–17—118n
31:20—149n
49:11—182n

Ezekiel
16:59–63—55
17:3–24—5
17:22–24—37
18:8—165n
18:13—165n
18:17—165n
31—37
33:31–32—137
34—148
34:6–8—73, 149

Daniel
4:10–12—37
4:20–27—37
7:13–14—114
9:14—71

Hosea
2—1
2:2—55
2:14–20—55
2:19–20—71
2:19—77, 83

6:6—119
6:6 (LXX)—132
10:1—52
11:1–4—149n

Joel
3:13—35

Amos
2:6–7—181
5:10–13—181

Micah
2:4—5

Habakkuk
2:6—5

Zechariah
9:9—116

Malachi
2:10—161

APOCRYPHA (DEUTEROCANONICAL BOOKS)

2 Esdras
12:7—190

Wisdom of Solomon
2:12–24—116
5:1–23—116

Sirach
1:16–18—90n
6:18–19 (LXX)—90n
11:19–20—178
31:12–32:13—140
37:22–23—90n

50:25–26—130

1 Maccabees
3:1–9—159
3:56—141
8:14—170

NEW TESTAMENT

Matthew
1:1—116, 117, 200
1:20—116, 117
1:23—69, 115, 203
2:1–12—116
2:2—117
2:13–14—117
2:17—91
2:19—196
2:23—91
3:1–4—91
3:2—207n
3:3—91
3:8—90, 207n
3:10—90
3:11—207n
3:17—116
4:1–11—116
4:14—91
4:17—77, 118, 175, 207

4:18–22—84, 86
4:23—71, 85, 118
5–7—64, 71, 201
5:1–11—98
5:1—201
5:6–7—119
5:6—71
5:9—203
5:10—71
5:11–12—121
5:12—91
5:13–16—120
5:13—121
5:14–16—103
5:14–6, 121
5:15–48, 65
5:16—121
5:17–48—96
5:17–20—79, 85, 199
5:17—91
5:20—71

5:21–48—71
5:21–22—178
5:22–24—111
5:29—83
5:43–46—83
5:44–45—203
5:44—192
5:45—202
5:48—79, 211
6:10—88
6:12—74, 78
6:15—78
6:22—82–83
6:24—163, 168
6:25–34—136
6:25–33—168, 203
6:30—72, 109
6:32—114
6:33—84
7:2—48, 65
7:3–5—111

7:7—75
7:10—203
7:12—76
7:15–23—79
7:15–20—90
7:15–18—104
7:21–23—104
7:21—69, 88, 91
7:22—91
7:24–27—137
7:24—178
7:28—65, 201
8:1–4—79
8:5–13—79
8:11–12—143
8:17—91
8:22—2
8:23–27—203
8:26—72, 109
9:9—175
9:11—79
9:13—119, 132
9:15—102
9:27—117, 119
9:35—71, 85, 118
9:37–38—80
10—13—117
10—64, 116, 121, 122, 201
10:5—117, 131
10:7—118
10:17–21—121
10:17–18—117
10:17—85
10:18—121
10:24—123, 203
10:25—203
10:26—2, 48, 65
10:39—142
10:40—111
10:42—72, 111
11—12—116
11:1—65
11:2–6—142
11:6—98

11:9—91
11:11—111
11:16—5
11:20–21—207n
11:25–30—201
11:25–27—116
11:28–30—203
11:30—2
12:7—119, 132
12:9—85
12:17–21—116
12:17—91
12:18–21—71
12:18–20—117
12:30—107
12:41—207n
12:46–50—64
12:49–50—111
12:50—88, 137
13—4n, 64–70
13:1–52—64
13:1–35—201
13:1–9—33–34
13:9—118
13:10–17—64
13:10—64
13:11—40n, 64, 66
13:12—66, 105
13:13—41n, 64
13:15–17—66
13:16–17—65
13:16—98
13:18—67
13:19—65
13:24–30—65, 67, 109
13:24–27—94
13:24—67
13:27—89
13:30—67
13:31–32—36–37, 65, 67
13:31—5
13:32—36, 63
13:33—5, 65, 67

13:35—65, 91
13:36–52—201
13:36–43—65, 68, 69, 104, 109
13:36—65, 66, 68
13:40—69
13:42—69
13:43—104
13:44–50—65
13:44–46—63, 68
13:44—8, 69
13:45–46—13, 17
13:47–50—69, 94
13:51–52—65
13:53–58—64
13:53—65
13:54—85
13:57—91
14:5–9—91
14:5—91
14:22—145n
14:28–32—201
14:31—72, 109
15:22—117, 119
16:8—72, 109
16:13–19—201
16:17—98
16:18–20—200
16:18—199
16:19—78
16:28—204
16:30–33—83n
17:15—119
17:20—72
17:22–23—83n, 84
17:24–27—201
18—64, 84, 147, 201
18:1–14—72
18:1–10—72
18:1–9—72
18:3—2
18:4—187
18:6—111
18:10–14—72, 99
18:10—111

18:12–14—17
18:13—148
18:14—73, 88, 111
18:15–35—72
18:15–20—72, 78,
   200
18:15—111
18:16—78
18:17—78, 100, 199
18:18–19—78
18:20—203
18:21–22—73
18:21—73, 111
18:22—73
18:23–35—8, 23, 24,
   70, 71, 72–79, 108,
   129, 133, 164
18:23–30—108
18:23–25—74
18:23—5, 94, 106,
   164
18:24—63, 74, 75,
   108
18:26—74, 75
18:27—74, 75, 77
18:28—74
18:29—24, 74, 75
18:30—74
18:31–32—74
18:31—24, 76
18:32—74, 108
18:32–33—74
18:33—74, 77
18:34—74, 76
18:35—73, 74, 77,
   111
19:1—20:16—70–72
19:1—65
19:10–12—103
19:28—84, 95n, 114,
   143
19:30—81, 84
20:1–16—13, 70, 72,
   79–85, 201

20:1–15—108
20:1–13—108
20:1–7—79
20:1—89
20:2—75, 80
20:4—80
20:7—80
20:8–11—79, 80
20:8—10, 80, 156
20:10—80
20:11–15—79
20:11—80
20:12–15—80
20:12—80, 82
20:13—80, 82
20:14—80
20:15—80, 108
20:16—80, 84
20:17–19—83n
20:17–18—84
20:28—125n
20:30–31—117
20:30—119
20:31—119
21:5—115
21:23–27—87
21:26—91
21:28—22:14—85–96
21:28–32—86, 87–89,
   201
21:28—87
21:30—91
21:31–32—87
21:31—90
21:32—71, 88, 91
21:33–45—4, 52, 87,
   89–92, 201
21:33–43—86
21:33—89
21:34—89, 91
21:35–36—89, 94
21:35—91
21:36—91
21:39—90

21:40–41—90
21:43—90, 97
21:46—90, 91
22:1–14—5, 86, 92–
   96, 201
22:1–2—102
22:2–4—93
22:5–6—141
22:6—94
22:7—94, 97, 142
22:11–14—93, 95
22:13—95n
22:15–40—129
22:34–40—71, 128
22:36—129
23—85, 86n, 96, 172,
   187
23:1–12—201
23:1–7—202
23:2–36—199
23:7–10—88
23:8–12—202
23:8–11—200
23:8–9—203
23:12—187
23:23—71, 78, 96
23:29–37—52
23:29–32—91
23:32–36—96
23:34–39—95
23:37–38—97
24—25—26, 64, 96–
   125, 201
24—122
24:1–36—97, 101
24:1—114
24:9–14—121
24:10–12—121
24:12—121
24:13—121
24:14—71, 114, 118,
   121
24:27—97
24:30—97

24:32–33—58
24:34–40—136
24:37—25:46—97, 114
24:37–39—98
24:37—97
24:40–41—98
24:42–44—97, 98
24:42—97
24:43—103
24:44—97
24:45—25:30—98
24:45–51—98–101
24:45—98, 178
24:46—97, 98
24:47—106, 108
24:48–50—100
24:48—97, 98, 113
24:49–50—106
24:50–51—99
24:50—97, 107
24:51—97, 100
25:1–13—63, 101–5
25:1—103n
25:2–24, 178
25:4—178
25:5—97
25:6—103
25:8—178
25:9—178
25:10—97
25:11–12—104
25:11—97, 103, 113
25:13—97, 101, 105
25:14–30—48, 53, 58, 99, 105–9, 154, 165
25:14—22, 59, 107
25:15—63, 106
25:19–24—108
25:19—74, 97
25:20—113
25:21—97, 106
25:23—97, 106

25:24—97, 106, 107, 113
25:29—48, 105
25:30—97
25:31–46—95, 98, 104, 109–25, 171
25:31–33—114n
25:31—97, 112, 113
25:32–33—112
25:32—110, 114
25:34–36—122
25:34—67, 94, 97, 113, 118
25:35–36—113
25:36—122
25:37—97, 113, 118, 119
25:38—113
25:39—113
25:40—72, 94, 113
25:42–43—113
25:44—97, 113, 114
25:45—72, 110, 113
25:46—97, 118, 119
26:1—65
26:2—125
26:13—71, 118
26:39—195
26:42—88
26:53—196
26:56—91
27:9—91
27:11—117
27:19—196
27:25—85, 199
27:29—117
27:37—117
27:42—117
27:51–54—200
28:10—111
28:16–20—66, 86, 91, 114–15, 201, 207
28:18–20—122

28:19–20—117
28:19—114, 115n
28:20—69, 202, 203

Mark
1:1—198
1:4—207n
1:7—48n, 49
1:8—198
1:9—48n
1:11—52, 198
1:14–16—59n
1:14–15—3, 34, 51, 59
1:14—46, 48
1:15—32, 46, 55, 59, 61, 175, 204, 207
1:16–20—47, 50
1:16–17—44
1:18—198
1:22—59
1:24—49, 198
1:25—42
1:27—49, 59, 196
1:29—60
1:31—139
1:34—42
1:37—43
1:39—48
1:41—195
1:43–45—42
1:43—195
2:1–22—172
2:1–12—60
2:7—196
2:10—59, 198
2:12—196n
2:13—40
2:14–15—47
2:14—175
2:19–20—28
2:19—102
2:21–22—28
2:27—3:5—197

2:28—198
3:5—195
3:6—56
3:11–12—42
3:13—192
3:13b–19—50
3:14–15—50
3:14—50
3:15—59
3:16—44
3:19–20—43
3:20–21—30
3:21—43, 195
3:22–30—30
3:23–30—43, 49
3:23–27—4, 28
3:23—28, 43, 58
3:24—32
3:28—49
3:31–35—30, 60, 64
3:31—43
3:32—43
3:34–35—43
3:34—45
3:35—137
4—29–32, 40n, 43,
   46, 49, 50, 51, 56,
   61
4:1–34—49, 52
4:1–20—29n
4:1–9—31, 39, 47, 61
4:1–2—29, 30, 31, 49
4:1—30, 40, 43
4:2—30, 32
4:3–9—28, 29, 30,
   31, 33–34, 40
4:3—30, 49
4:4—30, 33
4:5–6—33
4:5—34
4:7—33
4:8—10, 15, 34, 38,
   50
4:9—48, 49
4:10–25—32, 39–46

4:10–12—5n, 29, 30,
   31, 32, 39–46, 49,
   61, 64
4:10—30, 31, 39, 42,
   43, 66
4:11–32—31
4:11–25—29
4:11–12—30, 39, 42,
   44, 47
4:11—28, 30, 32, 39,
   42, 43, 58, 197
4:12—32, 39, 41, 44,
   50, 64
4:13–20—7, 28, 29,
   30, 31, 33, 39, 46–
   47, 48, 61
4:13—30, 32, 46, 48
4:14—46, 47
4:15—47, 50
4:16—50
4:17—47
4:18—50
4:19—47
4:20—47, 50, 61
4:21–25—28, 31, 32,
   39, 47–49
4:21–24—65
4:21–22—32, 48
4:21—30, 32, 48n,
   104, 121
4:22—48, 61
4:23–25—32
4:23—48, 49
4:24–25—48
4:24—30, 32, 48, 49
4:25—2, 64, 66, 105
4:26–34—39
4:26–32—31, 32
4:26–29—28, 29, 34–
   36, 61, 67
4:26—30, 32
4:27—35
4:28—35
4:29—35

4:30–32—28, 29, 36–
   37
4:30—5, 30
4:31—30, 36
4:32—15, 30, 36, 37,
   63
4:33–34—29, 31, 32,
   40, 42, 49
4:33—30, 32, 49
4:34—32, 42
4:35–41—49, 50
4:35—30
4:38—49
4:41—196, 198
5:4–6—195
5:7—196, 198
5:15—196n
5:20—196n
5:21–24—30
5:24—40
5:25–34—30
5:25–26—195
5:30–32—195
5:33—196n
5:35–43—30
5:39–43—60
5:42—196n
5:43—42
6:1–6—45, 64
6:1—48
6:2—47, 196
6:4—55
6:6—195
6:7–13—50
6:7—59
6:8–13—50
6:12—207n
6:14–29—59n
6:15—55
6:34—40
6:45—145n
6:50—196n, 198
6:51—196n
6:52—40
7:1–23—197

7:9–13—154
7:14–17—4, 50
7:14–15—28
7:15–17—5n
7:17–22—42
7:17—28, 60
7:18–40, 50
7:24—42
7:36—42
7:37—196n
8:11–13—19
8:12—195
8:17–21—40
8:18—50, 197, 198
8:26—42, 55
8:27–10:45—83
8:27—126, 196
8:29—196
8:30–9:1—51
8:30—42
8:31–32—40, 47,
  59n, 83n
8:31—45, 198
8:32—198
8:33—45
8:34—206
8:38—48
9:1—32, 204
9:7—52, 198
9:9—42
9:28—60
9:30–32—83n
9:30—42
9:31—59n, 198
9:32—198
9:33–37—72
9:33—126, 195
9:35—60
9:38–41—40
9:42–50—121
9:42–48—72
9:47—32
9:50—1, 121
10:10—60
10:13–16—197

10:14—32, 195
10:21—195
10:22—47
10:23–25—32, 47
10:24—196
10:25—28
10:26—196
10:28–31—60
10:30—47, 81
10:32–34—83n
10:32—126, 198
10:33–34—59n
10:42–45—197
10:44—60
10:45—48, 60, 62,
  125n, 139, 149
10:50–51—195
10:52—197
11:1—16:8—56
11:1—12:12—56
11:12–14—56
11:14—56
11:17—56, 60
11:18—43, 56, 196
11:20–21—56
11:27—52
11:28—196
12—52–57
12:1–11—4, 5, 28,
  52–57, 89
12:1–9—28
12:1—52, 54, 89
12:2–5—52
12:2—54, 59, 89
12:4–5—54
12:6—52, 53, 54
12:7–8—54
12:9—52, 53, 54, 55,
  56, 90
12:10–11—53, 55
12:12—41, 43, 52, 56
12:13–34—56, 56n,
  129
12:13–17—56
12:17—40, 196

12:18–27—56
12:28–34—56, 128
12:28–31—136
12:28—129
12:29—50
12:34—32
12:40—182n
13—29, 57–62
13:1–37—57
13:2—57
13:3–37—42
13:4—57
13:5–27—58
13:5—59
13:6—51, 57
13:7–8—57
13:9–23—57
13:9–13—50, 59n,
  121, 198
13:9—59
13:10—60
13:12—61
13:13—60, 61
13:21–22—51, 57
13:21—57
13:22—57, 61
13:23—59
13:24–27—57
13:24—57
13:26–27—49
13:26—51, 58
13:27—61
13:28–29—28, 58, 61
13:28—28, 58
13:29—58, 205
13:30–32—58, 61
13:31—58
13:32—61
13:33–37—53, 58–60,
  61, 99
13:33–36—58, 61
13:33—59
13:34–37—28
13:34—59
13:35—59, 103

13:37—59
14:1—43
14:20—135
14:27-28—47
14:28—198
14:34—59
14:35—195
14:36—45
14:37—59, 61
14:38—59
14:50—40, 47, 198
14:62—48, 49, 51, 56
14:65—197
14:66-72—198
14:68-71—44
14:71—40
14:72—197
15:2—197
15:15—196
15:16-20—196
15:26-39—198
15:32—19, 197
15:39—40, 197
15:42-43—197
16:1-8—197
16:5—196
16:6—62, 197
16:7—198
16:8—196

Luke

1:1-4—206
1:2—135
1:5—2:52—206
1:5-13—127
1:6—135n
1:8-23—135
1:10—191
1:14—150
1:16-17—207n
1:16—207
1:17—208
1:21—163
1:26-38—135

1:46-55—135, 192, 211
1:47—150
1:52-53—175
1:52—170
1:67-79—135, 192, 211
1:76-78—132
1:77-78—208
1:78—211
2:10-150
2:11—206
2:13-14—192
2:13—192
2:14—142
2:20—192
2:24—175
2:28-32—192
2:29-32—192
2:37—192
3:1—4:21—206
3:1-16—208
3:3—207n
3:7-12—205
3:8—207n
3:10—175, 210
3:20-21—192
3:21-22—191, 192
4:14-15—204
4:16-22—206
4:17-19—175
4:18—143
4:23—5
4:39—139
5:16—192
5:17-39—172
5:26—206
5:28—175
5:29—140
5:30—147
5:31-39—140
5:32—207n
5:33—192
5:34—102

5:36-39—5
6:12—192
6:20—142, 175
6:24-26—175
6:27—192
6:35—192
6:36—211
6:40—203
6:47-49—137
7:1-17—135
7:11-17—175
7:13—132, 163, 211
7:18-23—142
7:19—163
7:22—143, 175
7:31—5
7:33-34—140
7:36-50—140
7:36—140, 172
7:39—188
7:41-43—19, 126
7:44-46—135
8:5-8—33-34
8:14—136
8:15—135, 137
8:16—48, 121
8:18—105
8:21—137
9:3—127
9:18—192
9:23—206
9:27—204
9:28-29—192
9:51—19:27—26, 126, 128
9:51—18:14—126
9:51—10:20—128
9:51-56—128
9:51-55—131
9:51—127
9:57-62—128
9:57—127
10—4, 136-38
10:1-20—128

10:1—127, 163
10:2—127
10:5—142
10:9—205
10:11—205
10:13—207n
10:17—127
10:20–21—150
10:21—11:4—128
10:21–24—128
10:21–22—138, 192
10:23–24—65, 138
10:25–29—138
10:25–28—128–29, 134, 136
10:25—128, 129, 210
10:27—136
10:28—137
10:29–37—4, 8, 127, 129–34, 175, 209
10:29–36—127
10:29—129, 135
10:30–37—138
10:31—130
10:36—129
10:37—132, 210
10:38–42—134–39, 140
10:38—127
10:39—135, 137, 163
10:40—136, 139
10:41–42—136n, 139
10:41—163
10:42—135, 136
11:1–13—187
11:1–4—185, 192
11:1—127, 138
11:2–4—138
11:3—186, 192, 206
11:4—185, 192
11:5–13—185
11:5–8—103, 185–87, 192
11:5–7—186

11:5—186
11:7—185
11:8—186
11:9–13—186
11:13—127
11:23—107
11:28—137
11:32—207n
11:33—48, 104, 121
11:37–52—140
11:37—140, 172
11:39—163
11:41—175
12:1—13:9—176
12:1—176
12:2–12—176
12:11—136
12:12—187
12:13–21—128, 175, 176–78
12:13—176, 178
12:14–15—177
12:15–21—210
12:15—177, 180
12:16—177
12:17–19—177
12:17—188, 210
12:19—126, 177
12:20—178, 205
12:21—178
12:22–34—178
12:22–31—176
12:22—136, 176
12:25—136
12:33–34—128
12:33—175
12:35–56—59
12:37—139
12:41–48—168
12:41—176
12:42–46—98
12:42—163, 178
12:46—100n
12:47—137

12:49–56—205
12:50–51—142
12:54—176
13:1–5—185n
13:3—207n
13:5—207n
13:6—176
13:15—163
13:17—150
13:18–21—135, 147
13:18–19—36–37
13:19—36
13:22—127
13:29—140, 143
13:30—81, 127
13:31—172
13:32—206
13:33—127
13:34—52
14—16—140
14—144, 158
14:1–24—140
14:1–6—143
14:1—127, 140, 141, 144, 145, 172
14:7–14—140, 144
14:7–13—143
14:11—187
14:12–14—140
14:12–13—175
14:13—127, 143
14:14—143
14:15—141, 143
14:16–24—86, 92, 140–46
14:18–20—141
14:18—141
14:19—141
14:20—141
14:21—127, 141, 143, 175
14:23—141, 146
14:25–35—142
14:25–34—145

14:25—127
14:33—142
14:34—121
15—16—140, 173
15:1—16:31—174
15—146–62
15:1–10—23, 147–51
15:1–7—11
15:1–2—72, 79, 127, 162
15:1–5, 140, 147, 156
15:2—140, 147, 173
15:3–7—72, 140
15:4–10—135
15:4–7—18, 146, 149
15:4—148
15:5–7—149
15:5—148
15:6—148
15:7—150, 207n
15:8–10—140, 146, 149
15:8—149
15:9–10—149
15:9—148
15:10—150, 207n
15:11–32—5, 140, 146, 151–62, 167, 168
15:11–19—152, 153–54
15:11–22, 152, 167
15:13—154, 167
15:15–17—167
15:16—170
15:17–19—154, 167
15:17–18—210
15:17—126, 154, 188
15:18—154, 155
15:20–24—152, 154–56
15:20—15, 132, 152, 154, 155, 161n
15:21—155

15:22—152, 160
15:24—154, 159
15:25–32—12, 126, 152, 156–57
15:25—152
15:27—152
15:30—154
15:31—152
15:32—150, 154, 159, 167
16—158, 162–74
16:1–13—128, 140, 162
16:1–8—4, 13, 23, 107n, 126, 162–69
16:1–2—168
16:1—162, 163, 164, 165, 167, 177
16:3–4—167
16:3—126, 164, 167, 168, 188, 210
16:5—168
16:6—164, 165
16:7—163
16:8–13—162–63, 168
16:8—24, 163, 165, 167, 168, 178
16:9–13—162
16:9—163, 164
16:10—163
16:11—163
16:12—163
16:13—163, 168
16:14–31—169–74
16:14–18—172–74
16:14–15—162
16:14—162, 169, 172, 189
16:15—173
16:16–18—162
16:16—145, 173, 174
16:17—173
16:18—173

16:19–31—25, 112, 128, 140, 162, 169–72, 175
16:19–21—170
16:19—164, 177, 178
16:20—170
16:22–26—170
16:22–23—205
16:22—170
16:23—171
16:25—171
16:26—171
16:27–31—170
16:27—170, 171
16:29—173
16:30–31—171
16:30—171, 207n
16:31—171
17:3—207n
17:4—73, 207n
17:6—163
17:8—139
17:11–19—127, 209
17:11—127
17:16—127, 175
17:20–37—191
17:20–34—181
17:22–37—205
18—187
18:1–14—127, 135, 147, 180, 192
18:1–8—126, 175, 180–85
18:1—23, 180, 181, 185, 193
18:2–7—185, 187
18:2–6—181
18:2–5—180
18:2—183
18:3—182
18:4–5—126
18:4—182, 183, 184, 187, 188
18:5—183, 185
18:6–8—180

18:6—181, 183
18:7–8—181, 184–85
18:7—184
18:8—181, 185
18:9–14—19, 187–91
18:9—187
18:10–14—187
18:10—180
18:11—19, 188, 190
18:14—180, 187
18:15—180
18:18—210
18:35—127
19:1–10—128
19:1—127
19:5—206
19:7—147
19:8—175
19:9—206
19:10—138, 147, 150
19:11–27—58, 105–9, 154
19:11–12—105
19:11—105, 127, 205
19:12—59
19:26—105
19:27—105
19:38—142
20:9–18—52
20:21—127
20:46–47—182n
21:29–31—58
21:31—205
21:36—192
22:14–38—140
22:26–27—139
22:27—139
22:28–30—144
22:29–30—140, 143
22:31–34—192
22:32—207n
22:41—195
22:44–45—192
22:50–51—142

23:28–31—211
23:34—191, 192, 211
23:43—205
23:46—191, 211
23:48—190
24:19—55
24:20–49—140
24:27—172
24:28–49—143
24:30–31—192
24:34—163
24:44–49—207
24:44—172
24:47—127, 128, 145, 207n
24:48—209
24:49—208
24:51–52—191
24:52—150

John
4:7–10—130
6:25–33—100
8:48—130
10:1–18—148
11:1–40—134
12:2—134, 139
12:23–25—51
12:27–36—44
12:37–41—41
12:40—30, 44
13:16—203
14:26—187
15:2—90n
15:4—90n
15:5—90n
15:8—90n
15:16—90n
15:20—203
19:17—90

Acts
1:8–9—127
1:8—128, 145, 191, 205, 209

1:10—127
1:14—127, 191
1:22—209
1:24–25—191
2:1–4—191, 208
2:22—135
2:29—187
2:32—209
2:36—163
2:38–41—208
2:38—127, 207n, 209
2:41–47—175
2:41–42—208
2:42–47—193, 209
2:42—127, 192
2:43–45—128
2:44—179, 209n
2:46—150
3:1–10—127, 210
3:1—192
3:11–26—172
3:15—209
3:19–20—208
3:19—207n
4:4—46, 135
4:8—187
4:29–31—187
4:29–30—192
4:31—191
4:32–37—175, 193, 209
4:32–33—128
4:33—163
5:1–10—128
5:12–16—210
5:14—163
5:31—207n, 208
5:32—209
5:34—172
6:1–7—191
6:1–6—139
6:1–3—100
6:4—136
7:59–60—192
7:60—192

8:1–25—209
8:4—46
8:15—191
8:16—163
8:22—191, 207n, 208
8:24—191
8:25—127
8:26–40—210
9:1–30—210
9:2—127
9:11—192
9:31—135n
9:35—207n
10—144
10:1–45—210
10:2–4—191
10:2—175
10:4—175
10:9—191
10:30–31—191
10:31—175
10:39–41—209
10:43—127
11:3—144
11:5—191
11:18—207n
11:21–26—208
11:21—207n
12:5–12—192
12:5—192
13:1–3—191
13:24—207n
13:31—209
14:15—207n, 208
14:16—135n
14:23—191
15:19—207n, 208
16:13—192
16:14—179
17:30—207n, 208
18:27—179
19:4—207n
20:21—207n
20:36—192
21:5—192

22:3—135
22:15—209
23:6—172
24:17—175
26:2–24—208
26:16—209
26:18–20—207n
26:18—208
26:20—207n, 208
26:22—209
27:35—192
28:8—192
28:15—191
28:23–31—44
28:23—44
28:25–28—41
28:26—30
28:27—207n
28:31—187

Romans
1:24–25—177
1:29—177
2:13—137
3:24–25—125n
6:22—90n
7:4–5—90n
8:23—125n
9—11—159
9:6–13—159
9:16–29—41
10:16–21—41
11:7–10—41
11:17–24—52
11:25—44
12:6–8—60
12:11—109
13:14—95
16:2—147
16:25—44

1 Corinthians
1:23—44, 88
1:26–31—146
1:26–29—145
1:30—125n

2:1–2—44
2:7—44
3:2—100
3:5–10—52
3:5–9—12
3:7—52
4:1–2—99, 168
4:1—44
4:9–13—122
4:10—122
4:11—122
4:17—99
5:1–13—78
5:6–8—68
5:11—100
6:7–13—100
6:10—100
7:25–31—103
9:11—46
10:18—86n
11:17–22—100
11:21—100
11:26—144
12:4–11—60
15:35–36—52
15:42–43—52
15:58—60
16:10—60
16:19—60

2 Corinthians
4:7—122
4:8–9—122
6:4–5—122
6:5—59
8—9—174n
11:2—103n
11:23–29—122
11:23—122
11:27–28—59
11:27—122
12:9—122
12:10—122

Galatians
1:3–4—45

1:10—59
1:14—188
2:12-13—147
2:12—144
2:15—188
3:26-29—160
3:27—95
3:28—162
4:4-7—160
4:4-6—160
4:6—160
4:7—160
5:22-23—90n
6:6—46
6:16—86n

Ephesians
1:9—44
3:3—44
3:4—44
3:9—44
3:17—46
4:24—95
5:23-33—103n
6:21—99

Philippians
1:1—59, 95n
1:11—90n
2:5-11—14

2:5—193
2:29—147
3:4-6—188
4:17—90n

Colossians
1:6—90n
1:7—99
1:10—90n
2:7—46
2:8—46
3:5—177
3:12—95
4:5—105
4:7—95n
4:15—60

1 Thessalonians
1:6—46
4:16-17—103

1 Timothy
3:3—100
3:8—95n, 100
3:12—95n
4:4-5—170

Titus
1:7—100, 168
1:9—99

Philemon
9—122

Hebrews
5:12-14—100
12:11—90n
13:12—90
13:17—59

James
1:22—137
2:13—77
3:17-18—90n
5:19-20—73

1 Peter
2:21-25—125n
4:10—168
5:3—100

2 Peter
2:13—46

Revelation
3:20-21—142
6:6—132
18:1-20—203n
19:1-6—94
19:9—142
20-21—142n

PSEUDEPIGRAPHA AND EARLY PATRISTIC BOOKS

2 Baruch (Syriac
Apocalypse)
29:4-8—95
29:4—142n

1 Enoch
10:16-19—90n
13:5—190
39—71—5, 110
61:8—118
62:2—118

62:5—118
62:14—95, 142n
92—105—203n
99:10—135n

Psalms of Solomon
17:23—67n
17:26-42—118n

Gospel of Thomas
5—48n
6—48n

20—36n, 37
33—48n
64—92-93, 141
65—53
107—47-48

Gospel of Truth
31:35—32:9—148n

1 Clement
35:5—177

QUMRAN WRITINGS

1 QH (Thanksgiving Hymns)
7:34—189

1 QM (War Scroll)
7:4–6—144

1 QS (Manual of Discipline)
5:25—6:1—78n
6:24—7:25—78n
8:20—9:2—78n

1 QSa (Rule of the Congregation)
2:6–10—144

RABBINIC LITERATURE

Mishnah
Peah
8:7—153n

Sotah
8:1–7—141
8:2—141
8:7—142

Babylonian Talmud
Berakoth
28b—189

Jerusalem Talmud
Berakoth
2:8—82n

Midrash Rabbah
Numbers Rabbah
7:19—104
13:15–16—104n

Song of Songs
Rabbah
6:2—82n

OTHER ANCIENT SOURCES

Aristotle
Poetics 1450b—22
Poetics 1457b—6n
Poetics 1459a—7
Rhetoric 1405a–
   1407a—6n

Rhetoric 1411a–
   1413b—6n

Augustine
Quaestiones Evangeliorum 2.19—134n

Josephus
Jewish Antiquities
   18.2.2—130n

Strabo
Geography 16.2.41—
   130n

INDEX OF AUTHORS

Achtemeier, P., 51, 221

Bailey, K. E., x, 129, 130, 131, 141, 147, 151, 153, 154, 155, 157, 167, 176–77, 178, 180, 181, 182, 183, 184, 186, 188, 191, 220
Ballard, P. H., 141, 222
Barth, G., 66, 222
Batey, R., 103, 222
Best, E., 49–50, 222
Bird, P., 149, 222
Bonhoeffer, D., 51, 125, 222
Bornkamm, G., 66, 70, 203, 222
Boucher, M., x, 6, 11, 12, 28, 29, 44, 220
Bowker, J. W., 29, 222
Brandenburger, E., 112, 118, 125, 222
Breech, J. E., 3, 26, 220
Brooten, B., 174, 222
Brown, F. B., 222
Brown, R., 44, 79, 86, 130, 170, 199, 200, 222
Brown, S., 42, 44, 97, 180, 222
Bultmann, R., 21, 85, 94, 110, 119, 211, 222

Burlingame, E. W., 212, 222
Burnett, F., 97, 222
Bussmann, C., 110, 214, 222

Caird, G. B., 212, 223
Carlston, C., 4, 12, 29, 220, 223
Cave, C. H., 127, 223
Chilton, B., 26, 223
Ciardi, J., ix–x, 223
Collins, A. Y., 124, 203, 223
Collins, J., 69, 124, 223
Compton, J. E., 151, 223
Conzelmann, H., 144, 180, 204, 205, 209, 223
Cope, L., 65, 111, 223
Cousar, C., 57, 223
Creed, J. M., 164, 223
Crossan, J. D., x, 3, 8, 11, 15, 16, 26, 30, 33, 36, 43, 52, 53, 68, 69, 74, 92, 93, 130, 163, 220, 223

Dahl, N., 29, 224
Danby, H., 142, 153, 224
D'Angelo, M. R., 149, 224
Davies, S., 93, 224
Davies, W. D., 86, 224

Derrett, J. D. M., 81, 131, 132,
    141, 148, 154, 155, 159, 165,
    169, 224
Dewey, J., 23, 30, 224
Dibelius, M., 25, 224
Didier, M., 224
Dillon, R. J., 86, 224
Dodd, C. H., 5, 6, 8, 9, 11, 13, 17,
    33, 35, 134, 163, 214, 220
Donahue, J. R., 30, 45, 50, 56, 60,
    70, 92, 110, 115, 148, 195, 200,
    224
Donfried, K., 103, 104, 224
Dorr, D., 174, 224
Douglas, M., 144, 224
Drury, J., 63, 220
Duling, D., 117, 214, 224, 230
Dupont, J., 66, 174, 176, 225
Dupont-Sommer, A., 78, 225

Eagleton, T., 27, 225
Edersheim, A., 181, 225
Edwards, R., 29, 225
Evans, C. F., 127, 225

Farmer, W., 29, 225
Feldman, A., 212, 225
Feldman, E., 131, 225
Feldman, L., 130, 225
Fitzmyer, J., 29, 73, 85, 105, 107,
    120, 127, 136, 142, 144, 145,
    148, 152, 154, 162, 163, 165,
    172, 173, 174, 180, 181, 183,
    185, 188, 190, 191, 204, 205,
    207, 214, 225
Flender, H., 135, 225
Fletcher, A., 12, 226
Ford, J. M., 103, 142, 226
Fowler, R., 27, 226
Freyne, S., 212, 226
Fuchs, E., 211, 226
Fuks, A., 174, 232
Funk, R., x, 7, 8, 9, 12, 15, 30, 37,
    68, 92, 107, 133, 220, 226
Furnish, V., 122, 226

Garland, D., 86, 226
Gaventa, B. R., 207, 208, 226
Gelin, A., 174, 226
George, A., 174, 225
Gnilka, J., 46, 226
Goulder, M., 28, 63, 212, 226
Granskou, D., 220
Grayston, K., 57, 226
Grube, G. M. A., 6, 226
Gundry, R., 72, 87, 92, 95, 103,
    107, 115, 119, 120, 121, 226

Hamerton-Kelly, R., 161, 226
Hare, D., 86, 115, 226
Harrington, D., 115, 214, 226
Harrington, W., 64, 221
Haughey, J., 227
Held, J., 66, 222
Hellholm, D., 227
Hellwig, M., 211, 227
Herbert, A., 5, 227
Heschel, A., 55, 72, 227
Hooker, M., 57, 227
Horst, F., 185
Howe, Ilana W., 20, 227
Howe, Irving, 20, 227
Hunter, A., 221

Jeremias, J., x, 3, 8, 11, 26, 33, 35,
    41, 46, 51, 53, 58, 63, 67, 72,
    75, 81, 83, 87, 89, 94, 99, 101,
    102, 105, 129, 141, 146–47, 148,
    152, 153, 154, 155, 156, 158,
    163, 169, 182, 184, 185, 186,
    188, 189, 213, 221
Johnson, L., 172, 174, 209, 214,
    227
Johnston, R. M., 81, 82, 227
Jones, G. V., 7, 152, 221
Jülicher, A., 6, 7, 8, 11, 12, 221

Karris, R., 145, 176, 179, 227
Käsemann, E., 124, 194
Kealy, S., 214, 227
Kee, H. C., 194, 214, 227

Keegan, T., 27, 227
Kelber, W., 10, 28, 32, 43, 57, 194, 195, 227
Kellogg, R., 22, 24, 231
Kennedy, G., 207, 227
Kermode, F., 40, 134, 227
Kilgallen, J., 42, 227
Kingsbury, J. D., 4, 29, 42, 64, 66, 116, 200, 214, 221, 228
Kissinger, W., 221
Klauck, H-J., 12, 221
Kloppenborg, J., 29, 228
Koch, K., 124, 228
Kodell, J., 214, 228
Koenig, J., 144, 228
Kümmel, W. G., 29, 205, 228

Lambrecht, J., x, 4, 29, 30, 53, 97, 101, 105, 111, 112, 127, 221, 228
LaVerdiere, E., 111, 233
Légasse, S., 86, 228
Lewis, R. W. B., 166, 228
Linnemann, E., 18, 21, 75, 77, 83, 101, 103, 221
Lohfink, N., 174, 228
Luz, U., 66, 228

McArthur, H., 36, 228
McFague, S., 6, 10, 15, 27, 228
McLeod, N. B., 157, 228
Malbon, E. S., 60, 222, 228
Malina, B., 144, 212, 228, 229
Manson, T. W., 29, 65, 103, 104, 108, 151, 183, 229
Marcus, J., 29, 43, 229
Marrou, H., 207, 229
Marshall, I. H., 100, 136, 147, 148, 163, 173, 185, 229
Marxsen, W., 32, 229
Mays, J. L., 229
Mealand, D., 174, 229
Meier, J., 72, 79, 86, 101, 108, 115, 121, 200, 222, 229
Michie, D., 22, 23, 30, 230

Montefiore, H., 93, 229
Mott, S., 179, 229
Moule, C. F. D., 41, 229

Navone, J., 140, 147, 229
Neirynck, F., 29, 229
Neusner, J., 86, 229
Newman, L. I., 212, 229
Neyrey, J., 144, 229
Nickelsburg, G., 179, 203, 229
Norwood, F. A., 145, 229

Oesterley, W. O. E., 81, 157, 221
Ogawa, A., 86, 230

Patte, D., 70, 230
Pedersen, J., 71, 230
Perkins, P., x, 20, 23, 68, 101, 103, 114, 184, 221, 230
Perrin, N., x, 7, 9, 10, 32, 38, 51, 59, 93, 166, 194, 198, 211, 213, 214, 221, 230
Pesch, R., 32, 46, 57, 230
Pilgrim, W., 174, 179, 230
Polk, T., 5, 230
Posner, R., 103, 153, 230
Przybylski, B., 70, 230

Ramaroson, L., 147, 230
Reagan, C., 230
Rhoads, D., 22, 23, 30, 230
Riches, J., 3, 26, 213, 230
Ricoeur, P., ix, 10–11, 13, 15, 16, 148, 183, 194, 230
Ringe, S., 140, 230
Ringgren, H., 118, 161, 230
Rivkin, E., 85, 231
Robbins, V., 50, 231
Robertson, D., 20, 231
Robinson, J., 93, 231
Ruether, R., 231

Sanders, E. P., 213, 231
Sanders, J., 156, 231
Schillebeeckx, E., 213, 231

Schneiders, S., 161, 162, 231
Scholes, R., 22, 24, 231
Schottroff, L., 81, 231
Schottroff, W., 231
Schürer, E., 153, 231
Schüssler Fiorenza, E., 110, 138–
    39, 200, 231
Schweitzer, A., 123, 214, 231
Schweizer, E., 50, 79, 100, 152,
    231
Scott, B., 3, 26, 152, 166, 221, 231
Seccombe, D., 174, 231
Segbroeck, F. Van, 229
Segundo, J., 214, 231
Sellin, G., 135, 232
Shah, I., 212, 232
Sider, J. W., 5, 232
Sider, R., 111, 232
Soden, H. von, 111, 232
Sommer, F., 151, 232
Sparks, H. F. D., 67, 232
Stanton, G., 214, 232
Stegemann, W., 174, 231, 232
Stewart, D., 230
Stewart, R. A., 5, 232
Streeter, B. H., 29, 232

Talbert, C., 127, 194, 214, 232
Tannehill, R., 2–3, 50, 232

Taylor, V., 196, 232
Tcherikover, V., 174, 232
Theissen, G., 26, 93, 94, 199, 232
Thompson, W., 72, 111, 232, 233
Tolbert, M. A., x, 8, 11, 17, 23, 54,
    152, 221
Tracy, D., 110, 134, 233
Trible, P., 135, 149, 161, 233
Trites, A., 191, 233
Trocmé, E., 29, 233
Tuckett, C., 42, 233
Turner, H., 229

Vermes, G., 78, 189, 212, 233
Via, D. O., x, 11, 23, 74, 77, 83,
    102, 107, 108, 152, 166, 221
Via, E. J., 139, 233

Weder, H., 12, 221
Weeden, T., 51, 233
Wilder, A. N., x, 7, 8, 9, 14, 25,
    221, 233
Williams, J., 195, 233
Wimsatt, W., 14, 233
Wrede, W., 42, 233

Ziesler, J., 172, 233
Zumstein, J., 201, 233